IN MEMORIAM

Robert D. Barnes

b. Holden, Missouri, 1916
d. Sydney, New South Wales, 1999

Viking America

The First Millennium

Viking America

The First Millennium

GERALDINE BARNES

D. S. BREWER

First published 2001
D.S. Brewer, Cambridge

ISBN 0 85991 608 1

D.S. Brewer is an imprint of Boydell & Brewer Ltd
PO Box 9, Woodbridge, Suffolk IP12 3DF, UK
and of Boydell & Brewer Inc.
PO Box 41026, Rochester NY 14604–4126, USA
website: http://www.boydell.co.uk

A catalogue record for this title is available
from the British Library

Library of Congress Cataloging in Publication Data
Barnes, Geraldine.
    Viking America : the first millennium / Geraldine Barnes.
        p.   cm.
    Includes bibliographical references (p.) and index.
    ISBN 0–85991–608–1 (acid-free paper)
    1. American literature – Old Norse influences.   2. America
– Discovery and exploration – Norse – Historiography.   3. Old
Norse literature – History and criticism.   4. English literature –
History and criticism.   5. Geographical discoveries in literature.
6. Imperialism in literature.   7. Explorers in literature.   8.
Iceland – In literature.   9. America – In literature.   10. Vikings
in literature.   I. Title.
PS159.O44 B37 2001
810.9'355 – dc21   00–057215

This book is printed on acid-free paper

Printed in Great Britain by
St Edmundsbury Press Ltd, Bury St Edmunds, Suffolk

CONTENTS

Acknowledgments   vii

Introduction: Iceland, Greenland, Vínland, and the New World   ix

1. The Vínland voyages in saga narrative   1

2. Vínland in nineteenth-century history, criticism, and scholarship   37

3. The popular legacy: nineteenth-century theatre and polemic   60

4. Vínland in British literature to 1946   89

5. Vínland in American literature to 1926   117

Epilogue: Postcolonial Vínland   145

Bibliography   157

Index   183

And now came for him one of those moments in life, which, unlooked-for, undivined, send before them no promise of being different, in any way, from the commonplace moments that make up the balance of our days. . . . What such a moment holds within it, is something which has never entered our minds to go out and seek – the corner of earth, happened on by chance, which comes most near the Wineland of our dreams.

Henry Handel Richardson, *Maurice Guest* (1908)

ACKNOWLEDGMENTS

This book began as a short paper on Norse voyages to America, delivered at a one-day conference at the University of Sydney, in October 1992, to celebrate the Columbus quincentenary. Its development into its present form would not have been possible without the superlative resources of the Fiske Icelandic Collection at Cornell University and the professional expertise of its Curator, Patrick Stevens, whose manifold assistance and kindness over the last few years, which include the reading of a full-length early draft, constitute a debt which I can never repay. The brilliant sleuthing of the Interlibrary Loans staff at the University of Sydney Library, under the direction of Reingard Porges, tracked down and delivered further bibliographical riches with unfailing efficiency. A grant from the Australian Research Council in 1995–96 made it possible for me to benefit from the talents of two peerless research assistants, Judy Johnston (in 1995) and Jennifer Moore (in 1996), whose knowledge of, among much else, Victorian literature and nineteenth-century British periodicals contributed substantially to the shaping of Chapters 2 and 4. The same grant also helped to fund a short visit to the Fiske Collection and the archives of the Department of Scandinavian and Rare Book collection at the University of Wisconsin. A six-month period of sabbatical leave from the University of Sydney in the latter part of 1996 enabled me to complete the first full-length draft. I owe a special debt of thanks to Margaret Clunies Ross, who has been generous with her time, scholarship, pre-publication access to her recent work on the settlement of medieval Iceland and Old Norse literature in eighteenth-century Britain, and a constructively critical reading of an early draft. Bruce Gardiner supplied a treasure trove of bibliographical information on American Viking literature; Michael Wilding directed me to many early twentieth-century English Vínland texts and Adrian Mitchell to the Vínland reference in *Maurice Guest*; Justine Larbalestier and Louise Trott discovered and delivered some recent Vínland-inspired narrative. Richard Perkins very kindly drew my attention to an article by Ian McDougall before its publication, and Ian McDougall was equally kind in supplying me with a copy of it. Monique Rooney provided invaluable assistance with the compilation of the bibliography. Peter Wilson proved to be a gifted and tireless field assistant on the Maine/New Brunswick and Newfoundland expeditions of 1993 and 1995. The late Robert D. Barnes was, over a lifetime, an inspiring guide to American history and literature, and, especially during the last five years, to the early history of Virginia, the movement westwards to Kentucky and Missouri, the Civil War, and the trail which ended at Wounded Knee. The anonymous Boydell & Brewer reader provided salutary comment and criticism. Errors, infelicities, omissions, and excesses are entirely my own.

A Note on Names

Names of people and places as recorded in Old Icelandic sources are cited, with Icelandic letter forms and accents, in the nominative singular form (e.g. Leifr; Eiríkr; Guðríðr; Þorvaldr; Vínland). Proper nouns in works of post-medieval history and literature are cited in the form in which they appear in individual texts (e.g. Leif; Eric/Erik/Eirik; Gudrid; Thorwald; Vinland/Wineland).

Introduction:
Iceland, Greenland, Vínland,
and the New World

Medieval Iceland: New World or Old? Proto-republic or colony? Modern and medieval opinion offers a variety of viewpoints. The Icelandic explorer, Vilhjálmur Stefánsson, boldly titled one of his books *Iceland: the First American Republic* (1939) and, in the same work, claimed Greenland as the second.[1] In accordance with popular medieval conceptions of geography, an Anglo-Saxon map of the eleventh or twelfth century places Iceland beside Norway,[2] whereas Iceland is absent from the map of 'Europe and the surrounding lands in the High Middle Ages' which accompanies the Introduction to Robert Bartlett's *The Making of Europe* (1993).[3] The 'Vínland Map', allegedly a fifteenth-century map, although more likely a post-medieval construct imposed on the model of a medieval *mappa mundi*,[4] positions Iceland closer to mainland Scandinavia than to Greenland.

The settlement of Iceland, principally by Norwegians in the late ninth and early tenth centuries, established a Norwegian colony, according to Bartlett's definition of medieval colonialism, inasmuch as the purpose of its settlers was not the exploitation of raw materials but the replication of existing social structures.[5] The Icelanders brought with them the Norwegian institutions of local assemblies (*þing*) and priest-chieftains (*goðar*) but not allegiance to the kings of Norway, who nevertheless regarded themselves as the natural lords of Iceland during its 'Commonwealth' or 'Freestate' era from 930 to 1262. Despite its

---

1 *Iceland: The First American Republic* (New York, 1939), p. xxiii.
2 See Kirsten Hastrup, *Culture and History in Medieval Iceland. An anthropological analysis of structure and change* (Oxford, 1985), pp. 61, 63, and the references there.
3 *The Making of Europe. Conquest, Colonization and Cultural Change 950–1350* (London 1993). Map 1.
4 For discussion, see, for example, D. B. Quinn, 'The Vinland Map: A Viking Map of the West?', *Saga-Book of the Viking Society* 17 (1966), 63–72; P. G. Foote, 'On the Vínland Legends on *The Vinland Map*', *Saga-Book of the Viking Society* 17 (1966), 73–89; 'The Strange Case of the Vínland Map: A Symposium', *The Geographical Journal* 140 (1974), 183–216; T. A. Cahill, *et al.*, 'The Vinland Map, Revisited: New Compositional Evidence on Its Inks and Parchment', *Analytical Chemistry* 59 (1987), 829–33; Helen Wallis, 'The Vinland Map: fake, forgery or *jeu d'esprit*', *The Map Collector* 53 (1990), 2–6; *idem*, 'The Vinland Map: Genuine or Fake?', *Bulletin du bibliophile* 1 (1991), 76–83; Kirsten Seaver, 'The "Vinland Map": New light on an old controversy; who made it, and why?', *The Map Collector* 70 (1995), 32–40.
5 See Bartlett, *The Making of Europe*, pp. 306–9.

political independence from Norway, the Commonwealth of Iceland was, in some respects, a colony in the modern sense, in that its settlers owed certain legal obligations to their principal land of origin.[6] In the years leading up to and immediately following the conversion of Norway and Iceland to Christianity at the end of the tenth century, Icelanders established an offshoot settlement in Greenland and extended their territorial horizons to lands further west.

Whereas the Icelandic *Landnámabók* ('Book of Settlements'), a compilation probably begun in the early twelfth century[7] which records the arrival and *landnám* ('land-taking') by some 430 settlers and their families, relates the voyages of emigration to Iceland from Norway and the British Isles as a loosely collective enterprise, it recounts the settlement of Greenland as the initiative of one man, Eiríkr rauði ('the Red'). Eiríkr is forced into exile from Norway, and subsequently from Iceland, after committing a series of homicides shortly before the arrival of Christianity. *Landnámabók*'s account of these events forms the substance of the opening section of the two most extensive medieval accounts of Greenland's early history, the Icelandic *Eiríks saga rauða* ('Eric the Red's Saga') and *Grænlendinga saga* ('The Saga of the Greenlanders'),[8] the so-called 'Vínland sagas'. Eiríkr's search west of Iceland for new territory in which to re-establish himself is successful. Having undertaken a three-year survey of the land to establish its suitability for settlement and given it the deliberately enticing name of Greenland, he becomes its principal landowner and de facto ruler. A further push westward from Greenland in the early years of the eleventh century almost certainly reached the northeast coast of North America. The principal episode of both *Grænlendinga saga* and *Eiríks saga rauða*, and the inspiration for this book, is the discovery of and subsequent voyages to lands west of Greenland and the exploration and attempted settlement of the most attractive of these, which Eiríkr's son, Leifr, names Vínland.

Probably composed at the end of the twelfth century,[9] *Grænlendinga saga* sur-

---

6 Icelanders were, for example, according to a treaty with Óláfr Haraldsson (r.1014–30), liable to military service in Norway and obliged to pay land dues there in order to retain the status of free men. The treaty granted Norwegians the same status as Icelanders in Iceland, but the reverse did not always apply. See Jón Jóhannesson, trans. Haraldur Bessason, *A History of the Old Icelandic Commonwealth* (Winnipeg, 1974), pp. 109–17.

7 For a concise discussion, see Hermann Pálsson and Paul Edwards, trans., *The Book of Settlements. Landnámabók* (Winnipeg, 1972), pp. 4–6.

8 *Grænlendinga saga* and *Eiríks saga rauða* are abbreviated to *GS* and *ES* respectively in footnotes and quotation references. The latter, unless otherwise noted, are to the edition of *GS* by Matthías Þórðarson in Einar Ól. Sveinsson and Matthías Þórðarson, eds, *Eyrbyggja saga. Grænlendinga sögur*, Íslenzk fornrit 4 (Reykjavík, 1935) and, for *ES*, Ólafur Halldórsson, ed., *Eiríks saga rauða. Texti Skálholtsbókar. AM557 4to*, Íslenzk fornrit 4 (suppl.) Reykjavík, 1985). On the relationship between *Landnámabók* and *GS* and *ES*, and previous scholarship on the subject, see Ólafur Halldórsson, *Grænland í miðaldaritum* (Reykjavík, 1978), pp. 293–328; for a detailed examination of the manuscripts of *ES* and their relation to *Landnámabók*, see Sven B. F. Jansson, *Sagorna om Vinland. Handskrifterna till Erik den Rödes Saga* (Lund, 1944), pp. 82–91. See also the review, by Jeffrey Cosser, of *Grænland í miðaldaritum*, *Saga-Book of the Viking Society* 20 (1980), 222–7.

9 See Jón Jóhanneson, 'Aldur Grænlendinga sögu', *Nordaela* (Reykjavík, 1956), pp. 150–7; trans.

vives as a narrative embedded in *Óláfs saga Tryggvasonar en mesta* ('The Longest Saga of Óláfr Tryggvason'), a vast compilation dedicated to glorifying the missionary king of Norway, Óláfr Tryggvason (r.995–1000), preserved in *Flateyjarbók* (GkS 1005 fol.), a codex written by two Icelandic priests in the late fourteenth century.[10] *Eiríks saga rauða*, which is likely to be about a century younger than *Grœnlendinga saga*, survives as an independent narrative in two recensions.[11] The earlier is *Hauksbók* (AM 544 4to), which contains a number of encyclopedic, historical, and pseudo-historical works produced under the direction and partly in the hand of Haukr Erlendsson (1265–1334), an Icelander who rose to eminence in Norway. *Eiríks saga rauða* is also preserved in the late fifteenth-century collection of sagas and short narratives (*þættir*) known as *Skálholtsbók*.[12]

Whereas *Grœnlendinga saga* derives its account of the Vínland voyages from the oral report of Þorfinnr Karlsefni,

> Ok hefir Karlsefni gørst sagt allra manna atburði um farar ðessar allar, er nú er nǫkkut orði á komit.   (ch. 9: 269)

> Karlsefni has related more clearly than anyone else the events of all these voyages, which have now to some extent been told.

Eiríks saga rauða claims for itself no written or verbal authority but draws silently upon a range of written sources, which almost certainly include *Grœnlendinga saga* and encyclopedic material of the kind found in *Hauksbók*.[13]

Tryggvi J. Oleson, 'The Date of the Composition of the Saga of the Greenlanders', *Saga-Book of the Viking Society* 16 (1962), 54–66.

10 For a succinct description and history of *Flateyjarbók*, see Kolbrún Haraldsdóttir, '*Flateyjarbók*', *Medieval Scandinavia: An Encyclopedia*, ed. Phillip Pulsiano (New York, 1993), pp. 197–8.

11 On the extant texts of *ES*, see Arthur Middleton Reeves, *The Finding of Wineland the Good. The History of the Icelandic Discovery of America, edited and translated from the earliest records* (London, 1890), pp. 99–102; Sven B. F. Jansson, *Sagorna om Vinland. Handskrifterna till Erik den Rödes Saga* (Lund, 1944); Matthías Þórðarson, *Eyrbyggja saga. Grœnlendinga sǫgur*, pp. LXVII–LXXI.

12 See Dag Strömback, *The Arna-Magnæan Manuscript 557 4to containing inter alia the History of the first Discovery of America*, Corpus Codicum Islandicorum Medii Ævi, vol. XIII (Copenhagen, 1940), p. 9.

13 Cases from the plausible to the convincing have also been made for the influence on *ES* of Adam of Bremen, *Laxdœla saga*, an early thirteenth-century saga of Óláfr Tryggvason by Gunnlaugr Leifsson, and French epic. Halldór Laxness's suggestion concerning Adam of Bremen as a source for the description of Vínland in *ES* is cited by Richard Perkins in 'The Furðustrandir of *Eiríks saga rauða*', *Mediaeval Scandinavia* 9 (1976), 56, n. 1. Björn Þorsteinsson argues for *GS* and 'the general geographical knowledge common to educated men of his day' as likely influences ('Some Observations on the Discoveries and the Cultural History of the Norsemen', *Saga-Book of the Viking Society* 16 [1962–65], 185); Jón Jóhannesson for Gunnlaugr Leifsson's *Óláfs saga Tryggvasonar* and *GS* ('The Date of the Saga of the Greenlanders', pp. 63–6); Erik Wahlgren for *GS* and French epic ('Fact and Fancy in the Vinland sagas', in *Old Norse Literature and Mythology: a symposium*, ed. Edgar C. Polomé [Austin, Tx., and London, 1969], pp. 38, 45); Patricia Conroy for *Laxdœla saga* ('*Laxdœla saga* and *Eiríks saga rauða*: Narrative Structure', *Arkiv för nordisk filologi* 95 [1980], 123–5).

Where does the territory west of Greenland – Helluland, Markland, and, most famously, Vínland – fit into the medieval Scandinavian picture of the West Atlantic? From the broad perspective of the westward movement from mainland Scandinavia which began in the eighth century, Vínland and the other lands west of Greenland were the most distant points of a Norwegian sphere of influence which extended from the North Sea to the Atlantic. In the mid-eleventh century Adam of Bremen spoke of 'Winland' as the furthermost inhabitable island of the northern ocean, beyond which lay limitless ice and darkness. Adam cites the reliable oral authority of the Danish king, Sveinn Estriðsson (d.1076), and not 'fabulous report' (*non fabulosa opinione, sed certa comperimus relatione Danorum*) for his account of an island with vines and wild grain situated, along with Greenland and Iceland, in the ocean directly north of Norway:

> . . . quae dicitur Winland, eo quod ibi vites sponte nascantur, vinum optimum ferentes. . . . Post quam insulam, ait, terra non invenitur habitabilis in illo oceano, sed omnia, quae ultra sunt, glacie intolerabili ac caligine inmensa plena sunt.[14]

> . . . which is called Vinland because vines producing excellent wine grow wild there. . . . Beyond that island, he [Sveinn Estriðsson] said, no habitable land is found in that ocean, but every place beyond it is full of impenetrable ice and intense darkness.[15]

Helluland, Markland, and Vínland are mentioned in an Icelandic geographical treatise, probably originating from the thirteenth century and titled *Landafræði* ('Land Knowledge') by its first editor, Kristian Kålund, and in an extract from *Gripla*, an encyclopedic but no longer extant work of uncertain date preserved in the seventeenth-century compilation *Grænlands annáll*. *Landafræði* and *Gripla* anchor Vínland in a geographical frame of reference which includes Greenland, Helluland, and (in *Landafræði*) Markland, and extends to Africa. According to *Landafræði*:

> Sudr frá Grenlandi er Hellu-land, þá er Markland, þá er eigi langt til Vinlandz ens goda, er sumir menn e'tla at gangi af Affrika, ok ef svá er, þá er úthaf innfallanda à milli Vínlandz ok Marklandz.[16]

> South from Greenland is Helluland, then Markland; then it is not far to Vínland the Good, which some people think extends from Africa, and, if it is so, then the inland sea is between Vínland and Markland.

Gripla gives a similar account of the location of Vínland, but in this instance the lexis of Norse mythology replaces the *úthaf innfallanda* ('inland sea') between

---

14 Gesta Hammaburgensis ecclesiae Pontificum: Descriptio Insularum Aquilonis', in *Quellen des 9. und 11. Jahrhunderts zur Geschichte der Hamburgischen Kirche und des Reiches*, ed. Werner Trillmich (Berlin, 1961), pp. 488, 490.

15 Francis J. Tschan, trans., *Adam of Bremen: History of the Archbishops of Hamburg-Bremen* (New York, 1959), p. 219.

16 *Alfræði Íslenzk*, ed. Kr. Kålund (Copenhagen, 1908) I, 4. All references are to this edition.

Vínland and Markland, and *Ginnungagap*, the abyss which is said to form the bounds of ocean and earth, is located between Vínland and Greenland:[17]

> Nú er að segja hvað til móts við Grænaland gengur úr þeim botnum sem fyrr eru nefndir. Furðustrandir heitir land; þar eru frost mikil, so ekki er byggjanda so menn viti. Suður frá er Helluland; þat er kallað Skrælingjaland. Þá er skammt til Vínlands hin[s] góða, er sumir menn ætla að gangi af Affrica. Milli Vínland og Grænlands er Ginnungagap.[18]

> Now it will be told what lands opposite Greenland extend beyond those heads of land named above. There is a land called Furðustrandir; there are great frosts there, so it is not habitable, as far as people know. South from there is Helluland, which is called Skrælingjaland. Then it is a short way to Vínland the Good, which some people think extends from Africa. Between Vínland and Greenland is Ginnungagap.

By the fourteenth century Vínland and the other lands west of Greenland had been largely forgotten as parts of the Scandinavian world.[19] Of the three lands named by Leifr in *Grænlendinga saga* – Helluland, Markland, and Vínland – only Markland survives as a tangible destination in Icelandic chronicle after the twelfth century. An entry in the Icelandic *Konungsannáll* for 1121 says that *Eiríkr byskup af Grænlandi fór at leita Vínlands*[20] ('Bishop Eiríkr from Greenland went in search of Vínland') but not that he ever found it, or that he was ever seen again. On the other hand, the last recorded reference to Markland, in the *Skálholtsannáll* for the year 1347, suggests long-term acquaintance, possibly for the purpose of timber gathering:

> Þá kom og skip af Grænlandi . . . Þar voru á xvij menn og höfðu farið til Marklands, en síðan orðið hingað hafreka.[21]

> There also came also a ship from Greenland . . . There were seventeen men on board. They had made a voyage to Markland, but were afterwards storm-driven here.

---

17 On Ginnungagap, see Gustav Storm, 'Ginnungagap i Mythologien og i Geografien', *Arkiv för nordisk filologi* 6 (1890), 340–50; Fridtjof Nansen, trans. Arthur G. Chater, *In Northern Mists. Arctic Exploration in Early Times*, II (London, 1911), 239–41. For a succinct and helpful account of 'The Northern World-Picture' in the Middle Ages, particularly as it relates to points west of Greenland, see Gwyn Jones, *The Norse Atlantic Saga*, 2nd edn (Oxford, 1986), pp. 16–24.
18 Ólafur Halldórsson, *Grænland í miðaldaritum* (Reyykjavík, 1978), pp. 37–8.
19 On this point, see Rudolf Simek, 'Elusive Elysia or Which Way To Glæsisvellir?', in *Sagnaskemtmun. Studies in Honour of Hermann Pálsson*, eds Rudolf Simek, Jónas Kristjánsson, Hans Bekker-Nielsen (Vienna, Cologne, Graz, 1986), p. 252.
20 Guðni Jónsson, ed., *Annálar og Nafnaskrá* (Reykjavík, 1953), p. 13. Halldór Hermannsson comments: 'The verb *leita* can in this connection only have the meaning "to search for something which is undetermined, or lost" ' (Halldór Hermannsson, *The Problem of Wineland*, Islandica 25 [Ithaca and New York, 1936], 76). For a discussion of variants of this statement in the Icelandic annals, see P. G. Foote, 'On the Vínland legends on *The Vinland Map*', pp. 76–7.
21 Cited Ólafur Halldórsson, *Grænland í miðaldaritum*, p. 269. On the likelihood of such missions across the Davis Strait throughout the Middle Ages, see Kirsten Seaver, *The Frozen Echo. Greenland and the Exploration of North America ca. A.D. 1000–1500* (Stanford, 1996), p. 28.

In physical features and climate, the lands west of Greenland were not a New World for Norwegians, Icelanders, and Greenlanders, but simply an extension of an existing frame of reference. Voyages to lands west of Greenland were no more than a continuing part of the process of westward expansion which had begun centuries before. Whereas sixteenth-century European writers remarked on the difference of America and the difficulty of describing its dazzling diversity,[22] Vínland is represented in *Grænlendinga saga* as a land which is less Other than idealized familiar:

> ok sásk um í góðu veðri ok fundu þat, at dǫgg var á grasinu, ok varð þeim þat fyrir, at þeir tóku hǫndum sínum í dǫggina ok brugðu í munn sér ok þóttusk ekki jafnsœtt kennt hafa, sem þat var . . . Hvárki skorti þar lax í ánni né í vatninu, ok stœrra lax en þeir hefði fyrr sét. Þar var svá góðr landskostr, at því er þeim sýndisk, at þar myndi engi fénaðr fóðr þurfa á vetrum; þar kómu engi frost á vetrum, ok lítt rénuðu þar grǫs . . . ok gaf Leifr nafn landinu eptir landkostum ok kallaði Vínland.
>
> (*GS* ch. 3: 250, 251, 253)

> They went ashore and looked about them. The weather was fine. There was dew on the grass . . . and to them it seemed the sweetest thing they had ever tasted . . . There was no lack of salmon in the river or the lake, bigger salmon than they had ever seen. The country seemed to them so kind that no winter fodder would be needed for livestock: there was never any frost all winter and the grass hardly withered at all . . . Leifr gave the land a name in keeping with its choice qualities and called it Vínland.

Iceland, too, has waters teeming with fish and, although never with such unreserved enthusiasm, is lavishly praised by its early explorers.[23]

With grapevines and timber for the taking and a native population willing to barter unlimited supplies of furs for milk (*Grænlendinga saga*) or pieces of red cloth (*Eiríks saga rauða*), Vínland was a potential colony in the sense in which John Stuart Mill defined England's possessions in the West Indies:

> These are hardly to be looked upon as countries, carrying on an exchange of commodities with other countries, but more properly as outlying agricultural or manufacturing estates belonging to a larger community.[24]

For some, according to the Vínland sagas, the land was an appealing site of prospective permanent settlement; but others saw it primarily as a place where quick fortunes could be made by the export of raw materials. The fledgling west-of-Greenland colony is, however, abandoned in both sagas in the face of

---

22 J. H. Elliott, *The Old World and the New 1492–1650* (Cambridge 1970; Canto edn, 1992), p. 21.

23 'Þeir lofaði mjǫk landit; Garðarr . . . lofaði mjǫk landit', *Landnámabók*, ed. Jakob Benediktsson, Íslenzk fornrit, 1, i–ii (Reykjavík, 1968). I i (Sturlubók), 34, 36. ('They praised the land greatly; Garðarr . . . praised the land a great deal'.) All subsequent *Landnámabók* references are to this edition and to the Sturlubók manuscript.

24 *Principles of Political Economy*, III (Toronto, 1965), p. 693; cited Edward Said, *Culture and Imperialism* (London, 1993), p. 108.

escalating native hostility and, in *Grœnlendinga saga*, after a violent crime committed there by Eiríkr's daughter, Freydís. At the conclusion of both sagas, the narrative focus turns abruptly from Greenland and points west back to Iceland, where, through their many episcopal descendants, Þorfinnr Karlsefni, leader of the principal Vínland settlement expedition in both sagas, and his wife, Guðríðr Þorbjarnardóttir, gain a significant place in Icelandic church history.

It is not the importance of the Vínland story in the episcopal history of Iceland but its contentious claim to be the first chapter in the European history of America which has preoccupied nineteenth- and twentieth- century scholars. The question of the historicity of the Norse voyages west of Greenland and the likely location of Vínland have been their primary focus of interest. Some consider Vínland to be an entirely fictional construct. Fridtjof Nansen, for example, believed in the historical reality of Norse voyages to America but not in the substantiality of the Vínland of *Grœnlendinga saga* and *Eiríks saga rauða*, which he regarded as a rhetorical *locus amœnus* ('pleasant place'), probably derived from the island covered with richly laden grapevines in the ninth-century *Navigatio Sancti Brendani* ('Voyage of St Brendan').[25]

With its honey-sweet dew, fertile land, plentiful streams, frost-free winter, and unwithered grass, Leifr's Vínland in *Grœnlendinga saga* does have indisputable affinities with the universal rhetoric of paradise and promised lands.[26] To take some medieval Icelandic examples, paradise in *Landafrœði* is without frost or snow, and the forest in its midst is evergreen.[27] In *Eiríks saga viðfǫrla* (c.1300), a work influenced by encyclopedic and vision literature, streams of honey flow through the neo-paradise which Eiríkr enters through a dragon's mouth.[28] Two Scottish thralls despatched by Karlsefni in *Eiríks saga rauða* (ch. 8) to reconnoitre the land south of Markland, whence they return with grapes and wild wheat, have their biblical counterparts in the spies sent by Moses into Canaan in the Old Testament Book of Numbers, who bring back grapes, pomegranates, and figs.[29]

---

25 Fridtjof Nansen, *In Northern Mists*, i, 330–84; ii, 58–62. For support of Nansen's view, see John Honti, 'Vinland and Ultima Thule', *Modern Language Notes* 54 (1939), 168; and, more recently, Walter Baumgartner, 'Freydís in Vinland. oder Die Vertreibung aus dem Paradies', *Skandinavistik* 23 (1993), 16–35. The *Navigatio Sancti Brendani* was translated into Old Norse (ed. C. R. Unger, in *Heilagra Manna Sögur*, Christiania, 1877), although it exists only in fragments which lack both 'The Island of Grapes' and the account of the Earthly Paradise. For these two episodes, see Carl Selmer, ed., *Navigatio Sancti Brendani Abbatis, from Early Latin Manuscripts* (Notre Dame, 1959), pp. 53–5, 78–81. For a German translation of the Norse fragments, see Carl Wahlund, *Die altfranzösische Prosaübersetzung von Brendans Meerfahrt* (Uppsala, 1900), pp. xliv–xlvii.

26 See 'Earthly Paradises', in George Boas, *Essays on Primitivism and Related Ideas in the Middle Ages* (Baltimore, 1948), pp. 154–74. See also Anne Holtsmark, *Studier i Snorres Mytologi* (Oslo, 1964), pp. 46–7; Margaret Clunies Ross, *Skáldskaparmál. Snorri Sturluson's ars poetica and medieval theories of language* (Odense, 1987), pp. 165–6.

27 *þar er eigi frost ne snioR . . . þar fellr alldri lauf af vidi. Alfrœði Íslenzk*, I, 4.

28 Helle Jensen, ed., *Eiríks saga Viðfǫrla*, Editiones Arnamagnæanæ, Series B, Vol. 29 (Copenhagen, 1983), pp. 74, 75.

29 'And they came unto the borrok of Esh-col, and cut down from thence a branch with one cluster

Likely rhetorical influence on the construction of Vínland in *Grænlendinga saga* and *Eiríks saga rauða* does not necessarily preclude a basis in fact. As J. H. Elliott has pointed out, Christian and classical traditions provided yardsticks for sixteenth-century Europeans to measure the exoticism of the New World.[30] More recently, Mary Campbell has shown that Columbus's firsthand description of the New World is couched in the tropes of romance and paradise.[31] Elements of the monstrous and grotesque also appear in New World discovery narrative. Jacques Cartier, as Ramsay Cook observes, 'showed no scepticism'[32] towards the assertion by the Amerindian leader, Donnaconna, that people in another country which he has visited *n'ont que une jambe et aultres merveilles longues à racompter* (p. 96).[33] Spanish explorers of the Americas claimed to have discovered giants, and, early in the eighteenth century, the Jesuit missionary, Joseph Françoise Lafitauand, reported Cephalopod sightings by the Canadian Hurons.[34]

Whatever their fictional component, the accounts of voyages to lands west of Greenland in *Grænlendinga saga* and *Eiríks saga rauða* tally with the established facts of medieval Norse seamanship and the topography of the northeast coast of North America. Helluland is generally identified with the southern part of Baffin Island, and Markland either with the south coast of Labrador or the west coast of Newfoundland. Leifr's third and, in *Grænlendinga saga*, most extensively described landfall, eludes geographical pinpointing, although that saga gives sufficent topographical details of Vínland to invite continuing efforts to search for its precise location, currently favoured spots being the Maritime Provinces of Canada and northern New England.[35] The discovery, in 1960, by Helge

of grapes . . . and they brought of the pomegranates, and of the figs' (Numbers 13: 23). According to the interpretation by a thirteenth-century Icelandic prosodist, Óláfr Þórðarson, of a verse by the abbot Nikulás Bergsson (d.1159), the grapes (*vínber*) of Canaan and their juice represent the body and blood of Christ. Óláfr Þórðarson quotes the verse in that section of his *Third Grammatical Treatise* known as *Málskrúfræði*. See Björn Magnússon Ólsen, ed., *Den Tredje og Fjærde Grammatiske Afhandling i Snorres Edda Tilligemed de Grammatiske Afhandlingers Prolog og To Andre Tillæg* (Copenhagen, 1884), pp. 117–18. For an English translation and explanation of the verse, see G. Turville-Petre, *Origins of Icelandic Literature* (Oxford, 1953), p. 161. I am grateful to Margaret Clunies Ross for bringing Óláfr Þórðarson's interpretation of this verse as an example of the allegorical figure of *parabola* to my attention.

30 *The Old World and The New 1492–1650*, p. 25.

31 *The Witness and the Other World. Exotic European Travel Writing, 400–1600* (Ithaca and London, 1988), pp. 174–83.

32 Ramsay Cook, introd., *The Voyages of Jacques Cartier* (Toronto, Buffalo, London, 1993), p. xiv.

33 *Jacques Cartier: Relations*, ed. Michel Bideaux (Montreal, 1986), p. 177; 'whose inhabitants have only one leg and other marvels too long to relate' (Cook, *The Voyages of Jacques Cartier*, p. 82). Subsequent French references are to Bideaux, *Relations*, and English translations are taken from Cook, *Voyages*.

34 See Anthony Pagden, *European Encounters with the New World. From Renaissance to Romanticism* (New Haven and London, 1993), pp. 10, 28.

35 For example, Passamaquoddy Bay (an inlet of the Bay of Fundy), the site proposed by Edward Reman in *The Norse Discoveries and Explorations in America* (Berkeley and Los Angeles, 1949), pp. 77–86, for Leifr's landing, has more recently been supported by Erik Wahlgren in *The Vikings and*

Ingstad, and subsequent excavations from 1961 to 1968 led by Anne Ingstad, of a Norse site at Epaves Bay, near the village of L'Anse-aux-Meadows at the tip of the Great Northern Peninsula of Newfoundland, provide the only indisputable evidence of a Norse presence west of Greenland around 1000.[36] But there is no certainty that this was a Vínland community and some cause to think that it was not.[37] Newfoundland, for instance, is unlikely ever to have been hospitable to the grapes which are Vínland's defining characteristic in *Grænlendinga saga* and *Eiríks saga rauða*, or to the butternuts found in the excavations at L'Anse-aux-Meadows.[38]

Despite the acceptance by a majority of twentieth-century scholars of the validity of these accounts of New World landings, *Grænlendinga saga* and *Eiríks saga rauða* have generally been denied authorization as discovery narrative. Iceland itself went into a centuries-long period of economic decline from the fifteenth century, and Icelanders subsequently failed to lay public claim to the 'discovery' of America. Moreover, unlike the narratives of Cartier and Columbus, the Vínland sagas cannot claim the authority of eyewitness report. Although *Grænlendinga saga* names Þorfinnr Karlsefni as its chief source (ch. 10), both it and *Eiríks saga rauða* have been filtered through editorial hands and distanced by at least four generations from the events which they relate. Furthermore, the west-of-Greenland enterprise was both fleeting – according to the sagas themselves and the evidence of L'Anse-aux-Meadows – and unsuccessful. Moreover, the publication of the first modern edition of the Vínland sagas, by the Danish scholar Carl Christian Rafn in a volume entitled *Antiquitates Americanæ* (1837),[39] was seen by many Americans as a direct challenge to the pre-eminence of Columbus, and a number of its reviewers sought to downplay the significance of medieval Scandinavian landings on the American continent. In *The North American Review* (1838), for example, Edward Everett expressed the view that the lack of publicity given to the Vínland voyages in medieval Europe and the failure of the attempted Norse settlement to progress to

---

America (London, 1986), p. 164. Jones inclines towards northern Newfoundland in *The Norse Atlantic Saga* (1986), p. 126. Birgitta Linderoth Wallace identifies Vínland with the Gulf of St Lawrence area, and *Leifsbuðir* with L'Anse-aux-Meadows ('The Vikings in North America: Myth and Reality', in *Social Approaches to Viking Studies*, ed. Ross Samson [Glasgow, 1991], pp. 217–19). In 'The Vinland Sagas and Nova Scotia. A Reappraisal of an Old Theory', *Scandinavian Studies* 64 (1992), 305–35, Mats Larsson revives Gustav Storm's suggestion (in 'Studier over Vinlandreiserne, Vinlands Geografi og Ethnografi', *Aarbøger for Nordisk Oldkyndighed og Historie* (1887), pp. 293–372) that Vínland was in Nova Scotia.

36 See Anne Stine Ingstad, *The Discovery of a Norse Settlement in America: Excavations at L'Anse aux Meadows, Newfoundland, 1961–1968*, I (Oslo, 1977).

37 See Birgitta Linderoth Wallace, 'The Vikings in North America: Myth and Reality', pp. 215–16.

38 Butternuts flourish between New Brunswick and Georgia. See Alfred Rehder, 'Júglans', in *Cyclopedia of American Horticulture*, ed. L. H. Bailey, III (New York, 1975), p. 846.

39 *Antiqvitates Americanæ sive Scriptores Septentrionales Rerum Ante-Columbianarum in America. Samling af de i Nordens Oldskrifter indeholdte Efterretninger om de gamle Nordboers Opdagelsesreiser til America fra det 10de til det 14de Aarhundrede. Edidit Societas Regia Antiqvariorum Septentrionalium* (Hafniæ, 1837); rpr. Osnabrück, 1968.

full-scale colonization rendered them null and void as landmarks of either European or American history:

> The discovery by the Northmen . . . seemed, as far as we can judge, to produce no
> *sensation* in the world. It had no effect upon the mind of Europe at large. It led to
> no vigorous efforts at colonization; awoke no spirit of adventure; occasioned none
> of those mighty revolutions, which were caused by the discovery of Columbus;
> and was before long forgotten.[40]

Earlier this century the American philosopher, John Dewey, disqualified the
Norse voyages to America as 'discovery' because they led to no cultural
redrawing of the globe:

> The Norsemen are said to have discovered America. But in what sense? They
> landed on its shores after a story voyage; there was discovery in the sense of hitting
> upon a land hitherto untrod by Europeans. But unless the newly found and seen
> object was used to modify old beliefs, to change the sense of the old map of the
> earth, there was no discovery in any pregnant intellectual sense.[41]

For more recent commentators it is not the failure of the Vínland voyages to
make any impact on Europe at large but the absence of their imprint upon the
American continent or its people which disqualifies them as 'discovery'. Ivan
Sertima, for example, comments in *They Came Before Columbus* (1976):

> The Vikings brought no new plant, influenced no art, introduced no ritual, left no
> identifiable trace of their blood in the native American. Like waves, they broke for
> a moment on alien sands and then receded.[42]

In his article, 'Pre-Columbian Transoceanic Contacts' (1978), Stephen C. Jett
echoes the scepticism of many nineteenth-century Americans by labelling these
pre-Columbian voyages 'putative'. Like Sertima, Jett measures their inconsequentiality by their failure to leave their mark on Native American culture:

> Little will be said here regarding putative medieval voyages to America, since they
> seem unlikely to have had very important impacts on indigenous cultures
> (although this judgment may require reassessment in the future.[43]

Although the Vínland voyages became a controversial issue in North
America in the years leading up to the Columbus quatercentenary in 1892, the
spate of books on early European contacts with the New World published
around the quincentenary virtually ignored them. In *Cultures in Conflict* (1993)
Urs Bitterli acknowledges that, '[s]trictly speaking, the history of relations
between Europe and Canada begins with the Viking voyages around AD

---

40 *The North American Review* (1838), p. 194.
41 John Dewey, *Experience and Nature*, 2nd edn (London, 1929), p. 156.
42 *They Came Before Columbus* (New York, 1976), p. 77.
43 In Jesse D. Jennings, ed., *Ancient Native Americans* (San Francisco, 1978), p. 629.

1000',[44] but they pass unremarked in Felipe Fernández-Armesto's *Before Columbus. Exploration and Colonisation from the Mediterranean to the Atlantic 1229–1492* (1987); Mary Campbell's *The Witness and the Other World. Exotic European Travel Writing, 400–1600* (1988); Stephen Greenblatt's *Marvelous Possessions. The Wonder of the New World* (1991); the essays in Scott D. Westrem's, *Discovering New Worlds: Essays on Medieval Exploration and Imagination* (1991); and Anthony Pagden's *European Encounters with the New World* (1993). Pagden categorically asserts that:

> For all Europeans, the events of October 1492 constituted a 'discovery'. Something of which they had had no prior knowledge had suddenly presented itself to their gaze . . . America was also different from all other 'other' worlds in that until Columbus's landfall its very existence had been unknown.[45]

Vínland's geographical location is unlikely ever to be established with any certainty. Its position on the cultural maps of Iceland and America, as drawn and redrawn by scholars and creative writers from the medieval period to the late twentieth century, is nevertheless a rich field for investigation. This study attempts to turn the soil of that field by reading the Vínland sagas and their post-medieval reception as social history. The argument, in its broadest terms, is that, from the medieval period to the present day, the story has been shaped by a variety of vested interests, from dynastic pride to national identity. In *Grænlendinga saga* and *Eiríks saga rauða* it charts the cultural volatility which attended Iceland's transition from paganism to Christianity. In nineteenth- and early twentieth-century America, it becomes bound up with regional pride and national myths of foundation. In late nineteenth- and early twentieth-century English literature it is allied with the ethos of Empire. Retellings in the last years of the twentieth century address many of the questions about the impact of the Old World on the New which became the focus of the Columbus quincentenary in 1992.

This book makes no attempt either to evaluate the authenticity of the various North American artefacts claimed as Norse which have been comprehensively discussed by nineteenth- and twentieth-century scholars,[46] or to winnow 'fact' from 'fiction' in the Vínland sagas.[47] Chapter 1 considers *Grænlendinga saga* and *Eiríks saga rauða* as narratives of land-taking and colonization and examines the different ways in which Vínland is ultimately 'lost' in these and other Norse

---

44 Urs Bitterli, trans. Ritchie Robertson, *Cultures in Conflict. Encounters Between European and Non-European Cultures, 1492–1800* (Cambridge, 1993), p. 87.

45 Anthony Pagden, *European Encounters with the New World. From Renaissance to Romanticism* (New Haven and London, 1993), pp. 5, 11.

46 See, for example, Justin Winsor, 'Pre-Columbian Explorations', *Narrative and Critical History of America*, I (1889), 102–5; Birgitta Linderoth Wallace, 'The Vikings in North America: Myth and Reality', pp. 207–19.

47 For a detailed discussion, see Wahlgren, 'Fact and Fancy in the Vinland Sagas'; Else Ebel, 'Fiktion und Realität in den Vínlandsagas', in *Festschrift für Heinrich Beck*, ed. Heiko Uecker (Berlin and New York, 1994), pp. 89–100.

narratives. Chapters 2 and 3 discuss the reception of *Antiquitates Americanæ* in nineteenth-century England and America and the appropriation of the Vínland voyages to polemic and promotional ends. Chapters 4 and 5 look at reworkings of the story by British and American authors from the early nineteenth century to the end of World War II. The Epilogue surveys the evolution of Vínland from physical to metaphorical location in postcolonial treatments of the story in late twentieth-century British and North American poetry and prose.

CHAPTER ONE

The Vínland Voyages in Saga Narrative

Signalling the possibility of an approach to Vínland saga scholarship different from the questions of geography and historicity which had been its preoccupation since the nineteenth century, a little over thirty years ago Haraldur Bessason remarked that the author of *Grænlendinga saga* 'may have wished to endow his book with certain moral-social overtones'[1] and briefly speculated as to whether, despite the general tendency of scholars to concentrate on the Vínland voyages to the exclusion of the rest of the narrative, 'the commemoration of the explorers' noble descendants – the authors of the sagas about Vinland probably included – did not rather constitute the chief motivation for the writing of our two sagas'.[2] Those descendants constitute the episcopal dynasty founded by Guðríðr Þorbjarnardóttir and Þorfinnr Karlsefni, which is identified in the closing lines of *Grænlendinga saga* and *Eiríks saga rauða*. The couple's great-grandsons, Þorlákr Rúnólfsson and Bjǫrn Gilsson, became Bishop of Skálholt (1118–33) and Bishop of Hólar (1147–62) respectively; and a great-great-grandson, Brandr Sæmundarson, succeeded Bjǫrn at Hólar (1163–1201). Brandr Sæmundarson is the nominee of some scholars for the provider of the material of *Grænlendinga saga*, if not authorship of the saga itself.[3] An attempt made on behalf of Bjǫrn Gilsson in the last years of the twelfth century 'to find out whether he would pass muster as the patron saint of Hólar' may, as Ólafur Halldórsson suggests,[4] account for the idealization of

---

1 Haraldur Bessason, 'New Light on Vinland from the sagas', *Mosaic* 1 (1967–68), 53.
2 Bessason, 'New Light on Vinland from the sagas', p. 64.
3 'Bishop Brandr Sæmundarson . . . could well have been the author's authority for the material in the saga, or if not he, someone close to him' (Jón Jóhannesson, trans. Tryggvi J. Oleson, 'The Date of the Composition of the Saga of the Greenlanders', *Saga-Book of the Viking Society* 16 [1962], 66); 'the author seems to have been close to Bishop Brandr Sæmundsson . . . if the Bishop himself was not indeed the author' (Haraldur Bessason, 'New Light on Vinland from the sagas', p. 64).
4 Ólafur Halldórsson, 'Lost Tales of Guðríðr Þorbjarnardóttir', in *Sagnaskemmtun. Studies in Honour of Hermann Pálsson* (Vienna and Cologne, 1986), p. 243; cf. *idem*, *Grænland í miðaldaritum*, pp. 393–4. As the author also points out, predictions in both *GS* and *ES* use the register of hagiography to refer to Guðríðr's descendants, who, in *GS* (ch. 6: 260) will be *bjart ok ágætt, sœtt ok ilmat vel* ('bright and excellent, sweet and fragrant' [p. 64]) and, in *ES* (ch. 4: 413) *mun skína bjartr*

Guðríðr in both *Grænlendinga saga* and *Eiríks saga rauða*. The extension of this line of descent to Haukr Erlendsson himself in the *Hauksbók* version of *Eiríks saga rauða*[5] points strongly to a genealogical impetus for its inclusion in that volume.[6]

More recently, Walter Baumgartner, Teresa Pàroli, and William Sayers have pursued lines of investigation which directly address the Icelandic social and historical context of *Grænlendinga saga* and *Eiríks saga rauða*. For Sayers, these sagas are a 'narrativized justification' of Iceland's rejection of the pagan-heroic past in favour of a European-Christian future.[7] Baumgartner sees them, particularly *Grænlendinga saga*, as a turning away from the 'Wiking-Mentalität'.[8] Pàroli views them as works of dynastic glorification which directly connect the Vínland story with the conversion of Greenland and the prospering of Christian institutions in Iceland.[9] The following discussion takes as its springboard the insights of these three scholars. Situating *Grænlendinga saga* and *Eiríks saga rauða* ideologically on the cusp of the conversion of Greenland and Iceland, it argues that the narrative of both sagas is driven to a large extent by the performance of pagan and Christian ritual. The Vínland voyages are analyzed from two perspectives: first, as unrealized paradigms of the process of Icelandic *landnám* ('land-taking'); second, as the episode which steers *Grænlendinga saga* in the direction of Christian exemplum and *Eiríks saga rauða* towards the narrative mode of romance.

geisli ('there shall shine a bright light' [p. 83]) over them. Ólafur suggests that, in each case, the message is that Guðríðr will count a saint among her descendants.

5 'Dóttir Snorra Karlsefnissonar var ok Steinnun, er átti Einarr, sonr Grundar-Ketils, Þorvaldssonar króks, Þórissonar á Espihóli. Þeira sonr var Þorsteinn ranglátr; hann var faðir Guðrúnar, er átti Jǫrundr at Keldum. Þeira dóttir var Halla, móðir Flosa, fǫður Valgerðar, móður herra Erlands sterka, fǫður Hauks lǫgmanns.' Matthías Þórðarson, ed. *Eiríks saga rauta*, in Einar Ól. Sveinsson and Matthias Þórðarson, eds, *Eyrbyggja saga. Grænlendinga sǫgur*, Íslenzk fornrit 4 (Reykjavík, 1935), 237n. Subsequent *Hauksbók* references are to this edition. (The daughter of Snorri Karlsefnisson was Steinnun, who was married to Einarr, the son of Grundar-Ketill, the son of Þorvaldr krókr Þorisson of Espihóll. Their son was Þorsteinn 'the unjust'; he was the father of Guðrún, who was married to Jǫrundr of Keldur. Their daughter was Halla, the mother of Flosi, the father of Valgerðr, the mother of Herra Erlendr 'the strong', the father of Haukr the lawman.)

6 On genealogy as an inspiration for the composition of Icelandic narrative, see Margaret Clunies Ross, 'The Development of Old Norse Textual Worlds: Genealogical Structure as a Principle of Literary Organisation in Early Iceland', *Journal of English and Germanic Philology* [hereafter *JEGP*] 92 (1993), 372–85.

7 William Sayers, 'Vinland, the Irish, "Obvious Fictions and Apocrypha"', *Skandinavistik* 23 (1993), 1.

8 Walter Baumgartner, 'Freydís in Vinland oder Die Vertreibung aus dem Paradies', *Skandinavistik* 23 (1993), 22.

9 Teresa Pàroli, 'Bishops and Explorers. On the structure of the Vínland sagas', in *Sagnaþing helgað Jónasi Kristjánssyni sjötugum 10. apríl 1994*, eds Gísli Sigurðsson, Guðrún Kvaran, Sigurgeir Steingrímsson (Reykjavík 1994), pp. 641–52.

Christian rite and pagan ritual in Grœnlendinga saga *and* Eiríks saga rauða

The voyages west of Greenland coincide with the conversion of Iceland and Greenland. This, according to Ari Þorgilsson's *Íslendingabók* ('Book of the Icelanders'), a vernacular history of Iceland written in the early twelfth century, was a largely peaceful process initiated by the Norwegian king Óláfr Tryggvason, who despatched a missionary-priest there in 997.[10] Iceland adopted Christianity in 1000 and Greenland quickly followed suit. Codicologically anchored in the hagiographic juggernaut of the *Flateyjarbók* version of *Óláfs saga Tryggvasonar en mesta* ('The Longest Saga of Óláfr Tryggvason'), *Grœnlendinga saga* welcomes the arrival of Christianity in the North Atlantic with unreserved enthusiasm. In *Eiríks saga rauða* the discovery of Vínland is itself directly linked with the conversion of Greenland: in an episode without historical foundation but attributable to Gunnlaugr Leifsson's lost *Óláfs saga Tryggvasonar*,[11] Leifr Eiríksson is commissioned by Óláfr Tryggvason to convert the Greenlanders (*ES* ch. 5). Blown off course en route from Norway, he lands in new territory west of Greenland.

The coterminous establishment of the Greenland settlement and the conversion of Iceland and Norway probably accounts for the prominence of Christianity in other thirteenth-century Norse narratives in which Greenland plays a part, either as a backdrop to stories of Christian fortitude in the face of pagan opposition or as an illustration of Christian steadfastness in a sparsely populated land on the outermost fringe of Christendom. The Norwegian *speculum regale*, the *Konungs skuggsjá* ('King's Mirror'), for example, refers approvingly to the Greenlanders' institutionalization of Christianity:

> Fátt er folk aþvi [sic] lannde þvi at litit er þitt sva at byggiannde er en þat folk er cristit oc kirkiur hafa þeir oc kenni mænn . . . en þo hafa þeir ser nu byskup.[12]

> The inhabitants of that land are few in number, because little of it is habitable, but the people are Christian and have churches and clergy . . . and they now have a bishop to themselves.

Einars þáttr Sokkasonar (also known *Grænlendinga þáttr*), an independent narrative which, like *Grœnlendinga saga*, is preserved only in *Flateyjarbók*, tells the story of the ecclesiastical milestone in the history of Greenland to which the *Konungs skuggsjá* alludes here: the appointment, in 1124, of its first bishop. Among the *Íslendingasögur* ('Sagas of Icelanders'), Greenland is the locus for the testing of Christian faith in *Flóamanna saga* and, in *Fóstbræðra saga*, for an

---

10 *Íslendingabók*, ed. Jakob Benediktsson, Íslenzk fornrit I, i (Reykjavík, 1968), ch. 7. All references and quotations are from this edition.

11 See Jón Jóhannesson, 'The Date of the Composition of the Saga of the Greenlanders', pp. 60–1.

12 *Konungs Skuggsiá*, ed. Ludvig Holm-Olsen, rev. edn (Oslo, 1983), p. 30.

episode which demonstrates the superiority of Christianity over pagan superstition.

The ill-fated attempt in *Flóamanna saga* by an Icelander, Þorgils Ørrabeins-fóstri, an early convert to Christianity, to accept an invitation to visit Eiríkr rauði in Greenland takes place in the face of a vendetta waged against him by the pagan god, Þórr, who appears in dreams to predict that the enterprise will fare badly unless Þorgils reverts to his former beliefs (ch. 21).[13] Þorgils's disaster-fraught attempts to reach and settle in Greenland – he is becalmed for a long time, shipwrecked off the east coast of Greenland, disease kills many members of the group, his wife is murdered, his thralls abscond, and his son dies – can be read as a series of tests of faith in which Christian fortitude defies harassment from a powerful pagan deity.[14] Þorgils finally returns to Iceland with reputation enhanced and, like Guðríðr and Karlsefni in *Grœnlendinga saga* and *Eiríks saga rauða*, begets a line of bishops.

The pagan-Christian contest takes a contrastingly ludic turn in the Greenland episode of *Fóstbrœðra saga*. Two Icelanders, Þorgeirr and Þormóðr, pledge blood-brotherhood, a custom which the saga treats as a legacy of heathen 'bad habit' (*óvenja*, ch. 2: 125).[15] Þorgeirr is killed by Þorgrímr, a Greenlander. Þormóðr goes to Greenland, takes due vengeance on Þorgrímr, and then hides out in Eiríksfjǫrðr with an elderly couple named Gamli and Gríma. Þordís, Þorgrím's mother, enlists the aid of a band of men led by Eiríkr rauði's grandson, Þorkell Leifsson, to track down Þormóðr. Gríma forsees the arrival of Þordís, Þorkell, and company in a dream; she places a large chair, with a carving of Þórr on its pillars, in the middle of her sitting-room, instructs Þormóðr to be seated in it when they arrive, and then cooks a seal to fill the house with smoke. Þordís and Þorkell carry out a search but can see nothing in the smoky sitting-room apart from the chair occupied by what appears to be a carved image of the god. Gríma tells them that, although distance prevents her from going to church often, the fragility of this wooden image of Þórr reminds her of the superior power of God.

In *Eiríks saga rauða* the new faith asserts itself through active demonstration of its institutionalized practice, sometimes in direct confrontation or parallel display with pagan custom. The piety of Auðr djúpúðga ('the Deep-Minded'), a Christian matriarch who settles in Iceland via the British Isles, is, for example, manifested through prayer and the erection of crosses:

---

13 References are to the edition by Þórhallur Vilmundarson and Bjarni Vilhjálmsson in *Harðar saga*, Íslenzk fornrit 13 (Reykjavík, 1991).

14 As Richard Perkins has noted, the entire Greenland episode draws upon saints' lives, vision literature, and the Bible ('The Dreams of *Flóamanna Saga*', *Saga-Book of the Viking Society* 19 [1975–76], 197; *idem, Flóamanna saga, Gaulverjabær and Haukr Erlendsson*, Studia Islandica 36 [Reykjavík, 1978], 11–12).

15 References are to the edition by Guðni Jónsson in *Vestfirðinga Sǫgur*, Íslenzk fornrit 6 (Reykjavík, 1943).

Hon hafði bœnahald í Krosshólum; þar lét hon reisa krossa, þvíat hon var skírð ok vel trúuð. (*ES* ch. 1: 404)

She held prayers at Krosshólar, where she had crosses erected, because she was baptized and a true believer.

Eiríkr rauði's wife, Þjóðhildr, has a church built for Christian worship:

Hafði hon þar fram bœnir sínar ok þeir menn, sem við kristni tóku, en þeir váru margir. (*ES* ch. 5: 416)

She and those people who had accepted Christianity, and they were many, offered up their prayers there.

A mini-narrative of Leifr's conversion of Greenland is embedded into the saga,

Hann boðaði brátt kristni um landit ok almenniligia trú ok sýndi mǫnnum orðsendingar Óláfs konungs Tryggvasonar ok segir hversu mǫrg ágæti ok mikil dýrð þessum sið fylgði. (*ES* ch. 5: 415)

He soon preached Christianity and the catholic faith throughout the land; and he communicated King Óláfr Tryggvason's message to people and told them how much excellence and great glory there was in this faith.

and, in a second brief missionary narrative towards its end, Þorfinnr Karlsefni and his company baptize two natives of Markland (*ES* ch. 12).

There is less outward display of religious observance in *Grœnlendinga saga*. Christianity is nevertheless fully assimilated into the ethos and framework of the narrative. The conversion of Greenland is not itself an episode in *Grœnlendinga saga*, but *Flateyjarbók* immediately follows the saga's account of Eiríkr's settlement of Greenland (ch. 1) with a report of the unresisting conversion and baptism of Leifr and his companions, sixteen years later, by Óláfr Tryggvason.[16] References to the conversion in *Grœnlendinga saga* serve primarily as a means of dating and locating events. The departure of Eiríkr and the first fleet of settlers for Greenland takes place:

fimmtán vetrum fyrr en kristni var lǫgtekin á Íslandi. Á því sama sumri fóru útan Friðrekr byskup ok Þorvaldr Koðránsson. (*GS* ch. 1: 243)

fifteen years before Christianity was adopted by law in Iceland. That same summer Bishop Friðrekr and Þorvaldr Koðránsson travelled abroad.

When Bjarni Herjólfsson sets out on the trip from Iceland to Greenland which takes him within sight of previously unknown lands, the saga reports that *Heiðit var fólk á Grœnlandi í þann tíma* (*GS* ch. 2: 245–6) ('The people of Greenland were still heathen at that time'). When, mortally wounded on a Vínland expedi-

---

16 *Flateyjarbók. En Samling af Norske Konge-sagaer*, I (Christiania, 1860), p. 430. Matthías Þórðarson prints the episode as a footnote in his edition of *GS* (p. 243, n.14).

tion, Þorvaldr Eiríksson names the place where he asks to be buried as *Krossaness* ('Cross Ness'), the saga explains that *Grœnland var þá kristnat* (*GS* ch. 5: 256) ('Greenland was Christianized by then' [p. 61]); and when Þorsteinn Eiríksson sets out to retrieve Þorvaldr's body, *Þá var enn ung kristni á Grœnlandi* (*GS* ch. 6: 257–8) ('Christianity was then in its infancy in Greenland'). Eiríkr's daughter, Freydís, and her husband, Þorvarðr, are said to have lived at Garðar, *þar sem nú er byskupsstóll* (*GS* ch. 2: 245) ('where the bishopric is now').

The ascendancy of the new religion over the old is variously signalled in *Grœnlendinga saga*. Instead, for example, of a talismanic action like the carving and burning of 'surf runes' (*brimrúnar*) into the oars of the ship, as prescribed by the eddic poem *Sigrdrífumál*,[17] a Christian prayer ensures divine protection during Herjólfr Barðarson's voyage from Iceland to Greenland (*GS* ch. 2: 245).[18] Having acceded to Leifr's request, because of his reputed *heill* ('luck'), an innate quality signifying 'the conjunction of legitimation and the opportunity to appropriate land',[19] to lead an exploratory expedition to the lands sighted by Bjarni Herjólfsson, Eiríkr sustains a leg injury when his horse stumbles on the way to the ship, and he declines to make the trip (*GS* ch. 3: 249). Whereas Eiríkr construes the accident simply as a confirmation of his own opinion that he is getting too old for the rigours of travel, the incident can be interpreted as a signal that the pagan *heill* which attended his settlement in Greenland has weakened.[20] Christian Leifr Eiríksson, by contrast, is endowed with a form of luck free of pagan associations when he gains the epithet *inn heppni* ('the lucky') after rescuing fifteen people stranded on a reef off Greenland (*GS* ch. 4: 254; *ES* ch. 5: 415) on his return from the new lands. Þorsteinn svartr ('the Black'), who extends hospitality to Guðríðr and her second husband, Þorsteinn Eiríksson, on their unsuccessful trip to Vínland, indirectly indicates that his prospective guests are Christian, whereas he is not, and that this difference in faith may be a potential source of tension. At the same time, however, Þorsteinn acknowledges the superiority of the new religion: *annan sið hefi ek ok en þér hafið, ok ætla ek þann þó betra, er þér hafið* (*GS* ch. 6: 258) ('I have a faith

17 See Margaret Clunies Ross, 'Land-Taking and Text-Making', in Sylvia Tomasch and Sealy Gilles, eds, *Text and Territory. Geographical Imagination in the European Middle Ages* (Philadelphia, 1998), pp. 165–8.

18 For a discussion of this fragmentary poem, see Jakob Benediktsson, '*Hafgerðingadrápa*', in *Speculum Norroenum. Norse Studies in Memory of Gabriel Turville-Petre*, ed. Ursula Dronke *et al.* (Odense, 1981), pp. 27–32.

19 Clunies Ross, 'Land-Taking and Text-Making', p. 181.

20 In the account of the accident which prevents Eiríkr's joining the proposed exploratory expedition west of Greenland in *ES*, Eiríkr attributes the fall from his horse to his hiding of a chest filled with gold and silver (ch. 5: 416). This cryptic reading of the incident may be either an implicit acknowledgment of the merits of Christian teaching about greed, as Erik Wahlgren suggests ('Fact and Fancy in the Vinland Sagas', p. 67), or of the folly of Óðinn's law that wealth should be buried in the ground for use in Valhalla. For a discussion of this law here and other instances of the concealing of money in Icelandic narrative, see Matthías Þórðarson, 'Um dauða Skalla-Gríms og hversu hann var heygður (Egils-Saga, LVIII. Kap.)', *Festskrift til Finnur Jónsson* (Copenhagen, 1928), pp. 109–12.

other than the one you have, but I think that the one you have is better'). On the other hand, for all but the last chapter of *Eiríks saga rauða*, paganism and Christianity run on parallel or actively antithetical courses. Eiríkr, who according to *Grænlendinga saga* (ch. 4) died before the conversion,[21] becomes the focus of Christian–pagan opposition. Eiríkr's recalcitrant paganism has a deleterious effect on his personal alliances. It precipitates a cooling of his friendship with Þorgils in *Flóamanna saga* and, in *Eiríks saga rauða*, estrangement from his wife, Þjóðhildr.

The ritualistic side of pagan and Christian religious observance is foregrounded throughout *Eiríks saga rauða*, the importance of maintaining ceremonial proprieties in the practice of pagan prophecy and Christian burial becoming central issues. When anxiety over a famine in Greenland prompts an invitation to a seeress, Þorbjǫrg, to visit the home of Þorkell of Herjólfsnes (*ES* ch. 4), details of Þorbjǫrg's dress, preparations for her accommodation, reception, diet and the performance of the prophecy itself are the object of extended narratorial attention. The hostly concern of Þorkell and the deference of his guests to Þorbjǫrg underline the importance of proper performance to the success of the ritual.

Guðríðr's father, Þorbjǫrn Vífilsson, refuses to be present in the house while such *heiðni* ('heathenism') is in progress, but Guðríðr overcomes her Christian scruples and becomes a reluctant participant in this *seiðr* ('witchcraft'), because she is the only woman present who knows the prescribed incantations, *varðlokur* ('warlock songs'), which she has learned in Iceland from her foster-mother. Duly supplied with the prerequisites for the ceremony and assisted by Guðríðr's beautiful singing,

> Kvað Guðríðr þá kvæðit svá fagrt ok vel, at engi þóttisk fyrr heyrt hafa með fegri raust kveðit, sá er þar var. Spákona þakkar henni kvæðit; hon sagði margar náttúrur 'higat [sic] <hafa> at sótt ok þótti fagrt at heyra þat er kveðit var, er áðr vildi frá oss snúask ok oss øngva hlýðni veita. En mér eru nú margir þeir hlutir auðsýnir er áðr var bæði ek ok aðrir duldir.' (*ES* ch. 4: 413)

> Gudrid then sang the song so beautifully and well that no one thought that he had heard it delivered with a fairer voice. The seeress thanked her for the song. She said that many spirits, 'who previously wished to turn away from us and give us no obedience, have come hither and found it sweet to hear that which has been sung. And now many of those things which were previously concealed from both me and others are now clear to me'.

Þorbjǫrg makes a double prediction. The famine will end and Guðríðr will enjoy a distinguished future, in the course of which she will found a glittering family line back in Iceland:

---

21 Elsewhere in *Óláfs saga Tryggvasonar in mesta* it is said that he was *skirðr*, along with the rest of the Greenland populace. See Ólafur Halldórsson, ed., *Óláfs saga Tryggvasonar en mesta*, Editiones Arnamagnæanæ, Series A (Copenhagen, 1961), II, ch. 231: 200. (The manuscript used as the basis of this edition is AM 61 fol.)

vegar þínir liggja út til Íslands, ok mun þar koma frá þér ættbogi bæði mikill ok góðr, ok yfir þínum ættkvíslum mun skína bjartr geisli.   (*ES* ch. 4: 413)

your paths lead to Iceland; and there a lineage both great and good will descend from you, and over your family line will shine a bright light.[22]

In the *Hauksbók* text of *Eiríks saga rauða* Þorbjǫrg states that the radiance of Guðríðr's descendants will exceed her own powers of vision (p. 208), an acknowledgment which, as Margaret Clunies Ross puts it, makes 'the female functionary of the old religion . . . concede her Christian successor's greater glory (at least as it will be realized in the future) and to acknowledge graciously her own lesser powers in the face of the new religion which is to come, with its brighter spiritual radiance'.[23]

In a contrasting parallel to this scene two chapters later, Guðríðr serves once again both as the subject of an impressive prediction about her future and as linchpin in the consummation of a ritual in which singing is crucial. This time the ceremonial concern is the proper conduct of Christian burial. When her recently deceased husband, Þorsteinn Eiríksson, makes a request to speak to her, Guðríðr is advised to cross herself and pray, but she responds instead with a declaration of faith in God and calmly listens to the words of the dead man. Þorsteinn predicts that she will have a great destiny (*forlǫg mikil* [*ES* ch. 6: 420]), but his main reason for summoning her to this post-mortem dialogue is to deliver a lecture on the blessedness of those who observe the Christian faith properly and the failure of many in Greenland to do so, particularly in the matter of funeral rites. These, he says, are being carried out without the necessary *yfirsöngr* ('singing', 'service'):

Nú . . . mælti . . . at þeir menn væri sælir, er trúna heldu vel ok henni fylgði miskunn, ok hjálp ok sagði þó at margir heldi hana illa. – 'Er þatt engi háttr, sem hér hefir verit á Grœnlandi síðan kristni kom hér, at setja menn niðr í óvígða mold við litla yfirsǫngva.'   (*ES* ch. 6: 419)

Now . . . he said . . . that those men who held the faith which was attended by grace and salvation were blessed, but he then said that many observed it poorly. 'It

---

22 Dag Strömback, *Sejd. Textstudier i nordisk religionshistoria* (Lund, 1935, pp. 55–60) and Jón Jóhannesson, 'The Date of the Composition of the Saga of the Greenlanders' (pp. 58–9), both consider that the Þorbjǫrg episode is likely to be the product of authorial invention. On the other hand, Oddr Snorrason's *Saga Óláfs Tryggvasonar*, written in Latin in the late twelfth century but preserved only in Icelandic translation, may have provided a model for Þorbjǫrg in the figure of the queen-mother of Garðaríki (Novgorod), a *spákona*, who makes an annual yuletide prophecy. One year, she prophesies greatness for a king's son, recently born in Norway, who will become an outstanding man and glorious chieftain. Like Guðríðr Þorbjarnardóttir's progeny, this prince – the future Óláfr Tryggvason – will shine with greatness (*oc mun hann konungr vera oc skina með mikilli birti*), strengthen the kingdom of Garðaríki, and then, like Guðríðr herself, return to his own land. See Finnur Jónsson, ed., *Saga Óláfs Tryggvasonar af Oddr Snorrason munk* (Copenhagen, 1932), ch. 6, 21: 7 (the reference is to AM 310).
23 Margaret Clunies Ross, *Prolonged Echoes. Old Norse myths in medieval Northern society*, II (Odense, 1998), p. 172.

is not good custom, as has been practised here in Iceland since Christianity came here, to inter people in unconsecrated ground, with little in the way of funeral rites.'

The specific impropriety which agitates Þorsteinn, and which is explicated in a rare instance of authorial intrusion, is the Greenlanders' reported habit of burying the dead in unconsecrated ground. Their unorthodox custom, explains the narrator, is to mark the burial site with a stake driven into the ground and to postpone the funeral rites until the arrival of Christian clerics. Þorsteinn tells Guðríðr that he wants to be buried according to the offices of the Church. With the exception of a man called Garði, who has been blamed for some hauntings and is therefore ineligible for Christian funeral rites, Þorsteinn and others who have died in the outbreak of disease on his farm are duly interred with priestly *yfirsǫngvar*.

In a corresponding scene in *Grœnlendinga saga* the sole reason for the deceased Þorsteinn's desire to speak to Guðríðr is to reveal her glorious future in Iceland; her virtuous second widowhood as pilgrim, church-builder, and nun; and her distinguished descendants:

> En þat er þér at segja, Guðríðr, at þú munt gipt vera íslenzkum manni, ok munu langar vera samfarar ykkrar, ok mart manna mun frá ykkr koma, þroskasamt, bjart ok ágætt, sœtt ok ilmat vel. Munu þit fara af Grœnlandi til Nóregs ok þaðan til Íslands ok gera bú á Íslandi; þar munu þit lengi búa, ok muntu honum lengr lifa. Þú munt útan fara ok ganga suðr ok koma út aptr til Íslands til bús þíns, ok þá mun þar kirkja reist vera, ok muntu þar vera ok taka nunnu-vígslu, ok þar muntu andask.   (*GS* ch. 6: 260)

> But I say this to you, Guðríðr, that you will be married to an Icelandic man, and your voyage of life as a couple will be long, and many a man will descend from the two of you, vigorous, bright and excellent, sweet and fragrant. You two will go from Greenland to Norway and from there to Iceland and make your home in Iceland; there the two of you will dwell for a long time, but you will live longer than he. You will go abroad, on a pilgrimage to Rome and come back to Iceland, to your farm, and then you will have a church built there, and you will stay there and take the veil, and there you will die.

Like *Flóamanna saga*, *Eiríks saga rauða* pits Þórr against Christ in a demonstration of the ineffectiveness of the medium of invocation to the pagan god and the efficacy of Christian prayer. During the first harsh winter of Karlsefni's expedition west of Greenland, Eiríkr's close friend Þórhallr veiðimaðr ('the Hunter'), who is bad-tempered, uncouth, unpopular, and as unresponsive as Eiríkr to Christianity (*Hann hafði lítt við trú blandask síðan hon kom á Grœnland* [*ES* ch. 8: 423]; 'He had had little association with the faith since it had come to Greenland'), invokes Þórr in a ranting, three-day performance:

> fundu þeir Karlsefni ok Bjarni hann Þórhall á hamargnípu einni; hann horfði í lopt upp ok gapði hann bæði augum ok munni ok nǫsum ok klóraði sér ok klýpði sik ok þuldi nǫkkut.   (*ES* ch. 8: 425)

9

Karlsefni and Bjarni found Þórhallr on the peak of a crag; he was looking up at the sky, and he gaped with eyes and mouth and nostrils, and scratched and pinched himself and chanted something.

In the meantime, Karlsefni and his company have been praying to God for food during the first winter of the expedition, but when they eat the meat of the whale which appears in the wake of Þórhallr's incantations, they fall ill. After they discard the poisoned meat and commit themselves to God's mercy, the weather improves and they make an abundant catch of fish. Þórhallr suffers a grim end as a slave in Ireland, a fate which, as Richard Perkins suggests, seems 'more contrived to demonstrate how the heathen gods were powerless to help their devotees than to represent any sort of historical truth'.[24]

Despite the more strident nature of Christianity in *Eiríks saga rauða*, there is no resolution or rapprochement between the practice of the old faith and the new. Pagan Þorbjǫrg's prophecy about Guðríðr's glorious future in *Eiríks saga rauða* is as valid as that of the apparent convert, Þorsteinn Eiríksson. Eiríkr is apparently permanently estranged from Þjóðhildr. Contrastingly in *Grænlendinga saga*, the religious tensions which are played out in *Eiríks saga rauða* in competitive rituals of worship – prayer versus incantation; priestly rite versus necromancy – are quietly dispelled by the unreserved acknowledgment of the superiority of Christianity. *Grænlendinga saga* illustrates the peaceful displacement or modification of pagan by Christian custom, whereas *Eiríks saga rauða* keeps the two in competition with each other from beginning to end.

'Landnám' ('land-taking') west of Iceland

Although voyages of discovery and settlement, or attempted settlement, occupy the bulk of the narrative in both sagas, they contain little in the way of the traditions of *landnám*. As we have it, the account common to *Landnámabók*, *Grænlendinga saga*, and *Eiríks saga rauða* of Eiríkr rauði's settlement of Greenland is a compressed affair, and despite the reported ambition in *Grænlendinga saga* of Þorfinnr Karlsefni's expedition to establish a permanent settlement in Vínland (*þeir ætluðu at byggja landit, ef þeir mætti þat*; 'they intended to settle the land, if they could' (*GS* ch. 7: 261), the goal is never achieved. The abortive process of *landnám* west of Greenland further differs from the successful colonization of Iceland and Greenland in that it entails confrontation with an indigenous population. In *Grænlendinga saga* and *Eiríks saga rauða* this engagement with the ethnic Other follows a pattern regularly repeated in post-Columbian European discovery narrative.

---

24 'The Furðustrandir of *Eiríks saga rauða*', *Mediaeval Scandinavia* 9 (1976), 56. In *GS*, by contrast, there is no suggestion that either Þórr or God is directly responsible for the beaching of a large whale which provides Karlsefni and his company with good supplies of food after their arrival in Vínland (ch. 7).

As recorded in Icelandic tradition, the appropriation of land in the settlement period (AD 870–930) followed a set of actions intended to secure the direction and sanction of the gods. According to *Landnámbók* and a number of *Íslendingasögur*, sometimes the occupation of a permanent dwelling place does not take place until the high-seat pillars (*ǫndugissúlur*), brought by the settler from Norway and thrown overboard off the coast of Iceland, are retrieved from their divinely directed site.[25] Only at this point can the settler *nema land* ('take land') or *helga sér land* ('sanction land for himself'). Another supernatural element in the *landnám* process is the *landvættir* ('land-beings'), anthropomorphic beings thought to live in cliffs and mountains, which, although invisible, could be seen by people with second sight. Credited in *Landnámabok* and some *Íslendingasögur* with the capacity to protect lands and their human inhabitants from external aggressors, the *landvættir* were creatures not to be antagonized or unsettled, lest they turn against the settlers and evict them.[26]

The account of the settlement of Greenland in *Grænlendinga saga* (ch. 1), *Eiríks saga rauða* (ch. 2), and *Landnámabók* (i, 130–2) is devoid of invocation to supernatural direction and ritualistic gesture. With the exception of the standard formula to denote land-taking with supernatural authorization, *helga sér land* ('to sanction land for oneself'),[27] the same lexis of territorial establishment is used of Greenland as of Iceland elsewhere in *Landnámabók*: *byggja* ('settle'), *taka sér bústað* ('make a home for oneself'), *nema land* ('take land'). In *Eiríks saga rauða* Eiríkr first *tók sér þar bústað* in Eiríksfjǫrðr (*ES* ch. 2: 406); then he set out to *byggja landit* ('settle the land'). After Eiríkr's expedition to *byggja landit* in *Grænlendinga saga*, he *bjó í Brattahlíð í Eiríksfjǫrði* (*ES* ch. 1: 242). The first chapter of *Grænlendinga saga* ends with a list of nine men who travelled to Greenland with Eiríkr and who *námu land* there; the fjords or dales in which seven of them take up residence are named after them (Herjólfr/Herjólfsfjǫrðr; Ketill/Ketilsfjǫrðr; Hrafn/Hrafnsfjǫrðr; Sǫlvi/Sǫlvadal; Einar/Einarsfjǫrðr; Hafgrímr/Hafgrímsfjǫrðr; Arnlaugr/Arnlaugsfjǫrðr).

After Eiríkr's Greenland *landnám*, *Grænlendinga saga* and *Eiríks saga rauða* take separate paths in reporting voyages of discovery and attempted settlement further west. Whereas in *Eiríks saga rauða* the discovery of Vínland is briefly recounted as the result of Leifr's evangelizing mission to Greenland, in *Grænlendinga saga* it is the outcome of the observance of filial custom. Bjarni Herjólfsson, an Icelander in the habit of spending alternate winters in Norway and with his father in Iceland, arrives in Iceland one year to discover that Herjólfr has emigrated to Greenland. Bjarni decides to maintain his custom (*siðvenja* [*GS*

25 See Margaret Clunies Ross, 'Land-Taking and Text-Making', pp. 170–2; *idem*, 'Textual Territory: The Regional and Genealogical Dynamic of Medieval Icelandic Literary Production', *New Medieval Literatures* 1 (1997), 9–30.

26 See Bo Almqvist, *Norrön Niddiktning. Traditionshistoriska studier i versmagi*, I (Stockholm and Uppsala, 1965), pp. 148–50 (English summary, pp. 227–8); Clunies Ross, 'Land-Taking and Text-Making', pp. 162–3, 168–71, 177–9.

27 Clunies Ross, 'Land-Taking and Text-Making', p. 181.

ch. 2: 245]) by joining him. Blown off course on the unfamiliar seas between Iceland and Greenland, Bjarni sights but makes no gesture towards cognitive or material possession of three new lands. These preliminary acts of appropriation are left to Leifr, who, on a voyage of discovery and exploration prompted by Bjarni's report, names the new lands after their topographical features. He sees Bjarni's last land first and names it *Helluland* ('slab land'); Leifr's second landfall (*GS* ch. 3: 250), which, like Bjarni's, is *slétt ok skógi vaxit* ('flat and wooded') but not explicitly stated to have been the land which Bjarni saw, he names *Markland* ('forest land'). Leifr reaches a third land south of Markland, which the saga also fails to identify with any of Bjarni's sightings. The naming of this new land is postponed until it has been further explored. Not until Leifr is on the point of departure the following spring does he name it *Vínland*.

Although Leifr winters in Vínland in *Grænlendinga saga*, his only gesture towards proprietorship is the building of some *buðir* (*GS* ch. 3: 251), temporary stone and turf dwellings. When he and his thirty-five strong company decide to stay for the winter, they build *hús mikil* (*GS* ch. 3: 251) ('large houses'), but at no time is there an expressed intention to *taka bustað*. Although not so named by Leifr, the site of these dwellings is referred to in connection with the subsequent voyages of Þorvaldr and Karlsefni as *Leifsbúðir*. Leifr's refusal to give, although he says that he is prepared to lend, his Vínland houses to Karlsefni (*GS* ch. 7: 261) and Freydís (*GS* ch. 8: 264), nevertheless suggests that at some future time he proposes to make formal *landnám* there. The company of sixty men and five women who accompany Karlsefni to Vínland are said to intend to settle the land (*byggja landit* [*GS* ch. 7: 261]), but they engage neither in spoken nor performed rituals of *landnám*. By the beginning of their second summer at *Leifsbúðir*, however, Leifr's houses are denoted by the term used in Old Icelandic of permanent dwellings: *bær* (*GS* ch. 7: 262).

Leifr himself takes no active part in the process of naming in *Eiríks saga rauða*, and the saga implies that he spent no more time there than it took to gather evidence of his find. Off course on his missionary voyage from Norway to Greenland, he comes, it is briefly reported, upon lands of whose existence he has had no previous inkling (*ES* ch. 5: 415). Not until there is talk in Greenland of a westward expedition in the winter following Leifr's discovery does the saga refer to the land which Karlsefni and Snorri Þorbrandsson now determine to find as *Vínland*,

> léku miklar umrœður um vetrinn í Brattahlíð at þeir Karlsefni ok Snorri ætluðu at leita Vínlands. (*ES*, ch. 8: 422)

> There were great discussions during the winter at Brattahlíð concerning Karlsefni and Snorri's intention to go in search of Vinland. (p. 93)

and, in *Hauksbók* (p. 221), as *Vínland it góða* ('Vínland the Good'). It is Karlsefni's company which names Helluland, Markland, and other locations after their fauna (*Bjarney* 'Bear Isle'), tidology (*Hóp*, 'Tidal Lake', *Straumsey*, 'Stream Island', *Straumsfjǫrðr*, Stream Fjord'), detritus from previous voyages (*Kjalar-

ness, 'Keel Ness'); and, in the case of a long stretch of sandy coastline south of Markland which they call *Furðustrandir* ('Marvel Strands'), notable features of the landscape.

Although in *Eiríks saga rauða* Karlsefni spends three years in the lands west of Greenland with a company of 160 people – more than twice as many as on any other expedition in either of the Vínland sagas – the narrative contains no discourse of *landnám*. There is no mention of the construction of dwellings during the winter which he and his company spend at Straumsfjǫrðr, although it said they they *bjǫggusk* (*ES* ch. 8: 424) there; and, by the time Karlsefni decides to abandon the Vínland enterprise, the only buildings in this new territory are temporary: *búðir* (ch. 10: 428, 430) and *skálir* (huts') (ch. 10: 428).

Leifr's brother, Þorvaldr, leader of the second Vínland voyage in *Grænlendinga saga*, is the only figure in either saga who directly expresses a desire for *landnám* west of Greenland. Enacting a variation on such rituals of settlement as the claiming of land where the high-seat pillars are washed ashore, he sets up the storm-damaged keel of his ship on a headland and names it *Kjalarness* (*GS* ch. 5: 255). Then, having admired the beauty of a wooded promontory further along the coast, he expresses the verbal formula of intended *landnám*: *hér vilda ek bœ minn reisa* (*ibid.*). Mortally wounded shortly thereafter, Þorvaldr asks to be returned to his proposed homesite and buried there. At this point *landnám* ritual turns into Christian rite. Þorvaldr asks that the place be named *Krossaness* and, in place of the poles which sometimes mark out land claims in Icelandic *landnám* narrative,[28] requests that crosses be placed at his head and feet. Þorvaldr's proposed *bœr* thus becomes his Christian grave.[29] The significance of this modification of *landnám* ritual and Þorvaldr's dying quip that he intended to settle there only for a time (*þar búa á um stund* (*GS* ch. 5: 256) is underlined by its juxtaposition to a narratorial statement that Greenland had by then converted to Christianity.

One gesture which might be read as a formal reversal of *landnám* ritual in the closing chapter of *Grænlendinga saga* is Karlsefni's preparedness on his return to Norway to sell his ship's Vínland-made *húsasnotra*, a rare term, which Magnússon and Pálsson translate as 'carved gable-head',[30] for half a mark of gold (*GS* ch. 9). Karlsefni's conscious disengagement from the lands west of Greenland is further underlined by his statement that he does not know the type of wood from which the *húsasnotra* has been fashioned (the saga-writer says that it was *mǫsurr*, 'maple'). As Sayers observes, this action 'seems a clear release by Karlsefni of his New World attachment'.[31] The incident which triggered Eiríkr

---

28 See, for example, *Landnámabók* ii, 230–1; Clunies Ross, 'Land-Taking and Text-Making', p. 178.

29 On other Christian modifications of pagan practice in the ritual of *landnám*, see the introduction to Pálsson and Edwards, trans., *The Book of Settlements*, pp. 9–11.

30 Magnus Magnusson and Hermann Pálsson, trans., *The Vinland Sagas. The Norse Discovery of America* (Harmondsworth, 1965), p. 71. For a comprehensive discussion of the term, see Reeves, *The Finding of Wineland the Good*, p. 161.

31 'Vinland, the Irish', p. 10.

rauði's outlawry from Iceland offers something of a reverse parallel to this episode: a certain Þorgestr refuses to return the *setstokkir*, movable planks used to divide a Norse dwelling into different sections and considered of great value, which he has borrowed from Eiríkr. In *Eiríks saga rauða* and *Landnámabók*, the feud generated by this act of expropriation ends in the deaths of two of Þorgestr's son and a number of other men. *Grænlendinga saga* thus begins and ends with incidents which concern, in the first instance, the involuntary and, in the second, voluntary surrender of significant tokens of property ownership.

Cross-cultural encounters

Iceland and Greenland were to all intents and purposes *terra nullius* ('no one's land')[32] for their Scandinavian settlers. What were presumably a small number of Irish hermits are said in *Íslendingabók* to have vacated Iceland without a struggle upon the arrival of the Norsemen:

> váru hér menn kristnir . . . en þeir fóru síðan á braut, af því at þeir vildu eigi vera hér við heiðna menn. (*Íslendingabók*, p. 5; cf. *Landnámabók*, i, 31–2)

> There were Christian men here . . . but they then went away, because they did not wish to be here with heathen men.

There is no indication before the middle of the twelfth century[33] of the active presence of the natives of Greenland in either of the two Norse settlements, Ostrbyggð (Eastern Settlement) and Vestrbyggð (Western Settlement), although *Íslendingabók* reports that evidence was found there of boats and tools identical to those used by the people who had first settled Vínland. These people, says Ari Þorgilsson, are known to the Greenlanders as *Skrælingar* (*þess konar . . . es Vínland hefir byggt ok Grænlendingar kalla Skrælinga* [pp. 13–14]' 'that people . . . who had settled Vínland and whom the Greenlanders call Skrælings'). For Leifr the lands west of Greenland remain Edenic, but, for his successors, a land that initially appears to be so is gradually revealed to have prior occupants. After Þorvaldr Eiríksson has spent a winter in *Leifsbúðir* and explored the surrounding territory in *Grænlendinga saga*, he finds what appears to be a wooden granary (*kornhjálm af tre*, GS ch. 5: 255).[34] Otherwise his

---

32 The term *terra nullius* is widely used in Australia with reference to the nineteenth-century British claim that the Australian Aborigines were not that land's legal possessors. The concept of *terra nullius* was upheld by the Privy Council in 1889. See, for example, Alan Frost, 'New South Wales as *Terra Nullius*: the British Denial of Aboriginal Land Rights', *Historical Studies* 19 (1981), 513–23; Henry Reynolds, *Dispossession. Black Australians and White Invaders* (London and Sydney, 1989), pp. 67–8.

33 The *Historia Norvegiæ* refers to *homunciones* 'small people', unfamiliar with the use of iron, found in northern Greenland, who are called Skrælings (*Monumenta Historia Norvegie*, ed. Gustav Storm [Kristiania, 1880] p. 76).

34 See Reeves, *The Finding of Wineland the Good*, p. 185.

company *fundu hvergi manna vistir né dýra* (*GS* ch. 5: 255) ('found traces neither of man nor beast'). The first hint in *Eiríks saga rauða* that the lands west of Greenland have native populations comes after the first winter which Karlsefni's expedition spends in Straumsfjǫrðr.

Whatever the historical accuracy of the Vínland sagas, and whether or not their content derives from contemporary report or other sources,[35] *Grænlendinga saga* and *Eiríks saga rauða* provide the first written account of cultural contact, in Urs Bitterli's sense, of that 'initial, short-lived or intermittent encounter between a group of Europeans and members of a non-European culture'.[36] Both sagas prefigure the European habit of describing Native Americans in terms of their failure to conform to Old World ideals of beauty and custom[37] and follow the pattern of eyewitness reports of cross-cultural contact by later New World explorers: naming, contact, exchange, and the imposition of European values upon native peoples in terms of language, religion, and social practice.[38] The ignorance of technology on the part of the indigenes noted in *Grænlendinga saga* (ch. 7) and *Eiríks saga rauða* (ch. 11) is typical of such accounts. Just as the Spaniards' horses aroused terror among the natives of Central and South America,[39] so Karlsefni's roaring bull frightens the *skrælingar* (*GS* ch. 7; *ES* ch. 11).

Eiríks saga rauða treats these cross-cultural encounters in more ethnographic detail than *Grænlendinga saga*. Whereas *Grænlendinga saga* says nothing specific about their physical appearance, *Eiríks saga rauða* contains a description of the people encountered by the Norsemen which, in certain details of facial features and customs, is paralleled by accounts of the Beothuk of Newfoundland and the Micmac of Nova Scotia, New Brunswick, and Prince Edward Island.[40] According to this saga they are 'small' (*smáir*)[41] and 'ill-favoured' (*illiligir*), with 'unattractive hair' (*illt hár*), large eyes and broad cheekbones.[42] Lescarbot

---

35 Erik Wahlgren, for example, suggests that the encounters with the natives may draw upon 'three or four generations of intermittent or continual contact with the skrælings' ('Fact and Fancy', pp. 69–70).

36 Urs Bitterli, trans. Ritchie Robertson, *Cultures in Conflict. Encounters Between European and Non-European Cultures, 1492–1800* (Oxford, 1993), p. 20.

37 See, for example, Robert Berkhofer, *White Man's Indian. Images of the American Indian from Columbus to the Present* (New York, 1978), p. 23.

38 As demonstrated by Stephen Greenblatt in *Marvelous Possessions. The Wonder of the New World* (Oxford, 1991).

39 Bitterli, *Cultures in Conflict*, p. 24.

40 The case for the Micmacs as the *skrælingar* of *GS* and *ES* was first put by Gustav Storm, 'Studier over Vinlandsreiserne, Vinlands Geografi og Ethnografi', *Aarbøger for Nordisk Oldkyndighed og Historie* (1887), 352–4. For a recent discussion and a survey of scholarship, see Robert McGhee, 'Contact Between Native North Americans and the Medieval Norse: A Review of the Evidence', *American Antiquity* 49 (1984), 8, and the references there.

41 *Svartir* ('dark') according to the *Hauksbók* text (p. 227).

42 'Þeir váru smáir menn ok illiligir, ok illt hǫfðu þeir hár á hǫfði; eygðir váru þeir mjǫk ok breiðir í kinnum' (*ES* ch. 10: 428); ('They were small and ugly men, and they had unattractive hair on their heads; they were large of eye and broad of cheek').

observed that the Micmac were large-eyed;[43] and De Laet characterized the inhabitants of Newfoundland thus: 'The height of the body is medium, the hair black, the face, broad, the nose flat, and the eyes large'.[44] *Grœnlendinga saga*, on the other hand, lacks such physiognomic specificity and any indication that the indigenes look different from the Norsemen. All that it reports of the native Vínlanders' appearance is Karlsefni's assumption that a man who is *mikill ok vænn* (*GS* ch. 7: 263) ('tall and good-looking') must be their leader. In one particular detail *Eiríks saga rauða* has a more plausible scenario than *Grœnlendinga saga*: since there were no domesticated mammals in North America, the native Vínlanders' reported addiction in the latter saga to milk, for which they exchange a vast array of skins (*grávara ok safali ok alls konar skinnavara* [*GS* ch. 7: 261]; 'grey furs and sables and skins of all kinds'), must be fictional. *Eiríks saga rauða*, by contrast, has the *skrælingar* trade furs for progressively diminishing pieces of red cloth. The noisy sticks which salute Karlsefni and his company

> ok var veift trjánum . . . ok lét því líkast í sem í hálmþustum ok fór sólarsinnis.
>
> (*ES* ch. 11: 428)

> wood was waved . . . and it sounded just like flails, and it went sunwise.

may have been bull-roarers;[45] and the food described as *dýramerg dreyra blandinn* (*ES* ch. 11: 430) ('animal marrow mixed with blood') is almost certainly pemmican.[46]

The first recorded encounter between Europeans and a people who seem more likely to have been Amerindian than Inuit does not take place until the third reconnaissance trip, led by Þorvaldr Eiríksson, in *Grœnlendinga saga*. The unprovoked violence which the Norsemen inflict upon the natives on this occasion is reminiscent of, for example, Torres's report of his first contact in 1606 with the natives of New Guinea: 'we saluted them with our arquebuses and

---

43 *Histoire de la nouvelle France* (Paris, 1618), p. 804 (cited Storm, 'Studier over Vinlandsreiserne', p. 352).

44 *Novus Orbis* (1633) (cited in Hodge, ed., *Handbook of American Indians*, I, 142). Verrazzano, the first eyewitness chronicler of the natives of the east coast of North America, notes of the inhabitants encountered on the southernmost part of his voyage that: 'They are dark in color, not unlike the Ethiopians, with thick black hair . . . they are well proportioned, of medium height, a little taller than we are. They have broad chests, strong arms, and the legs and other parts of the body are well composed they tend to be rather broad in the face . . . They have big black eyes and an attentive open look' (Susan Tarrow, 'Translation of the Cellère Codex', in Lawrence C. Wroth, *The Voyages of Giovanni da Verrazzano 1524–1528* [New Haven and London, 1970], p. 134).

45 'This instrument consists of a rectangular slat of wood from six inches to two feet long and from a half an inch to two inches thick. The instrument has a cord attached to one end. The cord is held at one end and the wooden part is twirled above the head. The resulting sound is supposed to represent wind, thunder and lightning.' John L. Stoutenburgh, Jr., *Dictionary of the American Indian* (New York, 1960), p. 318.

46 'A food product usually made of deer meat dried in the sun or over a slow fire. The dried meat was pounded, and one part of melted fat mixed in' (Stoutenburgh, *Dictionary of the American Indian*, p. 41).

killed some'.[47] Having spent two winters at *Leifsbúðir* without encountering evidence of human or animal occupation, Þorvaldr and his company sail north and find nine men sleeping under three 'skin' boats (*húðkeipa* [*GS* ch. 5: 255]),[48] a custom noted by Cartier of the impoverished inhabitants of the Cape Gaspé area.[49] The Norsemen kill eight of them, but the ninth escapes and returns with a hostile force. Þorvaldr sustains a fatal arrow wound in the subsequent skirmish. A similar incident in *Eiríks saga rauða* (ch. 11) is related as a misreading of cultural signs: Karlsefni and his company unhesitatingly impose Norse values of social organization upon the aboriginal population by killing, without provocation, five men – probably on a hunting expedition – whom they find asleep along the coast, on the assumption that such an isolated company must be outlaws.[50]

Rituals of barter govern peaceful interchanges between Norsemen and natives in *Grænlendinga saga* and *Eiríks saga rauða* and preview, as Stephen Greenblatt puts it, '[t]he European dream, endlessly reiterated in the literature of exploration . . . of the grossly unequal gift exchange'.[51] When a large company of *skrælingar*, laden with furs of various kinds, take fright at Karlsefni's bull and seek refuge inside *Leifsbúðir* in *Grænlendinga saga*, the saga's narrator confidently interprets native motives and intentions. The *skrælingar*, he says, seek weapons in exchange for furs, although there is no indication as to how this desire might have been conveyed. Thwarted in this aim, they happily swap their valuables for milk:

> fór þar ór skógi fram mikill flokkr manna . . . Þá tóku Skrælingjar ofan bagga sína ok leystu ok buðu þeim ok vildu vápn helzt fyrir; en Karlsefni bannaði þeim at selja vápnin. Ok nú leitar hann ráðs með þeim hætti, at hann bað konur bera út búnyt at þeim; ok þegar er þeir sá búnyt, þá vildu þeir kaupa þat, en ekki annat. Nú var sú kaupfǫr Skrælinga, at þeir báru sinn varning í brott í mǫgum sínum, en Karlsefni ok fǫrunautar hans hǫfðu eptir bagga þeira ok skinnavǫru.
>
> (*GS* ch. 7: 262)

> a great crowd of men came from the wood . . . then the Skrælings put down their packs and untied them and offered them up, and they most preferred weapons in exchange, but Karlsefni forbade his men to sell arms. But then the idea occurred to him to tell the women to carry out milk to them; and as soon as they saw the milk they wanted to buy that, and nothing else. And the Skræling trading expedition

---

47 Cited Bitterli, *Cultures in Conflict*, p. 22.

48 It has been argued that the 'skin' boats mentioned in *GS* and *ES* indicate that the indigenous people described here were Eskimo, but, although they usually made birchbark canoes, moose hide was also sometimes used by the Micmac. For a survey of scholarship and further references, see Mats G. Larsson, 'The Vinland Sagas and Nova Scotia. A Reappraisal of an Old Theory', *Scandinavian Studies* 64 (1992), 317–18.

49 'Ils n'ont d'autre logis que soubz leurs *dites* barques qu'ilz tournent adans et se couchent sur la terre dessoubz icelles' (*Relations*, p. 115).

50 'þeir mundu gørvir landinu' (*ES*, ch. 11: 430); ('they must have been banished from the land').

51 *Marvelous Possessions*, p. 110.

went thus, that they carried their cargo away in their stomachs, and Karlsefni and his company had the packs and furs they left behind.

George Best reports a similarly unequal exchange during Martin Frobisher's first Arctic voyage in 1576, when the Inuit 'exchanged coates of seales, and beares skinnes, and suche like, with oure men, and received belles, looking-glasses, and other toyes in recompence thereof againe'.[52] In an episode related nearly three centuries later in *Tait's Edinburgh Magazine* (1838) an estimated crowd of some three hundred Chippewa on the southern shore of Lake Superior barter skins for bells, weapons, and trinkets:

> The establishment presented a scene of the utmost confusion, from the arrival of above three hundred Chippewa Indians, who had brought an immense quantity of racoon, beaver, and squirrel, skins, with a few bear and bison hides, which they were eagerly bartering for guns, knives, whisky, bells trinkets, &c. &c. They had also some very beautiful wild horses, of which I got my choice for a knife and two bottles of rum.[53]

The initial barriers to contact in *Grœnlendinga saga* are deliberately physical (*Karlsefni lét verja dyrrnar* [*GS* ch. 7: 262]; 'Karlsefni had the doors barred') and involuntarily linguistic (*Hvárigir skildu annars mál*; 'Neither of them could understand the other's language' [*GS* ch. 7: 262]), a frustration also reported by Columbus, Verrazzano, and Cartier.[54] In *Eiríks saga rauða* the semaphoric initiative remains with the indigenes. Confident, like Columbus, in the universality of European body language, the Norsemen try to interpret the gestures of an alien culture. Their first attempt at cross-cultural semiotics turns out to be more successful than Columbus's orders to his men to dance on the poop deck to persuade the natives of Trinidad to socialize, an action which they interpret as a hostile gesture.[55] Faced one morning with the sight of men in a flotilla, waving noisy sticks in a clockwise motion, Karlsefni asks what this means. His companion is reassuring and suggests a reciprocal display of signs:

52 *The Three Voyages of Martin Frobisher, in search of passage to Cathaia and India by the North-West, A.D. 1576–8*, ed. Richard Collinson (London, 1867), p. 73.

53 'Wild Sports of the Far West; or, a few weeks' adventures among the Hudson's Bay Company's fur traders, in the autumn of 1836', *Tait's Edinburgh Magazine* 5 (1838), 648.

54 Columbus wrote of his Third Voyage that: "Both the Indians and the Spaniards were much grieved that they did not understand one another" (J. M. Cohen, ed. and trans., *Christopher Columbus: The Four Voyages*, London, 1969, p. 214). Verrazzano noted that: 'Due to the lack of [a common] language, we were unable to find out by signs or gestures how much religious faith these people we found possess' (Tarrow, 'Translation of the Cellère Codex', p. 141). Cartier transcribes some words and 'aultres parrolles que n'entendions' (*Relations*, p. 110) in an encounter by sign communication with Amerindians in his voyage of 1534 and uses sign language to ask directions: 'Nous leur demandasmes par signes si c'estoit le chemyn de Hochelaga' (*Relations*, p. 149).

55 Cohen, *Christopher Columbus: The Four Voyages*, p. 210; Greenblatt, *Marvelous Possessions*, pp. 90–1.

Þá mælti Karlsefni: 'Hvat mun þetta tákna?' Snorri svara honum: 'Vera kann at þetta sé friðartákn ok tǫkum skjǫld hvítan ok berum í mót'.   (*ES* ch. 11: 428)

Then Karlsefni said, 'What can this signify?' Snorri answered him: 'It may be that this is a sign of peace, so let us take a white shield and carry it towards them'.

The gesture elicits a gratifyingly peaceable response. The indigenes approach and gaze in wonder (*undruðusk* [*ES* ch. 11: 428]) at the Norsemen, a reaction to Europeans commonly reported on the part of Native Americans in fifteenth- and sixteenth-century discovery narrative.[56] Verrazzano, for example, reports a similar reaction on the part of the natives of Carolina at the sight of Europeans: 'We reassured them with various signs, and some of them came up, showing great delight at seeing us and marveling at our clothes, appearance, and our whiteness'.[57] Similarly, Cartier often speaks of the natives of Canada as making 'signes de joye' when they set eyes on him.

Whereas indigenous peoples are often said in discovery narrative to attribute supernatural powers to Europeans or to perceive them as gods,[58] magical occurrences are primarily the province of the natives in the lands west of Greenland. After they have killed the eight men sleeping under their boats in *Grænlendinga saga*, Þorvaldr and his company are overwhelmed by an unexplained *hǫfga* ('drowsiness'), although an equally mysterious *kall* ('voice') alerts them in time to meet a counter attack (*GS* ch. 5: 256). Later in *Grænlendinga saga* (ch. 7) Guðríðr is confronted by the apparition of a pale, large-eyed woman dressed in black, who calls herself Guðríðr and disappears at the moment when Karlsefni kills a *skræling* who is attempting to steal a weapon. In *Eiríks saga rauða* (ch. 11) two forces simultaneously attack Karlsefni and his company, one from the shore and another, which proves to be illusory, from inland. William Sayers suggests that such 'hallucinatory' experiences, which bear similarities to magically contrived ocular disturbances in other *Íslendingasögur*, may be instances of 'malign native magic'.[59] Baumgartner points to sleep induced by the waters of a magic spring in the *Navigatio Sancti Brendani* as a possible model for the *hǫfga* of *Grænlendinga saga*.[60] But, whatever their ultimate origins, these supernaturally assisted actions can be accommodated to Norse traditions of territorial encounter if they are read as the manifestations of the power of the resident *landvættir*. The unprovoked attack by Þorvaldr's company upon the *skrælingar* in

---

56 Bitterli, *Cultures in Conflict*, pp. 24–5.
57 Tarrow, 'Translation of the Cellère Codex', p. 134.
58 Bitterli, *Cultures in Conflict*, pp. 15–16, 24–6.
59 Sayers, 'Vinland, the Irish', pp. 6, 7.
60 Baumgartner, 'Freydís in Vinland', p. 18. See Carl Selmer, ed., *Navigatio Sancti Brendani Abbatis, from Early Latin Manuscripts* (Notre Dame, 1959), p. 27; J. F. Webb, trans., 'The Voyage of St Brendan', in *Lives of the Saints* (Harmondsworth, 1965), p. 44. Dag Strömback identifies a similarity between the unidentified *kall* and the awakening of King Fróði by a strange voice in *Hrólfs saga kraka*. (See *The Arna-Magnæan Manuscript 557 4to containing inter alia the History of the first Discovery of America*, Corpus Codicum Islandicorum Medii Ævi, vol. 13 [Copenhagen, 1940], p. 38).

Grœnlendinga saga immediately follows his expressed desire to take possession of the land, a combination of word and deed which, in addition to being a direct assault on its human inhabitants, might be seen as a challenge to its spiritual guardians. Although not explicitly said to be endowed with second sight, Guðríðr is said to be an innately wise (*vitr*) woman (*GS* ch. 6: 258). That wisdom and her earlier encounter with a talking corpse may be indications that she has the capacity to see human manifestations of *landvættir*, in the shape of her vanishing Doppelgänger.

In the climactic encounter of *Eiríks saga rauða* a non-illusory force of *skrælingar* attacks the Norsemen with an extraordinary weapon of much discussed but uncertain origin. The device is hoisted and catapulted over their heads:

> Þat sjá þeir Karlsefni ok Snorri at þeir fœrðu upp á stǫngum, Skrælingarnir, knǫtt mikinn [*Hauksbók*: því nær til at jafna sem sauðarvǫmb], ok blán at lit ok fló upp á land yfir liðit ok lét illiliga við þar er niðr kom. (*ES* ch. 11: 429)

> Karlsefni and Snorri saw that the Skrælingar were hoisting up a large ball on a pole [*Hauksbók*: it was almost like a sheep's stomach], dark blue in colour, and it flew up to the shore, over the company, and made a frightful noise when it landed.

It has been postulated that the weapon is a large club, known from ancient Algonquian tradition,[61] although its head appears to be a missile rather than a thickened stick. The association of different ethnicity with the supernatural in Scandinavian tradition might suggest that the device is 'a supernatural artifice rather like Odin's spear, which paralyzes an opposing army with fear when thrown over them'.[62] There may also be resonances here of Norse traditions of aggression involving poles topped by detachable animal heads, which are displayed in order to arouse local *landvættir* to outrage and expel enemies.[63] The most famous example of this form of incitement comes in *Egils saga* (ch. 57: 171–2), when Egill Skallagrímsson raises a *níðstǫng* ('pole of insult') crowned by a horse's head and directed towards the Norwegian king, Eiríkr blóðøx ('Blood-axe'), and the country's *landvættir* to provoke the latter to expel Eiríkr and his queen.[64]

A small act of Christian imperialism completes the European-native encounter in *Eiríks saga rauða*. In Markland, on their journey back to Greenland, Karlsefni and his company meet five *skrælingar*, a 'bearded man' (*einn skeggaðr* [*ES* ch. 12: 233]),[65] two women, and two children. The children are

---

61 See Gwyn Jones, *The North Atlantic Saga*, p. 133 (Jones here cites Henry Schoolcraft, *Indian Tribes of the United States* [Buffalo, 1851], I, 85). For a review of opinion on the subject, see also Ólafur Halldórsson, *Grœnland í miðaldaritum*, p. 373.

62 John Lindow, 'Supernatural Others and Ethnic Others: A Millenium of World View', *Scandinavian Studies* 67 (1995), 13.

63 Clunies Ross, 'Land-Taking and Text-Making', p. 169.

64 See Almqvist, *Norrön Niddiktning*, 89–118 (English summary, pp. 215–21).

65 [S]*keggaðr* is probably to be taken metaphorically as signifying 'adult'. But, if it is meant literally,

captured, taught Icelandic,[66] and baptized in an act which Greenblatt, writing of Columbus and later European explorers, calls 'kidnapping language'[67] for the purpose of imposing religion. As Columbus expressed it: 'there in Castile, learning the language, they will much more readily receive baptism and secure the welfare of their souls'.[68] Verrazzano reports a similar encounter with an old woman, a teenage girl, and five children, in which the male child is abducted and taken back to France: 'We took the boy from the old woman to carry back to France'.[69] Cartier collected two young male natives as human souvenirs of his first voyage and used them as guides and interpreters on his second.[70]

But the colonial paradigm is not fulfilled, the process of *landnám* is abandoned, and the lands west of Greenland elude appropriation. Never formally taken in the first place, all future claim to Vínland is symbolically surrendered by Karlsefni at the conclusion of *Grœnlendinga saga*; Leifr alone asserts any material form of proprietorship, in the tenuous form of *Leifsbúðir*. In *Eiríks saga rauða* Vínland itself remains solely the property of Leifr's gaze. No one else in this saga take definitive cognitive possession, or, as it happens, ever gets the opportunity to lay any other sort of claim to it. By the conclusion of both narratives, the discovery, naming, and exploration of the lands west of Greenland has not positioned them within the Norse sphere of trade, colonization, or influence, and Greenland itself is abandoned for Iceland by Karlsefni and Guðríðr.

How the West was Lost: exemplum and romance

The historical reasons for the abandonment of the Vínland enterprise early in the eleventh century are not in dispute. The Norsemen had the seamanship but not the ships to transport supplies and settlers in the quantities necessary for

---

it is perhaps a mark of fiction. Many writers note the beardlessness of the natives of America, although a German woodcut (c.1505), based on a report of Vespucci and 'usually claimed to be the first picture showing Native Americans (the Tupinambas of coastal Brazil) in some ethnographic detail' gives its subjects beards (Berkhofer, *The White Man's Indian*, p. 139, plate 2). Alvarez Chanca, a member of Columbus's second expedition, notes that the Caribbean natives are 'completely beardless' (Antonello Gerbi, trans. Jeremy Moyle, *Nature in the New World. From Christopher Columbus to Gonzalo Fernández de Oviedo* [Pittsburgh, 1985], p. 25; cf. p. 37).

66 Interestingly, later explorers comment on the facility of the natives of the New World in learning English and Spanish. See Greenblatt, *Marvelous Possessions*, pp. 105, 108. On language as an instrument of establishing cultural power, see Pagden, *European Encounters with the New World*, pp. 118–19.

67 'From the very first day, in 1492, the principal means chosen by the Europeans to establish linguistic contact was kidnapping' (Greenblatt, *Marvelous Possessions*, p. 106). As Greenblatt puts it: 'Columbus's ultimate hope is that Spanish language will, as it were, carry with it Spanish religion: "there in Castile, learning the language, they will much more readily receive baptism and secure the welfare of their souls" (Ii.88)' (*Marvelous Possessions*, p. 107).

68 Cited Greenblatt, *Marvelous Possessions*, p. 107.

69 Tarrow, 'Translation of the Cellère Codex', p. 136.

70 Bideaux, *Relations*, pp. 117, 137; Cook, *Voyages*, pp. 27, 49.

colonization.[71] The Vínland sagas, however, tell it from different perspectives. On the face of it, in both sagas continuing opposition from the native inhabitants of the lands west of Greenland drives away the would-be settlers. In *Grœnlendinga saga* the implication is that Þorfinnr Karlsefni is tired of being harassed and withdraws. After three years of searching for Leifr's idyllic Vínland in *Eiríks saga rauða*, Karlsefni concedes that native hostility will forever dog him and make permanent settlement an impossibility:

> þótt þar væri landskostir góðir, at þar mundi jafnan ófriðr ok ótti á liggja af þeim er fyrir bjuggu. (*ES* ch. 11: 430)

> although there was choice land there, there would always be hostility and danger from those who had previously settled it to oppress them.

For a late twentieth-century reader in Australia, where acknowledgment of aboriginal proprietorship prior to white settlement is the subject of vigorous public debate, the reference to those *er fyrir bjuggu* ('who [had] previously settled') is striking. Whereas Ari Þorgilsson says in *Íslendingabók* that *menn Kristnir* ('Christian men') – probably Irish hermits – simply 'were' (*váru*) in Iceland when the Scandinavians arrived, he refers to the indigenous people of Vínland as having 'settled' or 'inhabited' (*byggt*) that land:

> Þá váru hér menn kristnir . . . þar hafði þess konar þjóð farit, es Vínland hefir byggt ok Grœnlendingar kalla Skrælinga. (*Íslendingabók* ch. 1: 5; ch. 6: 13–14)

> There were Christian men here . . . that kind of people, who had settled Vínland and whom the Greenlanders call *skrælingar*, had been there.

Ari's lexical distinction between the landed status of the presumably transient Christians of pre-Norse Iceland and the natives of Greenland and Vínland reinforces the impression that the author of *Eiríks saga rauða* is giving linguistic validation to a prior right of claim by the *skrælingar* to the lands west of Greenland.

Implicitly in *Eiríks saga rauða* and explicitly in *Grœnlendinga saga*, internal ructions further inhibit the feasibility of settlement. No social structures are established, even in microcosm, to support or regulate the embryonic society west of Greenland. Despite the substantial number of people on Karlsefni's three-year expedition in *Eiríks saga rauða*, there is no indication that, apart from Guðríðr and Karlsefni, and Freydís and Þorvarðr, they include married couples. Apparently as a result of sexual frustration, strife breaks out among the company in *Eiríks saga rauða* during their last winter in Straumsfjǫrðr:

> Gengu menn þá mjǫk sleitum; sóttu þeir er kvánlausir váru í hendr þeim her kvángaðir váru. (*ES* ch. 11: 432)

---

71 See, for example, Thomas H. McGovern, 'The Vinland Adventure: A North American Perspective', *North American Archaeologist* 2 (1980–81), 287–8, 296–8, 300–1.

Then the men engaged in much squabbling; those who were wifeless annoyed those who were married.

Vínland is finally abandoned in *Grænlendinga saga* after a nightmarish expedition led by Freydís, who reneges on a promise to share the profits of the undertaking with her partners, the Icelandic brothers, Helgi and Finnbogi. Rules and regulations break down from the beginning of this fatal venture. Freydís contravenes the agreement that each party will have thirty men by smuggling five extra men aboard her ship before they leave Greenland. When they reach an apparently uninhabited Vínland, she turns Helgi and Finnbogi out of *Leifsbúðir* (*GS* ch. 8: 265), and mercantile partnership disintegrates into frontier lawlessness. The bargain with Helgi and Finnbogi is broken; ill-feeling between the two parties increases; Freydis eventually engineers the killing of most of the men and axes five women to death herself.

Defiling the paradisial dew of Vínland which had ravished Leifr and his companions, Freydís uses it as prop for a homicidal plot. On the morning when she sets out early to make an offer which she has no intention of keeping – to exchange ships with Helgi and Finnbogi and to leave Vínland – she goes outside in heavy dew without her shoes. Returning to the marital bed, she tells Þorvarðr that her cold and wet feet are the result of rough handling by the brothers. Þorvarðr is galvanized into retributive action, and Freydís completes the massacre herself. The saga (*GS* ch. 9: 267) calls her action evil (*þat it illa verk*), outrageous (*ódáðir*), and cruel (*illska*). In contravention of Icelandic law,[72] Freydís does not report the killings but instead, with threats and bribes, obtains the complicity of her companions in her story that the victims have decided to stay in Vínland. On their return to Greenland, the conspiracy of silence breaks down, and Leifr tortures the true version of events out of three of these accessories after the fact (*Leifr . . . píndi þá til sagna um þenna atburð allan jafnsaman* [ch. 9: 267–8];[73] 'Leif . . . tortured them into telling everything about that incident'). He declines to punish Freydís herself, but her descendants earn his curse. The narrative abruptly turns to the post-Vínland life of Guðríðr and Karlsefni, who are waiting in Greenland for a favourable wind to sail to Norway when the survivors of the Freydís expedition return.

The ultimate significance of the Vínland voyages diverges in the two sagas. In Baumgartner's moral-allegorical interpretation of *Grænlendinga saga* the loss of Vínland is the punishment for Freydís's sin. Baumgartner reads the saga as a misogynist exemplum in which Freydís, a woman who usurps the male role by leading an expedition and goads her husband into unjustified killing, is the antithesis of the Pauline ideal. Guðríðr, conversely, is its embodiment, and Iceland's transition from a pagan-Viking to Christian society is symbolized by

---

72 As Baumgartner notes in 'Freydís in Vinland', p. 26.
73 The verb *pína* is unusual in saga literature, although common in religious works; the formula *pína til sagna* is used in *Grágás* of the right to interrogate outlaws in some circumstances. See *The Laws of Early Iceland. Grágás I*, trans. Andrew Dennis, Peter Foote, Richard Perkins (Winnipeg, 1980), p. 171.

the episcopal dynasty which she and Karlsefni found in Iceland on their return from the west.[74] *Grœnlendinga saga* lends itself to a reading as exemplary narrative from another viewpoint, if it is interpreted as a powerful illustration of a lesson which potentially underlies all the Vínland voyages in that saga: that *radix malorum est cupiditas* ('greed is the root of evils'). The Vínland voyages have, as *Grœnlendinga saga* reminds us in the opening sentence of chapter 8 (p. 264), resulted in and gained a reputation as sources of worldly fame and fortune (*sú ferð þykkir bæði góð til fjár ok virðingar* ('that voyage was considered favourable to both wealth and reputation'). All the Vínland explorers in *Grœnlendinga saga* return to Greenland laden with valuable cargo: Leifr with grapes and timber (ch. 4), Þorvaldr's companions with grapes and vines (ch. 5), Karlsefni with vines and grapes and pelts (ch. 7), and Freydís with as big a load of the land's resources as her companions and their ship can carry (ch. 8). Leifr, says the sagas's narrator, *varð nú bæði góð til fjár ok mannvirðingar* (ch. 4: 254) ('was enhanced both in wealth and reputation') after his Vínland voyage. A further indication of the saga's preoccupation with wealth is the information, early in the narrative, that Freydís has been married off to the unimpressive Þorvarðr *til fjár* (ch. 2: 245) ('for his wealth').

The first reaction to Leifr's report of his discoveries in *Grœnlendinga saga* is enthusiasm for further exploration, but, after the death of Þorvaldr Eiríksson, commercial aims supersede the spirit of discovery, and the stated object of the next expedition, by the merchant Þorfinnr Karlsefni, is profit and settlement: *Þeir hǫfðu með sér alls konar fénað, því at þeir ætluðu at byggja landit, ef þeir mætti þat* (*GS* ch. 7: 261); ('They had all kinds of livestock with them, because they intended to settle the land, if they could manage it'). Subsequent voyages to the lands west of Greenland bring steadily increasing gains. By the time Karlsefni leaves Greenland for Norway, it is the general opinion that *eigi mundi auðgara skip gengit hafa af Grœnlandi* (*GS* ch. 8: 267) ('no ship would have departed from Greenland more richly laden').

The ill-gotten gains of Freydís take profit to gross and unlawful excess when she returns with the murdered Helgi and Finnbogi's large boat laden with as much *gæði* as it and her companions can carry. The wages of this sinful misappropriation of Vínland's riches are calumny of self, family, and descendants, and, by implication, the loss of paradise itself. The Freydís episode retrospectively casts previous voyages to Vínland in a moralizing light and becomes part of a larger exemplum about *caritas* and *cupiditas*, which dominates the narrative as it draws to a close with a marked shift of interest from the commercial to the spiritual: from profit-making ventures west of Greenland to journeys east, of Christian purpose. The last chapter of *Grœnlendinga saga* juxtaposes the positive example of the life of Guðríðr to the negative example of Freydís. Freydís's unholy voyage to Vínland, her subsequent disgrace back in Greenland, and accursed succeeding generations are countered by Guðríðr's pilgrimage to

---

74 Baumgartner, 'Freydís in Vinland', pp. 28–9.

Rome; her model widowhood in Iceland as nun and anchoress in the church built by her Vínland-born son, Snorri; and her distinguished clerical descendants. In the final analysis, as Sayers argues, *Grœnlendinga saga* lends itself to interpretation as an encoding of the rejection of Iceland's pagan past in favour of the new faith. *Grœnlendinga saga*, whose codicological framework situates it within a broad perspective of Christian endeavour, can also be interpreted on a universal Christian level as a moral lesson about the wisdom of forsaking materialist adventures in alluring new lands for spiritual riches. Freydís's *cupiditas* leads to a curse upon her line; Guðríðr's *caritas* to familial fame and glory.

In *Eiríks saga rauða*, on the other hand, Vínland is not so much 'lost' as never decisively found. Neither the reader nor Leifr's successors ever lay eyes directly upon it. All that we hear of Vínland is the laconic report of Leifr's unexpected landfall on a difficult voyage from Norway to Greenland. The land is distanced from both narrative and audience by being neither topographically described nor, unlike the new lands in *Grœnlendinga saga*, actively sighted and named. Devoid of the rhetoric of paradise, it is simply a source of vines, grain, and grapes:

> Leifr . . . hitti hann á lǫnd þau er hann vissi áðr ǫngva ván í. Váru þar hveitiakrar sjálfsánir ok vínviðr vaxinn; þar váru ok þau tré er mǫsurr heita, ok hǫfðu af ǫllu þessu nǫkkur merki. (*ES* ch. 5: 415)

> Leifr . . . came upon those lands of which he had previously had no inkling. There were fields of self-sown wheat there, and vines growing; there were also those trees which are called maples, and they took some samples of all these.

Export of the rich resources of the new lands never materializes beyond the samples (*merki*) of flora which Leifr takes back after his briefly and indirectly recounted visit. Karlsefni is not said to return to Greenland laden with produce after his three-year expedition in *Eiríks saga rauða*, although the lands which he explores are rich in wheat, grapes, fish, and abundant other game, and he has engaged with the *skrælingar* in trade for furs on highly favourable terms.

In *Grœnlendinga saga* the ultimate but failed aim is settlement, and the Greenland–Vínland route apparently well established. Although further Vínland voyages by Leifr's siblings, after his happy winter there, are less successful, they remain geographically on track. Neither Þorvaldr, Karlsefni, Freydís, Helgi, nor Finnbogi has any trouble in locating *Leifsbuðir*. Only Þorsteinn Eiríksson, on a mission to recover the body of his brother, Þorvaldr (*GS* ch. 6), fails to reach his destination because of bad weather. The primary goal of *Eiríks saga rauða*, on the other hand, becomes the quest for Vínland itself. The verb most often used of departures for Vínland in this saga, *leita* ('to search'), and the chance nature of Leifr's discovery makes the romance topos of *aventure* the motive for subsequent Vínland voyages. The talk back in Greenland is not of exploration or of settlement but of seeking this still anonymous land: *Á því gerðisk orð mikit at menn mundu leita lands þess er Leifr hafði fundit* (*ES* ch. 5: 416) ('There was much discussion about people going to search for this land which Leifr had discovered'). Only after Þorsteinn Eiríksson's failed expedition (*ES* ch. 5), not to recover his brother's body, but to find Leifr's land, is it identified as Vínland, and in *Hauksbók* as 'Vínland the Good'. Qualified by idealizing epithet, possibly on the model of the *Frakkland hit góða* (*la dulce France*) formula of *Karlamagnús saga*,[75] Vínland is thus formally signified as the object of quest.

Two years after the death of Þorsteinn Eiríksson and now married to his widow Guðríðr, Karlsefni leads a company which includes Þorvaldr Eiríksson, Bjarni Grímólfsson, Freydís, Þorvarðr, and Þórhallr veiðimaðr ('the Hunter') 'to search' for Vínland (*at leita Vínlands, ES* ch. 8: 422). After their expedition reaches land west of Greenland, the indications are that the goal is within their grasp when two Scottish thralls, Haki and Hekja, return from a three-day reconnoitre (*ES* ch. 8: 425) with grapes (*vínber*) and 'self-sown' grain (*hveiti sjálfsáit*). But, seduced by the summer climate of Straumsfjǫrðr, a beautiful and fertile mountainous area south of Markland, the company fail to make provision for what turns out to be a severe winter:

> Fjǫll váru þar, ok fagrt var þar um at litask. Þeir gáðu einskis nema at kanna landit.
>
> (*ES* ch. 8: 425)

> There were mountains there, and the surroundings were fair to look at. They gave heed to nothing except exploring the land.

Food runs short and hunting fails. The reader is teased. Is this Vínland or is it not? Is there an implicit moral here about heedlessness of long-term needs in the midst of short-term plenty?

The following spring, a rival quest for Vínland is undertaken by a frustrated breakaway group led by Þórhallr veiðimaðr, who heads north in a vain attempt to *leita svá Vínlands* (*ES* ch. 9: 426). Þórhallr eventually gives voice to doubts about Vínland's very existence in a verse which expresses scorn for the substitution of water for the wine he was expecting:

> Hafa kváðu mik meiðar
> malmþings er komk hingat,
> mér samir láð fyrir lýðum
> lasta, drykk inn bazta.
> Bílds hattar verðr byttu
> Beiðityr at reiða;
> heldr er svá at ek krýp at keldu,
> komat vín á grǫn mína.   (*ES* ch. 9: 426)

> Men told me that I would have the best of drinks when I came hither, but it befits me to condemn the land in public. The

---

75 'Such phrases in the romantic sagas as *Frakkland hit góða* have exerted influence retroactively. The expression likely derives from *Karlamagnus saga* and is a rendering of *la dulce France, France dulce*, and so on, not least in immediate association with textual references to the fair forests and fields, the fruit trees, ample pasturage, and impressive grapevines of gracious France' (Wahlgren, 'Fact and Fancy', p. 45).

helmet-wearer must wield a bucket; no wine has reached my
lips; I kneel at a well instead.

Þórhallr's quest for Vínland ends in disaster. Driven east by fierce winds, he and
his crew are enslaved in Ireland, where he dies.

In the meantime, Karlsefni and his company travel south to an attractive
estuary which they name Hóp. With its wild grain, grapes, abundance of fish
and game, and snowless winter, Hóp's surrounding landscape is strikingly
similar to Vínland's in *Grœnlendinga saga*:

> Þar fundu þeir sjálfsána hveitiakra þar sem lægðir váru, en vínviðr allt þar sem
> holta kenndi. Hverr lœkr var þar fullr af fiskum. Þeir gerðu þar grafir sem landit
> mœttisk ok flóðit gekk efst; ok er út fell váru helgir fiskar í grǫfunum. Þar var
> mikill fjǫlði dýra á skógi með ǫllu móti . . . Nú váru þeir þar þann vetr. Þar kom
> alls engi snjár, ok allr fénaðr gekk þar úti sjálfala. (*ES* ch. 10: 427–8)

> They found fields of wild wheat where the ground was low, and grape vines could
> be seen all over the ridges. Every brook was full of fish. They dug trenches where
> the land and the tide met at the highest point; and when the tide went out there
> were halibut in the trenches. There was a great number of animals of all kinds in
> the woods . . . Then they stayed there that winter. No snow came at all, and all the
> livestock managed for themselves outdoors.

But whether Hóp is to be conclusively identified with the land discovered by
Leifr, *Eiríks saga rauða* declines to say. Only after Karlsefni finally decides to
return to Greenland does the *Hauksbók* version of the saga remark, in a seem-
ingly self-contradictory reference, that *þeir sigldu af Vínlandi* (p. 233) ('they
sailed from Vínland'), when the company leave Straumsfjǫrðr, the very place
from which Þórhallr set out on his ill-fated quest for Vínland. According to
Skálholtsbók, Karlsefni simply sets sail from Straumsfjǫrðr *sunnanveðr* (*ES* ch. 12:
432) ('before a wind from the south').

As the object of constant but unfulfilled quest in *Eiríks saga rauða*, Leifr's
briefly visited land of wild grain, maple trees, and vines becomes something of a
geographic Holy Grail. Framing this quest are two other motifs typical of
romance: the wooing of a woman of higher station and the prospect of travel to
fantastic destinations. The staginess of other episodes of the saga, such as the
seiðr of Þorbjǫrg, the actions of Freydís in the face of a *skræling* assault, and the
fabulous lands and people in the west-of-Greenland orbit, reinforce the impression of a saga-author consciously operating in the dimension of fiction and
learned literature. The arrow which kills Þorvaldr in *Grœnlendinga saga* is, for
example, not fired in *Eiríks saga rauða* by a *skræling* but by a uniped (*einfœtingr*,
ES ch. 12: 431), an African phenomenon which derives from Isidore of Seville's
encyclopedic *Etymologies*.[76]

---

76 Unipeds are described in the *Hauksbók* text 'Heimslýsing ok helgifrœði' ('Worldly and Sacred
Learning'): Ein fætingar hafa sua mikinn fot við iorð at þeir skykgia ser i suefní við solo . . . Su þioð
er i Afrika (p. 166: 25–7); 'Unipeds have such a large foot upon the ground that they shade

The thrice-widowed Guðríðr Þorbjarnardóttir is never actively wooed in *Grænlendinga saga*. The first reference to her in the saga is brief and indirect: she is the unnamed wife of a certain Þórir, one of fifteen people rescued from a reef by Leifr on his return trip to Greenland from Vínland (*GS* ch. 4). When Guðríðr next appears, Þórir is dead and she has married Þorsteinn Eiríksson (*GS* ch. 6).[77] After Þorsteinn's death, her union with Karlsefni is a matter of brief, offstage negotiation:

> Brátt fell hann hug til Guðríðar ok bað hennar, en hon veik til Leifs svǫrum fyrir sik. Síðan var hon honum fǫstnuð ok gǫrt brúðlaup þeira á þeim vetri.
>
> (*GS* ch. 7: 261)

> He soon fell in love with Guðríðr and proposed to her, but she turned to Leifr for an answer on her behalf. Then she was betrothed to him, and their wedding took place that winter.

In *Eiríks saga rauða*, by contrast, Guðríðr is introduced as an unmarried woman who is the object of an unsuccessful proposal back in Iceland by a man called Einarr Þorgeirsson. Einarr himself is signified as a potential romance hero: he is good-looking, accomplished, and presentable (*vænn maðr ok vel mannaðr ok skartsmaðr mikill* [*ES* ch. 3: 407]) ('a handsome and well-mannered man and a great dandy'). His father is wealthy but a freedman. When Einarr falls instantly in love with the exceptionally beautiful and gifted Guðríðr (*kvenna vænst ok hinn mesti skǫrungr í ǫllu athæfi sínu* [*ES* ch. 3: 407]; 'the most beautiful of women and the finest person in every aspect of her conduct'), the stage is set for a low-born man to prove that nobility is not simply a matter of birth.

The episode is given dramatic immediacy by being conducted largely in dialogue between Einarr and Ormr, Guðríðr's foster-father, and her father, Þorbjǫrn. Einarr announces his intention to seek her hand and lectures Ormr on the advantages of the match for the deteriorating fortunes of Þorbjǫrn. Ormr warns Einarr that his prospects are not good. Although Einarr is a persistent suitor, Þorbjǫrn, himself the grandson of a slave (*ES* ch. 1), refuses to marry his daughter to the son of one. Einarr disappears from the narrative without further ado, and Þorbjǫrn's continuing financial straits prompt him to take up Eiríkr rauði's invitation to settle in Greenland, whither he departs with Guðríðr and thirty others.

Eiríks saga rauða has another unsatisfactory love affair which initially raises

---

themselves from the sun with it while they are asleep . . . That species is in Africa'. For an ingenious reading of the verse which recounts Karlsefni's company's unsuccessful pursuit of the *einfœtingr* (*ES* ch. 12: 432) as a pen riddle, see Ian McDougall's article, 'The enigmatic einfœtingr of Eiríks saga rauða', in *Frejas Psalter: en psalter i 40 afdelinger til brug for Jonna Louis-Jensen på tresårsdagen den 21. oktober 1996*, ed. Bergljót S. Kristjánsdóttir and Peter Springborg (Copenhagen, 1997), pp. 128–32.

77 'Þat hafði gǫrzk til tíðenda meðan á Grœnlandi, at Þorsteinn í Eiríksfirði hafði kvángazk ok fengit Guðríðar Þorbjarnardóttur' (p. 257); ('In the meantime in Greenland, it had happened that Þorsteinn of Eiriksfjǫrð had married and taken to wife Guðríðr Þorbjarnardóttir').

expectations of a marriage between an accomplished but non-noble man and a woman of higher station. Newly introduced to the narrative and fresh from a stay in Norway with Óláfr Tryggvason, the promising (*efniligr*) Leifr Eíriksson is blown off course twice on his return to Greenland. He makes his discovery of previously unknown lands on the second occasion. On the first (*ES* ch. 5) he is driven to the Hebrides, where he spends most of the summer waiting for favourable winds and engages in a love affair with a woman of noble birth (*kona ættstór*) named Þorgunna. When the time comes for Leifr to leave the Hebrides, Þorgunna suggests that Leifr abduct her. Mindful, he says, of the likely hostility of her kinsmen, he declines. Having announced that she is pregnant, Þorgunna takes over the narrative in prophetic mode. In a contrasting parallel with Þorbjǫrg's *seiðr* in the previous chapter of the saga, she predicts that she will give birth to a son, that she will send him to Greenland to be raised by Leifr, that Leifr will not welcome the child, and that she herself will eventually come to Greenland. Leifr makes no response to Þorgunna's declaration, but he showers her with valuable gifts: a gold ring, a Greenland cloak, and a belt of ivory. Whereas Þorbjǫrg delivers a fulfilled prophecy about Guðríðr, Þorgunna spins a tale about her future which becomes one of many loose narrative threads in the saga. The saga-writer confirms some of her story but never completes it: Þorgunna's son was, he says, named Þorgils, came to Greenland, was acknowledged by Leifr, was thought by some to have gone to Iceland in the summer before the *Fróðáundr* ('Frodriver marvels') – a string of weird incidents involving hauntings which are recounted in *Eyrbyggja saga* (chs 51–4) – and was considered somewhat strange throughout his life (*ES* ch. 5: 414). Like Einarr Þorgeirsson, Þorgunna simply disappears from the narrative upon the failure of her suit.

Whereas *Grænlendinga saga* contrasts Guðríðr and Freydís as positive and negative exemplars of womanhood, in *Eiríks saga rauða* the distinction is, argu-ably, between heroine of romance (Guðríðr) and epic (Freydís). The beautiful Guðríðr is wooed, fulfils the dazzling prophecy about her, and lives happily ever after with Karlsefni back in Iceland. In both sagas, Freydís is a woman who transgresses the traditional boundaries of gender; but whereas she is monstrously evil in *Grænlendinga saga*, dauntlessness is her style in *Eiríks saga rauða*. In the most spectacular piece of theatre in *Eiríks saga rauða* she metamor-phoses into a combination of the Norse mythological and literary figures of fertility goddess, warrior woman, whetter,[78] and, perhaps, the Amazon of Greek mythology[79] in her expression of scorn for the feebleness of the menfolk when the *skrælingar* attack Hóp (*ES* ch. 11). Hampered by advanced pregnancy, she faces down the enemy by exposing her breast and slapping it with a sword, actions which send the aggressors scurrying back to their boats. It is more diffi-cult to see Freydís's behaviour here as the enactment of ancient Germanic tradi-

---

78 For a recent investigation of these female types in Icelandic literature, see Jenny Jochens, *Old Norse Images of Women* (Philadelphia, 1996).
79 See Kirsten Wolf, 'Amazons in Vínland', *JEGP* 95 (1996), 480–5.

tion,[80] since it has no parallel elsewhere in Icelandic literature, than as sheer performance, under authorial direction and staged in the same histrionic mode as the shamanistic actions of Þorbjǫrg and Þórhallr.

The last six chapters of *Eiríks saga rauða* fracture into journeys of different kinds in different directions, and the saga oversteps the boundaries of geographical plausibility. The discourses of romance and encyclopedia intersect here, such that, by the end of the narrative, *Eiríks saga rauða* has signalled its potential to become a veritable *Mandeville's Travels of the North*. After Þórhallr leads his party on a northward quest for Vínland, Karlsefni and the rest of the company continue south to Hóp. The following spring they set out from Straumsfjǫrðr in search of Þórhallr and find themselves in a wild wasteland where they encounter the uniped which kills Þorvaldr Eiríksson. Heading north in pursuit of the creature, they catch sight of a land which they assume to be *Einfætingaland* ('Unipedland'). Topographically, this imaginary land is linked with the 'real' world of Helluland, Markland, and Straumsfjǫrðr, since its mountains are assumed to belong to the same range as those of Hóp. Karlsefni's party calculate that Hóp and Einfætingaland are equidistant from Straumsfjǫrðr:

> Þeir ætluðu ǫll ein fjǫll þau er í Hópi váru ok þessi er nú fundi þeir ok þat stœðisk mjǫk svá á ok væri jamlangt ór Straumsfirði beggja vegna. (*ES* ch. 12: 432)

> They estimated that the mountains which were in Hóp and these which they now could see were one range, and they thus established that both sides of it were the same distance from Straumsfjǫrðr.

Considering it prudent not to investigate any further, they return for a final winter in Straumsfjǫrðr.

As the hazards of the lands west of Greenland escalate, so does the reported bizarreness of their inhabitants. The people of a land called *Skrælingaland* are said by a family of native Marklanders to be ruled by two kings, Avaldamon and Valdidida,[81] and to live in caves or holes in the ground. When, after two

---

80 As suggested by A. Lodewyckx, 'Freydís Eiríksdóttir rauða and the Germania of Tacitus', *Arkiv för nordisk filologi* 70 (1955), 182–7. Björn Þorsteinsson notes that Freydís here 'is a heroine endowed with the appearance of a fertility goddess' ('Some Observations on the Discoveries and Cultural History of the Norsemen, p. 185). Judith Jesch calls her '[o]ne of Saxo's warrior women' (*Women in the Viking Age* [Cambridge, 1991], pp. 182–5). For a discussion of possible sources in Irish and Lapp tradition, see Stefán Einarsson, 'The Freydís-Incident in Eiríks Saga Rauða, ch. 11', *Acta Philologica Scandinavica* 13 (1938–39), 246–56. In a private communication, Margaret Clunies Ross has suggested to me that 'a common-sense interpretation of such a gesture, and a reason why it might have sent the attackers back to their boats, is that it says: "breasts are usually for non-militant things, nourishing children etc. However, by slapping mine with a sword, I give notice that I negate my role as a nurturer in favour of one as a warrior/potential killer. So look out!"'
81 Oddr Snorrason's *Saga Óláfs Tryggvasonar* (see n. 22) offers a tenuous parallel between these names and those of the king and queen of Garðaríki, Valdamarr and Allogia (ch. 8, 23: 14–15). On the other hand, Inuit or Micmac origin has been suggested for these and for the names of the parents, Vethildi and Óvægi, of the captured Markland boys. In 'Contact Between Native North Americans and the Medieval Norse: A Review of the Evidence', *American Antiquity* 49 (1984) Robert McGhee cites (p. 10) William Thalbitzer's suggestion in 'Four Skræling Words from

members of this family are captured, the rest escape by sinking into the earth, it looks as if Markland and Skrælingaland may have merged into one. A fourth land west of Greenland whose existence is alleged in *Eiríks saga rauða* is *Hvítramannaland* ('White Men's Land'). There is, say the two Markland captives, a land opposite their own, inhabited by shouting, white-clad, pole-carrying men. This, the saga says, is thought to have been Hvítramannaland:

> ok gengu menn þar í hvítum klæðum ok œpðu hátt ok báru stangir ok fóru með flíkr. Þat ætla menn Hvítramannaland. (*ES* ch. 12: 432)

> And people went around there in white clothes and shouted loudly and carried poles with rags. That is thought to be Hvítramannaland.

The *Hauksbók* recension of *Eiríks saga rauða* identifies Hvítramannaland with *Írland it mikla*, 'Greater Ireland' (p. 234), as does *Landnámabók* in its report of a certain Ari Mársson, who is driven off course to a Christian land called Hvítramannaland. According to *Landnámabók* this land is known by some as *Írland it mikla* and is located 'westward in the sea near Vínland the Good' (*þat liggr vestr í haf nær Vínlandi enu goða*).[82] Many ingenious explanations have been offered for the description in *Eiríks saga rauða* of the people of Hvítramannaland,[83] but, as Hermann Pálsson has pointed out,[84] *Hauksbók*'s encyclopedic text 'Heimslýsing ok helgifrœði' ('Worldly and Sacred Learning') provides a plausible common origin for Hvítramannaland and Einfœtingaland. In the section of that text headed 'Her segir fra marghattaðum' ('Here different types of people are discussed'), there are descriptions of unipeds and a people called *Albani* ('Albinos'), who are said to have hair and skin as white as snow (*huítir sem snior beði a hars lit oc a horund*).[85]

Karlsefni finally gets back to Greenland, but the narrative continues to postpone his return to Iceland by interrupting it to tell the story of the disastrous homeward voyage of his partner on the Vínland expedition, Bjarni Grímólfsson (*ES* ch. 13). In a spectacular display of death-defying heroism as his ship goes down in the *Maðksjór* ('Maggoty Sea'), Bjarni surrenders the place in the lifeboat which he has drawn by lot to a fearful young Icelander and goes down

---

Markland (Newfoundland) in the Saga of Erik the Red (Eirikr Rauði)', *International Congress of Americanists. Proceedings of the XVIII Session* (London, 1912), pp. 88–93, that all four names are transcriptions of Inuit words. Storm ('Studier over Vinlandsreiserne', pp. 349–50) argues to the contrary but suggests that the names could be of Micmac origin. On their much disputed linguistic origin, see also Reeves, *The Finding of Wineland the Good*, pp. 177–9; Ólafur Halldórsson, *Grœnland í miðaldaritum*, pp. 355–6.

82 *Landnámabók*, i, 162.

83 Gwyn Jones, for example, suggests that the description could possibly derive from 'the white chamois or buckskin dancing robes of the Naskaupi' (*The Norse Atlantic Saga*, p. 133). Storm thought that Hvítramannaland was a fiction derived from Irish traditions ('Studier over Vinlandsreiserne', pp. 359–60).

84 'Íslenzkar fornsögur og Isidor frá Seville', *Tímarit Þjóðræknisfélags Íslendinga* 49 (1968), 35–8.

85 Finnur Jónsson, *Hauksbók*, 166: 27–8.

with his worm-eaten ship.[86] The survivors eventually reach land (Ireland, according to *Hauksbók* [p. 235]), and the narrative abruptly concludes with a brief account of Karlsefni's and Guðríðr's return to and later life in Iceland and the names of their episcopal descendants. Karlsefni's mother's initial opinion that he has a made a poor choice of bride (*ES* ch. 13: 434) signals a return from the world of marvels and adventure, where Guðríðr's dazzling qualities speak for themselves, to the conventional prejudices of everyday life.

Although both Vínland sagas conclude with Karlsefni and Guðríðr ascendant in Iceland, in contrast to the neatly sutured recital of *Grœnlendinga saga*, *Eiríks saga rauða* winds up in a degree of structural and ideological inconclusiveness. Normally the *Íslendingasǫgur* give brief details about the later life of the surviving characters, but Leifr Eiríksson – missionary, explorer, and acclaimed rescuer of shipwrecked seamen – vanishes without trace long before the saga is over. We last hear of him, indirectly and retrospectively, as having given the thralls Haki and Hekja to Karlsefni for his Vínland expedition (*ES* ch. 8). Whether Þorgunna ever fulfilled her promise to come to Greenland remains an unanswered question. The reason for Þorgils Leifsson's adult reputation for strangeness is never explained, nor is there any further mention of the child which Freydís is carrying when she makes her heroic stand against the *skrælingar*. Vínland remains out of reach, its existence validated only through indirect report and the samples of grain, vines, and maple which Leifr is said to have taken back to Greenland. Whereas *Grœnlendinga saga* operates within a framework of geographical and ethical certainty, *Eiríks saga rauða* poses questions on both scores. Where is the land which Leifr discovered? What of the kings of Skrælingaland, Avaldamon and Valdidida, and their cave- and hole-in-the-ground-dwelling subjects? Would Hvítramannaland correspond to the bizarre account of its inhabitants related by the captured boys in Markland? What adventures might be had in Einfœtingaland? What narrative purpose does the story of Bjarni Grímólfsson serve? Is he a model of pagan heroism or of Christian selflessness? Or are his actions, like Þjorbjǫrg's *seiðr* and Freydís's heroics, simply another piece of theatre? And although *Vínland it góða* remains forever out of sight both for the reader and Karlsefni, the implication is that it is not so much a paradise lost as one still there for the taking.

Having returned to Iceland by their separate routes, the twin conclusions of *Grœnlendinga saga* and *Eiríks saga rauða* actively celebrate the consolidation of the ecclesiastical history of Iceland, through the illustrious family of Guðríðr and Karlsefni, and passively spell out the dynastic failure of Eiríkr rauði. Þorvaldr and Þorsteinn Eiríksson are dead (*Grœnlendinga saga* and *Eiríks saga rauða*), Freydís's descendants cursed (*Grœnlendinga saga*), and Leifr apparently without issue in *Grœnlendinga saga* and encumbered with an unpromising son

---

86 On possible sources for this episode as an exemplum to illustrate the equality of free people, see Bjarni Einarsson, 'On the Status of Free Men in Society and Saga', *Mediaeval Scandinavia* 7 (1974), 52–5; Peter Foote, 'A Question of Conscience', *Opuscula Septentrionalia. Festskrift til Ole Widding*, ed. Bent Chr. Jacobsen *et al.* (Copenhagen, 1977), pp. 11–18.

in *Eiríks saga rauða*. Either lopped off or accursed in *Grænlendinga saga*, if the branches of Eiríkr's family tree flower in *Eiríks saga rauða*, they do so in textual wilderness.[87]

West of Greenland in post-classical Norse narrative

Tacitly forfeited in *Grænlendinga saga*, indefinitely postponed in *Eiríks saga rauða*, and briefly mentioned in *Eyrbyggja saga* as the place where Snorri Þorbrandsson is killed in combat with the *skrælingar*,[88]

> En Snorri fór til Vínlands ins góða með Karlsefni; er þeir bǫrðusk við Skrælinga þar á Vínlandi, þá fell þar Snorri Þorbrandsson, inn rǫskvasti maðr.
>
> (ch. 48: 135)

> And Snorri went to Vínland the Good with Karlsefni; and they fought there in Vínland with the Skrælings, when Snorri Þorbrandsson, the bravest of men, died.

the quest for Vínland was simply abandoned by subsequent generations of saga-writers. The last reference to Vínland among *Íslendingasögur* is the nickname 'Vínlendingur' ('Vínland traveller') which the early fourteenth-century *Grettis saga* gives to Þorhallr Gamlason, Bjarni Grímólfsson's partner in *Eiríks saga rauða*.[89] The arena of knightly romance, the most popular form of narrative in late medieval Iceland, lay in the opposite direction, in Ireland, England, and points east and south to the Holy Land. Of all the lands west of Greenland in *Grænlendinga saga* and *Eiríks saga rauða*, only Helluland, the bleakest and most northerly, appears in later saga narrative. As a forbidding wasteland, situated sometimes in the vicinity of Norway and sometimes that of Greenland,[90] desolate, rocky, and glacial Helluland lends itself to an eastward shift, to the terrain of the legendary north in the fourteenth- and fifteenth-century narratives of ancient Viking times known as *fornaldarsögur*.

In the fifteenth-century manuscript tradition of *Ǫrvar-Odds saga*, for example, Oddr, who during his long life visits every corner of the world, travels to the wastes of Helluland (*Hellulands úbygðir*), which are situated southwest of the *Grænlands haf* ('Greenland Sea'), between Greenland and Iceland).[91] In *Hálfdanar saga Brǫnufóstra*, another *fornaldarsaga*, which dates from around 1300, the wastes of Helluland are areas of flat sand and glaciers, which appear

---

87 Despite the intimations in both *GS* and *ES* that Eiríkr's line is headed for extinction, there is an implication that he has founded a hereditary ruling dynasty in *Fóstbrœðra saga* (ch. 20: 223), where a certain Þorkell Leifsson is said to be chieftain over Eiríksfjǫrðr.

88 In *ES* he survives and returns to Greenland with Karlsefni, but his son, Þorbrandr, is killed in an attack by *skrælingar* (*ES* ch. 11).

89 *Grettis saga Ásmundarsonar*. Ed. Guðni Jónsson, Íslenzk fornrit 7 (Reykjavík, 1936), chs 14, 30.

90 See Perkins, 'The Furðustrandir of *Eiríks saga rauða*', p. 54; Storm, 'Studier over Vinlandsreiserne', pp. 328–32.

91 See *Ǫrvar-Odds saga*, ed. R. C. Boer (Leiden, 1888), pp. 131–2.

to be west of mainland Scandinavia and not far from the British Isles.[92] In the excerpt from *Gripla* which is incorporated into the seventeenth-century *Grœnlands annáll*,[93] Helluland is recognizable as its namesake in *Grœnlendinga saga* and *Eiríks saga rauða*, situated as it is west of Greenland, south of Furðustrandir, and in the vicinity of Vínland. On the other hand, in the late thirteenth- or early fourteenth-century *Íslendingasaga*-cum-*fornaldarsaga*, *Bárðar saga Snæfellsáss*, Helluland is an island in the *Dumbshaf*, a sea north of Norway.[94] In *Gunnars saga Keldugnúpsfífls*, a saga of similar type and date, Helluland seems to be west of Iceland, in the same location as in *Qrvar-Odds saga*,[95] but in *Hálfdanar saga Eysteinssonar*, a *fornaldarsaga* probably composed in the mid-fourteenth century,[96] it occupies the Arctic seas of Norway.[97]

Vínland otherwise survives in 'post-classical' Old Norse literary narrative only in a Faroese stanzaic poem of uncertain date: the ballad of *Finnur hin fríði* ('Finn the Fair').[98] Here Vínland comes with all the trappings of medieval chivalric romance: palaces, kings, a flying dragon, and a bride-quest. Finn, younger son of an Upland jarl and desirous of a bride, learns that the maiden most eligible is Ingibjørg, daughter of the king of Ireland, and sets out in princely splendour to win her. The Irish king declares the proposed match unequal, and, after a skirmish between Finn's retinue and the king's, Finn is imprisoned. Released through the good offices of Ingibjørg and the brute strength of his brother, Hálvdan, Finn undertakes the task imposed upon him by Ingibjørg to prove himself worthy of their union: to subdue the kings of Vínland. Steering a swift and straight course under silken sail to his destination, he enters an imposing palace, where the kings of Vínland are guarded by five hundred warriors, and then finds himself confronted by an army of twelve hundred. After two days of fierce battle, in which he kills two of the Vínland kings, Finn is fatally poisoned by a flying dragon. Hálvdan kills the third king and races

---

92 *Hálfdanar saga Brǫnufóstra*, ed. Guðni Jónsson, *Fornaldar sögur Norðurlanda* IV (Reykjavík, 1954), ch. 4: 297.

93 See above, 'Introduction', p. xii.

94 *Bárðar Saga*, ed. and trans. Jón Skaptason and Phillip Pulsiano (New York, 1984), chs 14: 98; 15: 102.

95 *Gunnars saga Keldugnúpsfífls*, ed. Jóhannes Halldórsson, Íslenzk fornrit 14 (*Kjalnesinga Saga*), chs 5–6.

96 Ed. Guðni Jónsson, *Fornaldar Sögur Norðulanda*, IV. On these regions in saga narrative, see Simek, 'Elusive Elysia', pp. 257–8.

97 This bifurcation of Helluland is noted by the compiler of the *Grœnlands annáll*, who identifies two separate lands by that name: the *Hellulandsóbyggðir*, which 'we call the northern wastes of Greenland and North Greenland or Great Helluland', and *Litla-Hellulands* or *Markland* (köllum vær norðuróbyggðir Grænlands og Norður-Grænland og Helluland hið mikla'; 'Litla-Hellulands eður Marklands'). See Ólafur Halldórsson, *Grænland í miðaldaritum*, pp. 43, 48.

98 References are to *Føroya Kvæði. Corpus Carminum Feroensium*, eds N. Djurhuus and Chr. Matras (Copenhagen, 1951–63), I, Version A, 534–9. For an English translation, see Joshua Toulmin Smith, *The Discovery of America by the Northmen in the Tenth Century* (London, 1839), pp. 199–210. The ballad is printed with a Latin translation in *Antiquitates Americanæ*, pp. 320–35.

back to Ireland, where Ingibjǫrg refuses to accept him as a substitute for Finn and dies of grief.

*

Greenland's and Iceland's surrender of autonomy to Norway in 1261–62 and a simultaneous deterioration in weather conditions severed the Iceland–Greenland nexus. As drift ice encroached on Greenland from the late thirteenth century, travel west of Iceland became hazardous and infrequent. The vision of Eiríksfjǫrðr harried by trolls and monsters during the winter after Eiríkr's arrival there in *Bárðar saga Snæfellsáss* (ch. 5) suggests that, for the author of this late thirteenth- or early fourteenth-century saga, things did not bode well for the settlements. Progressively abandoned by both Norway and Rome, Ostrbyggð and Vestrbyggð were defunct by 1500.[99] From as early as the mid-fourteenth century, the learned Icelandic record of the Vínland venture is one of failure. In the version of *Landafræði* in the manuscript AM 194 8vo (written in 1387),[100] a brief résumé of the West Atlantic voyages is added to the geographical information about Helluland, Markland, and Vínland common to other *Landafræði* texts:[101]

> Þat er sagt, ath Þorfidr karls-efni hioGi husa-snotro tre ok feri sidan ath leita Vinlandz ens goda ok kiemi þar er þeir etludu þat land ok nadu eigi ath kanna ok eingum landz-kostum. Leifr hinn hepni fann fystr Vinland, ok þa fann hann kaup-menn i hafinu illa stadda ok gaf þeim lif med guds miskunn.
>
> (Alfræði Íslenzk, I, 12)

> It is said that Þorfinn Karlsefni felled fine timber for *husasnotra* and then went to search for Vínland the Good. He and his companions arrived where they assumed that land to be, but did not succeed in exploring it or in obtaining any of its resources. Leifr the Lucky was the first to discover Vínland, and when he found some merchants in a difficult situation at sea, he saved their lives with God's mercy.

The writer appears to be familiar with the material of *Grænlendinga saga* and *Eiríks saga rauða*, although perhaps not with the extant texts. Karlsefni's *husas-notra* are mentioned, but only in connection with their manufacture before he goes in search of Vínland the Good, not with their sale after he has returned to Norway. The emphasis of this *Landafræði* account is, explicitly, upon the

---

99   See Jones, *The Norse Atlantic Saga*, pp. 87–114. For a recent discussion, which hypothesizes that Norse Greenland was abandoned at the end of the fifteenth century in favour of the New World, see Kirsten A. Seaver, *The Frozen Echo. Greenland and the Exploration of North America ca. A.D. 1000–1500* (Stanford, 1996).

100   Rudolf Simek, *Altnordische Kosmosgraphie. Studien und Quellen zu Weltbild und Weltbeschreibung in Norwegen und Island vom 12. bis zum 14. Jahrhundert* (Berlin and New York, 1990), p. 428.

101   Ólafur Halldórsson, *Grænland í miðaldaritum*, p. 386; Simek, *Altnordische Kosmographie*, pp. 428, 432; *Alfræði Íslenzk*, I, xx.

35

inability of Karlsefni's company to explore or to reap any benefit from the land after they reach its presumed location.

Prompted by the voyages of Columbus, expeditions in search of the 'lost colonies' of Greenland were sponsored by the kings of Denmark from the late sixteenth to the early nineteenth centuries,[102] but it was not until the middle of the nineteenth century that the scholarly quest for Vínland commenced in earnest. Launched by the first modern edition of the Vínland sagas in the volume *Antiquitates Americanæ* (1837), its effect was to remove Vínland from the geographical, historical, and literary landscape of Scandinavia and relocate it wholly within the orbit of North America. So situated, and variously embraced, disputed, denied, and relegated to the realms of myth, the Vínland voyages were to be appropriated by the nineteenth-century literary and historical imagination of England and America. Variously rerun as tales of national foundation and colonial adventure, their framing narratives of conversion and ecclesiastical consolidation were refashioned by a vociferous international coterie of church historians in a spurious discourse of New World episcopal history.

---

102 See Marijke Spies, *Arctic Routes to Fabled Lands. Olivier Brunel and the Passage to China and Cathay in the Sixteenth Century* (Amsterdam 1997), p. 18, and the references there.

CHAPTER TWO

Vínland in Nineteenth-Century History, Criticism, and Scholarship

Whereas the ultimate concerns of *Grœnlendinga saga* and *Eiríks saga rauða* lie in Iceland, and the discovery of land to the west of Greenland failed to grip the imagination of later saga-writers, virtually the sole focus of interest in the Vínland sagas throughout the nineteenth century was the question of their authenticity as accounts of the 'discovery' of America. The next two chapters of this study trace the fortunes of the Vínland voyages in nineteenth-century America, in terms of their impact on historiography and Old Norse scholarship, the subject of this chapter, and the popular and polemic 'American Viking' discourses which are addressed in the next.

Many reviewers of *Antiquitates Americanæ* (1837), the first modern edition of the Vínland sagas, saw the work as a challenge to the image of America as a land unseen, unnamed, and otherwise without mortal creator before 1492. Uncontroversial in England, in America the Vínland sagas impinged upon questions of national history and identity. With increasing fervour in the years leading up to the Columbus quatercentenary, Leifr Eiríksson was trumpeted as the true 'discoverer' of America by a diverse group of partisan commentators. Although the language and even the contents of *Grœnlendinga saga* and *Eiríks saga rauða* were largely irrelevant to those with an ideological barrow to push, for a small number of New England scholars in the late 1830s the Vínland sagas became, briefly, a focus for the serious study of Old Norse. Two commemorative events later in the century stimulated further interest in the Vínland voyages: the Centennial (1876) and the Columbus quatercentenary (1892). By 1892, a statue of Leifr had been unveiled in Boston; Viking 'finds' were proliferating throughout New England; and Vatican records were being trawled for evidence of a pre-Columbian Christian colony of Vínland.

Vínland and the North in America to the mid-1830s

Knowledge of journeys from Iceland to lands west of Greenland in the tenth and eleventh centuries had circulated in Scandinavia since the seventeenth. The Swedish scholar, Johannes Peringskiöld, incorporated *Grœnlendinga saga* (chs 2–9), with Swedish and Latin translations, into his 1697 edition of

Heimskringla.[1] Thormod Torfæus, the Iceland-born historiographer to Frederick IV of Denmark and Norway, published his *Historia Vinlandiæ Antiqvæ* in 1705. The Vínland voyages remained largely the province of Northern European scholars until the closing decades of the eighteenth century,[2] when Thomas Percy, who had whetted the English appetite for 'Viking gothic'[3] in *Five Pieces of Runic Poetry* (1763), introduced his readers to the Vínland voyages in *Northern Antiquities* (1770),[4] a translation and revision of the 1763 edition of Mallet's *L'Histoire de Dannemarc*.[5] Further reports of the Vínland story appeared in England a few years later in the reviews, published in *The Critical Review* (1786) and *The Monthly Review* (1787), of *History of Discoveries and Voyages made in the north* (1786), the English translation of Johan Reinhold Foerster's *Geschichte der Entdeckungen und Schifffahrten im Norden* (1784). The piece in *The Critical Review* concludes with an extract from Foerster's account of the discovery of 'Winland dat Gode', which he based on the account in *Grænlendinga saga*. It notes that 'the facts are, on the whole, well established in various authors; and we must allow, that probably some parts of the American coast were seen by the Normans five hundred years before the reputed discovery'.[6] Similarly, although *The Monthly Review* adopts a note of caution about certain 'discoveries . . . lately . . . made . . . from ancient manuscripts', it takes the view that 'Dr. Forster is fully justified, and we esteem ourselves much obliged to him for making these curious and interesting particulars more public than they were before'.[7] In his 'Preliminary Dissertation' to George Mackenzie's *Travels in the Island of Iceland* (1812), Henry Holland offered a two-page summary of the Vínland voyages which refers readers to additional information in medieval Icelandic sources such as *Landnámabók* and *Eyrbyggja saga* and, 'among more modern writings', Thormod Torfaeus.[8] John Barrow's 1818 account of the settlement of Iceland

---

1 For the background to this, see Samuel Laing, *The Heimskringla; or, Chronicle of the Kings of Norway. Translated from the Icelandic of Snorro Sturleson*, 3 vols (London, 1844), III, 343–4.

2 For a useful and comprehensive account of Vínland scholarship in the seventeenth and eighteenth centuries, see Matti Enn Kaups, 'Shifting Vinland – Tradition and Myth', *Terrae Incognitae* 2 (1971), 32–7. See also William Stetson Merrill, 'The Vinland Problem Through Four Centuries', *The Catholic Historical Review* 21 (1936), 26–9.

3 On the influence of Icelandic poetry in eighteenth-century England, see J. A. W. Bennett, *The History of Old English and Old Norse Studies in England from the Time of Francis Junius till the end of the Eighteenth Century*, unpubl. D.Phil. thesis, University of Oxford, Bodl. MS D.Phil. d. 287 (1938), pp. 214–16; Frank Edgar Farley, *Scandinavian Influences in the English Romantic Movement*, Studies and Notes in Philology and Literature 9 (Boston, 1903); Margaret Omberg, *Scandinavian Themes in English Poetry, 1760–1800*, Acta Universitatis Upsaliensis, Studia Anglistica Upsaliensia, 29 (1976), 134–46, 62–85; Margaret Clunies Ross, *The Norse Muse in Britain, 1750–1820* (Trieste, 1998).

4 *Northern Antiquities: or, a Description of the Manners, Customs, Religion and Laws of the Ancient Danes, And other Northern Nations*, 2 vols (London, 1770), I, 286–305.

5 *Introduction à l'histoire de Dannemarc, ou l'on traite de la Réligion, des Loix, des Mœurs & des Usages des Anciens Danois* (Copenhagen, 1755).

6 *The Critical Review* 62 (1786), 337.

7 *The Monthly Review or Literary Journal* 76 (1787), 621.

8 Henry Holland, M.D., 'Preliminary Dissertation on the History and Literature of Iceland', in

and Greenland included a brief recital of Leifr's voyage to Helluland, Markland, and Vínland and a more detailed botanical consideration of Vínland's grapes.[9]

Whereas scholarly interest in Old Norse had begun in England in the late seventeenth century,[10] and translations of Icelandic heroic poetry were popular in the eighteenth among English lovers of a characteristically 'gothic' blend of beauty and terror, the only documented evidence of interest in Old Icelandic language or literature in eighteenth-century America is Thomas Jefferson's unsuccessful proposal to the Virginia Assembly that one of eight professorships designated by a committee appointed in 1776 to revise the constitution of the College of William and Mary should be in 'ancient languages, including Oriental (Hebrew, Chaldee, Syriac) and Northern Tongues (Mœso-Gothic, Anglo-Saxon, Old Icelandic)'.[11] The 'gothic' conception of Scandinavia never took hold in America, where the arbiters of literary taste were predominantly lawyers and clergymen, whose criteria for literary excellence were social conservatism, optimism, and a lack of obscurity in thought and action.[12] The first Americans who undertook the study of Old Norse language and literature and the history of medieval Scandinavia were likewise, for the most part, trained as lawyers, their interest sparked both by the common origins of Germanic legal institutions and languages[13] and the notion, which goes back to seventeenth-century England, that the Goths – in the tribal sense – were the champions of liberty.[14] A generation earlier, after the defeat of his bill to amend the constitution of the College of William and Mary, Jefferson had justified his views on the importance of the study of Northern languages and literature for Americans on similar grounds in his *Notes on the State of Virginia* (1785): '[t]o the professorships usually established in the universities of Europe it would seem proper to add one for the ancient languages and literatures of the north, on account of their connection with our own language, laws, customs, and history'.[15]

Reviews of the first major history of early Scandinavia by an American, *History of the Northmen, or Danes and Normans, from the earliest times to the*

Sir George Steuart Mackenzie, *Travels in the Island of Iceland during the summer of the year MDCCCX* (Edinburgh, 1812), p. 45.

9   John Barrow, *A Chronological History of Voyages into the Arctic Regions* (London, 1818), pp. 7–9.

10 Bennett, *The History of Old English and Old Norse Studies in England*, pp. 214–16; *idem*, 'The Beginnings of Norse Studies in England', *Saga-Book of the Viking Society* 12 (1937–1945), 35–42; Farley, *Scandinavian Influences*, pp. 19–25; Omberg, *Scandinavian Themes*, pp. 17–120; Judy Quinn and Margaret Clunies Ross, 'The Image of Norse Poetry and Myth in Seventeenth-Century England', in *Northern Antiquity*, ed. Andrew Wawn (Enfield Lock, 1994), pp. 189–210.

11 Cited Herbert Baxter Adams, *Thomas Jefferson and the University of Virginia*, U.S. Bureau of Education, Circular of Information No. 1 (Washington, 1888), p. 42 (from *Sundry Documents on the Subject of a System of Public Education for the State of Virginia* [Richmond, 1817], p. 60).

12 See William Charvat, *The Origins of American Critical Thought 1810–1835* (Philadelphia, 1936).

13 See Adolph B. Benson, 'The Beginning of American Interest in Scandinavian Literature', *Scandinavian Studies and Notes* 8 (1924–25), 135–7.

14 See Reginald Horsman, *Race and Manifest Destiny. The Origins of American Racial Anglo-Saxonism* (Cambridge, Mass., 1981), pp. 15–24.

15 *Notes on the State of Virginia*, ed. Thomas Perkins Abernethy (New York, 1964), pp. 144–5.

Conquest of England by William of Normandy (1831) by Henry Wheaton, eminent jurist and chargé d'affaires to Denmark from 1827 to 1835,[16] demonstrate the contrasting perceptions of medieval Scandinavia in the minds of English and American readers in the early 1830s. Wheaton's expressed intention was to position Scandinavia's history in the context of the development of the monarchies of Europe (Preface, p. v). His reviewer in *The Westminster Review* applauded that measure of 'Gothic blood and Gothic affection' which had inspired the author of a work devoted to 'the history of our forefathers – the progenitors of our own blood – the history of one great branch, and that the most adventurous, of our renowned Gothic race'.[17] The *American Monthly Review*, on the other hand, voiced approval of Wheaton's historical method[18] but made no reference to the glories of Gothic ancestry. Wheaton's account of pre-Christian Scandinavians was deeply satisfying to *The Athenæum*, which heartily endorsed his comparison of the Icelandic Commonwealth with Ancient Greece,[19] but *The American Quarterly Review* was less impresssed ('They presented very few of the features of a regular government . . . Of this singular state of society or barbarism, Mr. Wheaton gives an animated picture')[20] and would have preferred that a history of the Northmen place more emphasis upon their influence on the evolution of European institutions by undertaking

> an inquiry into the origin of the laws, customs, language, and forms of government, which long existed in Europe, for in all of them may be distinctly seen, as it is strongly marked, the impression made by these barbarians upon the institutions of the countries which they overran.   (p. 312)[21]

Wheaton himself had elsewhere remarked upon the ultimate Northern source of 'our origin, our language, and our laws',[22] but his interests went beyond the Anglo-American Teutonic legacy to the linguistic ties which bind 'the great family of man, from the banks of the Ganges to the shores of Iceland' (*ibid.*).

References to the likelihood of a Scandinavian landing west of Greenland occasionally appear in American letters of the latter part of the eighteenth and

---

16 On Wheaton's Scandinavian scholarship see Adolph B. Benson, 'Henry Wheaton's Writings on Scandinavia', *JEGP* 29 (1930), 546–61.
17 *The Westminster Review* 15 (1831), 442.
18 *The American Monthly Review* (March, 1832), 245–56.
19 *The Athenæum* 194 (July, 1831), 454.
20 *The American Quarterly Review* 10 (1831), 317, 318.
21 Wheaton's *The American Quarterly Review* reviewer indicates a lack of familiarity with the literature of medieval Scandinavia in stating that the sagas are 'compositions in verse, each of which relates the story of some distinguished king or chieftain' (*ibid.*, p. 329), a misconception which persisted in some quarters until the end of the century. The 1895 issue of *Poet-lore* declares that: 'All the old poems of the Norsemen are called "Sagas"' (P.A.C., 'School of Literature. Poems Illustrative of American History: Whittier's "The Norsemen"', *Poet-lore* 7 [1895], 107). A short, anonymous piece in *The Atlantic Monthly* (1887) claims that Icelandic was the 'court language in Norway, Sweden, Denmark, England, and at Rouen' (p. 856) in the time of Leifr Eiríksson and that Icelandic merchants spoke Latin and Italian (*ibid.*).
22 'Scandinavian Literature', *The American Quarterly Review* (1828), 490.

early nineteenth centuries. In the account of his travels to Canada published in 1751,[23] John Bartram of Philadelphia noted the short distance between Davis Strait and the American continent and speculated that:

> it is scarce possible to think, that of the numerous fleets with which the *Danes* and *Norwegians* terrified continually the rest of Europe, none tempted by the hopes of gain, or drove by stress of weather, should ever fall in with the coasts of *Newfoundland* or *Gulph of St. Lawrence*. If it be objected that the navigators of those times were too unskilfull to attempt such a discovery, does it not furnish us with a reason to account for its being made by chance.   (pp. 75–6)

In a letter to Samuel Mather written in 1773, Benjamin Franklin remarked that, despite his initial scepticism in the face of the claim, a handwritten account concerning the Norse discovery of America produced for him some twenty-five years earlier by the Swedish botanist, Peter Kalm, had a 'great Appearance of Authenticity'.[24] An anonymous article, 'The discovery of Vinland, or America, by the Icelanders', translated from Mallet's *Histoire de Dannemarc* (1763) and endorsing that scholar's sources as 'of most unquestionable credibility', appeared in two issues of *The American Museum* in 1789–90.[25] Citing David Crantz and the Norwegian bishop, Erik Pontoppidan (1698–1764), as his authorities in the first volume of his *American Biography* (1794), Jeremy Belknap credited 'Biron' (Bjorn Herjolfsson) with the accidental discovery of '*Winland* . . . supposed to be a part of the island of *Newfoundland*'.[26] In his summary of the Vínland voyages, based upon Torfæus and Peringskiold, in *History of the Northmen* Wheaton permitted himself a qualified footnote conjecture that Vínland 'must have been in the latitude of Boston'.[27]

Other late eighteenth- and early nineteenth-century English and American writers had also canvassed the possibility of Scandinavian landings in the New World. The Scottish historian, William Robertson, raised it in *The History of America* (1788).[28] In his *Historical Account of Discoveries and Travels in North America* (1829) the English writer, Hugh Murray, declared himself prepared to accept that the voyages had taken place but, on the evidence of his reading of Torfaeus and Peringskiold, located Vínland in Greenland rather than America.[29] On the cited authority of Torfæus and Mallet, Hugh Williamson remarked in *The History of Carolina* (1812) that '[t]he eastern coast of North America was

---

23 *Observations on the Inhabitants, Climate, Soil, Rivers, Productions, Animals, and other matters worthy of Notice made by Mr. John Bartram, In his Travels from Pensilvania to Onondago, Oswego and the Lake Ontario, In Canada* (London, 1751).

24 *The Papers of Benjamin Franklin*, ed. Leonard W. Labaree *et al.*, 34 vols (New Haven and London, 1959–98), Vol. 20, ed. William B. Willcox (1976), 288.

25 *The American Museum* 6 (August, 1789), 159–62; 7 (June, 1790), 340–4.

26 Jeremy Belknap, *American Biography* I (1794), 47.

27 *History of the Northmen*, p. 24n.

28 *The History of America*, III, fourteenth edn (London, 1821), 311–13.

29 *Historical Account of Discoveries and Travels in North America* (London, 1829), pp. 19–21.

visited by Erick a Norwegian, near one thousand years ago'.[30] In *History of the State of New York* (1824) Joseph Moulton declares that 'the Scandinavian voyagers . . . clearly visited our coast several centuries before any southern European nation had discovered America'[31] and provides a lengthy excursus on the subject translated from an article published in 1818 by the Swedish scholar, Johan Schröder.[32] Moulton permits himself 'the bold flight of a licensed fancy' (p. 115) to follow Leifr's itinerary east or west of Long Island Sound. However, in possibly the first expression of what was to become a major point of contention in the 'Leifr vs. Columbus' debate later in the century, he takes issue with Schröder's conclusion that Columbus must have been familiar with Scandinavian reports of land to the west of Greenland, because it 'tends to the prejudice of the great modern European discoverer of this continent' (p. 123).

The first sustained evidence of scepticism about the validity of reports of voyages to the west of Greenland in Old Norse sources appears in reviews of Wheaton's *History of the Northmen*. *The Westminster Review* (1831) argued that the author should have ignored Peringskiold's *Grænlendinga saga* material, which did not have the authority of Snorri Sturluson, as 'unworthy of credence' (p. 445). The report of the land called Vínland 'cannot', states the writer, 'refer to the American continent' (p. 446). For reasons which had nothing to do with the disputed authenticity of medieval sources, American readers had by this time become less hospitable than Benjamin Franklin and Jeremy Belknap to the notion of a pre-Columbian Norse presence. Wheaton's reviewer in the *American Monthly Review* (1832) had conceded that the distance between Greenland and America was not great; that there was nothing in Wheaton's sources 'which does not in its general features agree with the northerly regions of this continent' (p. 249); and, moreover, that 'the merits of Columbus and of Cabot are not impaired by this fact of previous transient settlement on the shores of this continent' (p. 250). *The American Quarterly Review*, on the other hand, seemed reluctant to acknowledge the existence of Vínland, let alone that it might have been in America: accounts, says Wheaton's reviewer, of expeditions there and other places south of Greenland 'are indistinct, and uncertain' (1831, 323). Unsurprisingly, Washington Irving ignored the question altogether in his favourable review of Wheaton's book for *The North American Review* (1832).

Washington Irving himself had a lot to do with this post-1830 reluctance to entertain the notion of a pre-Columbian Viking presence in America. The publication of *Antiquitates Americanæ* shifted allegations of prior landings and temporary settlements from the sphere of rumour and conjecture to tangible record, thereby conceivably posing a threat to the growing pre-eminence of Columbus. Irving's admiring – some would say hagiographic – biography, *The*

---

30 *The History of Carolina*, I (Philadelphia, 1812), p. 6.
31 *History of the State of New York*, I (New York, 1824).
32 'Om Skandinavernes Fordna Upptåcktsresor Till Nordamerika', *Svea* 1 (1818), 197–226. Schröder derives his information from Torfæus and the chapters from *GS* in Peringskiold's *Heimskringla* ('Om Skandinavernes Fordna', pp. 201, 202).

Life and Voyages of Christopher Columbus, had been published in 1828 to a generally rapturous reception in America,[33] where it inspired a veritable cult of Columbus as architect of the nation's genesis. 'What', as Edward Everett asked with rhetorical flourish a few years later, 'can a mortal man do, which approaches so near the work of his Creator, as to bring an unknown world to the knowledge of his fellow-men?'[34] Some English reviewers of *The Life and Voyages* were less enthusiastic. 'On the whole, we consider this book to be unnecessary', sniffed *The Athenæum* reviewer. '[H]e has imbued his pages with far more of the colouring of mere romance, than of authentic narration', sneered *The Monthly Review.*[35]

Irving had previously aired his views on the Vínland voyages in *Knickerbocker's History of New York* (1809), in which the Norsemen appear only as bit players in the burlesque of scholarly enterprise which serves as the prelude to the founding of the city:

> I shall neither inquire whether it [America] was first discovered by the Chinese, as Vossius with great shrewdness advances; nor by the Norwegians in 1002, under Biorn . . . I pass over the supposition of the learned Grotius . . . that North America was peopled by a strolling company of Norwegians . . . Nor shall I more than barely mention, that father Kircher ascribes the settlement of America to the Egyptians, Rudbeck to the Scandinavians, Charron to the Gauls, Juffredus Petri to a skating party from Friesland.[36]

In the opening paragraph of *The Life and Voyages* the Vínland voyages are dismissed again. The sagas are mere 'legends'. Vinland is 'mysterious' and unlikely to have been within the borders of the United States:

> if the legends of the Scandinavian voyagers be correct, and their mysterious Vinland was the coast of Labrador or the shore of Newfoundland, they had but transient glimpses of the new world, leading to certain or permanent knowledge, and in a little time lost again to mankind.[37]

Irving nevertheless accorded the voyages of the Norsemen more detailed and serious attention in the essay 'Voyages of the Scandinavians', based largely on

---

33 See, for example, *The American Quarterly Review* 5 (March, 1828), 173–90; *The North American Review* 28 (January, 1829), 125–34. For a late twentieth-century assessment of the work, which argues that Irving is ambivalent towards his hero, see John D. Hazlett, 'Literary Nationalism and Ambivalence in Washington Irving's *The Life and Voyages of Christopher Columbus*', *American Literature* 55 (1983), 560–75.

34 *The North American Review* 46 (1838), 162. On the evolution of Columbus as hero and martyr, see Kirkpatrick Sale, *The Conquest of Paradise. Christopher Columbus and the Columbian Legacy* (London, 1991), pp. 235–40, 325–60.

35 *The Athenæum* 10 (26 February 1828), 151; *The Monthly Review* 7 (1828), 419.

36 *A History of New York, from the beginning of the world to the end of the Dutch dynasty*, The Works of Washington Irving, I (London, 1883), pp. 15, 18.

37 *The Life and Voyages of Christopher Columbus*, ed. John McElroy, The Complete Works of Washington Irving, 9 (Boston, 1981), p. 9.

the relevant section of Foerster's *Northern Voyages*, which appears in the Appendix (Part XIV) to *The Life and Voyages*. With evident reluctance, he conceded that, despite his conviction that the evidence was flimsy,

> There is no great improbability . . . that such enterprising and roving voyagers as the Scandinavians may have wandered to the northern shores of America.[38]

Such landings, however, he judged to be of no greater consequence 'than would the interchange of communication between the natives of Greenland and the Esquimaux', even in the minds of the Scandinavians themselves:

> The knowledge of them appears not to have extended beyond their own nation, and to have been soon neglected and forgotten by themselves.   (*ibid.*)[39]

Neglected it may have been, but the notion of a Viking presence in America around the year 1000 arguably extended the course of the continent's European history by five hundred years and placed a Christian hero from an Atlantic 'republic' at its helm. Moreover, according to *Eiríks saga rauða*, Leifr was bound on a mission worthy of Columbus himself: the conversion of Greenland. Moulton's 'bold flight of fancy' in the early 1820s, which has Leifr winter in New York, suggests a preparedness to admit the Vínland voyages to the myth of national foundation and Leifr to its sparsely populated pantheon of legendary heroes. The revelation in *Antiquitates Americanæ*, less than ten years after the publication of Irving's *The Life and Voyages*, of eleventh-century Scandinavian landfalls west of Greenland was, however, seen by many as an affront, or even a threat, to the pinpointing of Columbus's landing at San Salvador on 12 October 1492 as the moment of national creation.

The reception of Antiquitates Americanæ

Issued under the aegis of the Royal Danish Society of Northern Antiquaries,[40] *Antiquitates Americanæ*[41] was financed to a large extent by its principal author and publicist, the Danish scholar Carl Christian Rafn (1795–1864).[42] The work comprised editions, with Danish and Latin translations, and notes and commentary in Latin, of *Grænlendinga saga* and *Eiríks saga rauða*; related

---

38 *The Life and Voyages of Christopher Columbus; together with the Voyages of His Companions*, author's revised edn, 2 vols, The Works of Washington Irving, 6 (London, 1883), II, 843.
39 For an analysis of Irving's treatment of Scandinavians in *Knickerbocker's History of New York* and *The Life and Voyages of Christopher Columbus*, see Adolph B. Benson, 'Scandinavians in the Works of Washington Irving', *Scandinavian Studies and Notes* 9 (1926), 207–23.
40 The Society was founded in 1825 by Rafn and Rasmus Rask.
41 Henceforth abbreviated in footnotes to *AA*.
42 On Rafn's financial contribution to *AA*, see the review in *The American Monthly Magazine* 11 (1838) 366; Thomas H. Webb, 'Communication on Professor Rafn', *Proceedings of the Massachusetts Historical Society* 8 (1865–65), 189.

material in Latin and Norse; compendious background information; an English summary of the Vínland voyages; identification of place-names in *Grœnlendinga saga* and *Eiríks saga rauða* with specific New England locations;[43] and a detailed report on alleged Viking remains in Massachusetts with maps and drawings. Widely publicised and reviewed in America, its reception in England, where Old Norse studies were well established and the book's concerns of no great national interest, was more muted.

English translations of sections of *Antiquitates Americanæ*, mainly from Rafn's Latin and Danish versions of *Grœnlendinga saga* and *Eiríks saga rauða* but in some instances from the Icelandic itself, were nevertheless published on both sides of the Atlantic. Extended extracts appeared in Joshua Toulmin Smith's *The Northmen in America* (London and Boston, 1839) and Nathaniel Ludlow Beamish's *The Discovery of America by the Northmen in the Tenth Century* (London, 1841). George Webbe Dasent included passages, although not ones which concerned the Vínland voyages, from Rafn's edition of *Grœnlendinga saga* and *Eiríks saga rauða* in *Antiquitates Americanæ* among the 'Extracts in Prose and Verse by way of Praxis' in his *A Grammar of the Icelanders* (London, 1843).[44] Excerpts from *Grœnlendinga saga* relating the westward voyages of Leifr, Þorvaldr, and Þorsteinn Eiríksson, 'Translated from the Icelandic' by Elihu Burritt, appeared in the inaugural issue of *The American Eclectic* (1841).[45] The Reverend Benjamin De Costa's *The Pre-Columbian Discovery of America, by the Northmen* (1868) contained English versions, based on *Antiquitates Americanæ*, of material relating to voyages west of Greenland in *Grœnlendinga saga*, *Eiríks saga rauða, Landnámabók*, and *Eyrbyggja saga*.[46]

Antiquitates Americanæ was a large, expensive, and generally grandiose production, whose showmanship was ultimately to the detriment of its otherwise sound scholarship. Based archaeologically and geographically on some-

---

43 Nantucket, for example, is identified with the shallows encountered by Leifr in *GS* (ch. 3); *Kjalarnes* is Cape Cod; the *Furðustrandir* are Nauset Beach, Chatham Beach, and Monomoy Beach; *Straumfjǫrðr* is Buzzard's Bay; *Straumey* is Martha's Vineyard; *Krossaness* 'is probably Gurnet Point' (p. XXXV); *Hóp* is Mount Hope's Bay (pp. XXIV–XXXV).

44 *A Grammar of the Icelanders or Old Norse Tongue translated from the Swedish of Erasmus Rask* (London, 1843), pp. 257–63.

45 'The Narrative of Thorstein Ericsson', *The American Eclectic: Selections from the Periodical Literature of all Foreign Countries* 1 (1841), 109–111.

46 De Costa's cited sources are the relevant extracts from *Landnámabók* in *Grönlands Historiske Mindesmærker* (Copenhagen, 1838–45) and *Antiquitates Americanae*. The extent of his command of Icelandic is not clear. Of Danish and Icelandic he says, somewhat confusingly, in the Preface: 'In everything relating to the latter tongue, the author has had the invaluable assistance and advice of one who has spoken it from childhood. He has also had most important and indispensable aid in connection with the Icelandic' (*The Pre-Columbian Discovery of America, by the Northmen, with translations from the Icelandic sagas*, 2nd edn, Albany 1890, p. 7). As De Costa's reviewer in *The North American Review* 109 (1869, 267) indicates, most of his material from *GS* is taken, almost entirely verbatim and without acknowledgment, from Samuel Laing's translation of the 'Norse' of Jacob Aal (see Samuel Laing, *The Heimskringla; or, Chronicle of the Kings of Norway* [London, 1844], Preface, p. v).

what shaky premises, the work's scholarly reputation ultimately foundered on them. From the time of its publication to the end of the nineteenth century, however, *Antiquitates Americanæ* attracted the attention of serious scholars as well as the more eccentric fringes of learning. Concurrent in the 1830s with George Perkins Marsh's Jeffersonian interest in the shared origins of the Germanic languages and institutions, for example, was the enthusiastic excavation of a spurious Viking past by members of the Rhode Island Historical Society, who warmly embraced the notion of Leifr Eiríksson as New England traveller. In the second half of the nineteenth century there were attempts, largely but not wholly outside the mainstream of scholarship, to incorporate the Vínland voyages directly into New England's 'gothic' lineage and even to construct a centuries-long colony of Vínland.

In addition to the evidence of the Vínland sagas themselves, Rafn added a new dimension to the notion of Norse voyages to America by offering precise, and utterly unfounded, geographical pinpointings for Viking landings in New England. In the course of his research he corresponded with the historical societies of Rhode Island and Massachusetts.[47] The latter were polite but never fully convinced. The former responded to his requests for evidence of a Viking presence with an avalanche of spurious Vínlandia. This ranged from the 'Dighton Rock', which had been found in the previous century beside the Taunton River, in Massachusetts, and whose inscriptions Rafn's co-editor, Finnur Magnússon, confidently identified as runic,[48] to an edifice in Newport, Rhode Island, which Rafn claimed, on the strength of a lithograph sent to him by Thomas Webb, Secretary of the Rhode Island Historical Society, as an eleventh-century Scandinavian church.[49] Rafn, the tenor of whose exchanges with James Bartlett of the

---

47 For Rafn's correspondence with the Society from 1829 to 1852, see *Massachusetts Historical Society, Proceedings* 1 (1791–1835), 425 (Rafn accepts election to the Society); 2 (1835–55), 29–30 (report of letter received from Rafn concerning completion of *AA*); 85–6 (Rafn sends prospectuses for *AA* and solicits subscribers; seeks American members for the Royal Society for Northern Antiquaries); 97–8 (Rafn seeks assistance in increasing the circulation of *AA* and says that 'monuments' in Massachusetts and Rhode Island have been confirmed as North European by Finnur Magnússon); 107–9 (T. M. Harris, Corresponding Secretary of the Massachusetts Historical Society, declines election to the Royal Society of Northern Antiquities on the grounds of age and infirmity; has sent prospectuses of *AA* to the editor of *The North American Review* and copies of *AA* to subscribers); 125–6 (T. M. Harris will forward parcels from Rafn to their designated recipients; expresses disappointment in the lack of acknowledgment of his letter of the previous year concerning the delivery of copies of *AA*); 500–1 (Rafn sends a short article on the Norse discovery which he asks the Society to publish and distribute). For Rafn's correspondence with Thomas Webb, see *AA*, pp. 356–404; Benedict Grøndal, ed., *Breve fra og til Carl Christian Rafn, med en Biographi* (Copenhagen, 1869), pp. 130–75; *Proceedings of the Massachusetts Historical Society* 8 (1864–65), 189–98 (this last includes a lengthy tribute to and defence of Rafn's researches on the Vínland voyages).

48 *AA*, pp. 378–82.

49 See 'Bemærkninger om en gammel bygning i Newport', *Annaler for nordisk Oldkyndighed* (1840–41), pp. 37–51. For a succinct review of the history of the Dighton Rock and the Newport Tower, see Stephen Williams, *Fantastic Archaeology. The Wild Side of North American Prehistory* (Philadelphia, 1991), pp. 213–17.

Rhode Island Historical Society[50] and letters to the Massachusetts Historical Society suggests that he was a somewhat demanding correspondent, also enlisted the voluntary services of a retinue of well-placed New Englanders, among them George Perkins Marsh, to obtain subscribers, reviews, and the wide distribution of *Antiquitates Americanæ*. By 1849 no less an authority than Alexander von Humboldt had recanted the doubts expressed in his *Examen critique de l'histoire de la geographie du nouveau continent* (1836)[51] and, with a reference to the 1845 edition of *Antiquitates Americanæ*, acknowledged the Norse landing as fact.[52] The American historian, William Hickling Prescott, was prepared to concede, in a footnote to his classic *Conquest of Mexico* (1843), that the evidence of the sagas was convincing in principle, if not in geographical particulars:

> Whatever skepticism may have been entertained as to the visit of the Northmen, in the eleventh century, to the coasts of the great continent, it is probably set at rest in the minds of most scholars since the publication of the original documents by the Royal Society at Copenhagen. (See, in particular, Antiquitates Americanæ (Hafniæ, 1837), pp. 79–200.) How far south they penetrated is not so easily settled.[53]

On the other hand, although a leading proponent of the notion that the origins of liberty were Teutonic, Prescott's equally eminent friend and fellow Bostonian, George Bancroft, found no room for a Viking presence in his country's history.[54] Despite a polite exchange of letters with Rafn in the early 1830s, in which he expressed his eagerness to read the published results of the Danish scholar's research, Bancroft steadfastly consigned the Vínland sagas to the realm

---

50 In an anxious-sounding letter to Rafn of 19 February 1837, Bartlett, for example, says that he is having trouble in getting subscriptions to *AA* because the two copies of the prospectus which he received have been lost, and that he cannot distribute the prospectus and other promotional material because winter has caused the closure of rivers and canals. By June 1839, Rafn was telling Bartlett that he was about to send him 2,000 more copies of the prospectus. Rafn asked both Bartlett (Rafn to Bartlett, 22 September 1838) and Longfellow (Rafn to Longfellow, 18 October 1838) to send him all the 'notices' of *AA* which they could procure. Fiske Icelandic Collection, Cornell University. See Þórunn Sigurðardóttir, *Manuscript Material, Correspondence, and Graphic Material in the Fiske Icelandic Collection. A Descriptive Catalogue*, Islandica 48 (Ithaca and London, 1994), Item 81.

51 Alleged discoveries of America prior to Columbus 'ne sont pas tous également avérés ou bien interprétés, tels que le repport d'un prêtre bouddhiste, Hoeïchin sur le Fousang et Tahan (l'an 500), les découvertes du Groenland, du Vinland, et de l'embouchure du Saint-Laurent, par Erik Rauda (985), Bjoern (1001), et Madoc ap Owen (1170)', *Examen critique le l'histoire de la geographie du nouveau continent et des progrès de l'astronomie nautique aux quinzième et seizième siècles*, I (Paris, 1836), 29.

52 *Cosmos: A Sketch of a Physical Description of the Universe*, translated from the German by E. C. Otté, II (London, 1849), 603–5.

53 William H. Prescott, *History of the Conquest of Mexico*, ed. Wilfred Harold Munro (Philadelphia and London, 1904) I, 226, n.8.

54 See David Levin, *History as Romantic Art: Bancroft, Prescott, Motley, and Parkman* (New York and Burlingame, 1959), ch. IV (pp. 74–92).

of legend through the many editions of his *History of the United States*, the first volume of which appeared in 1834. A prominent exponent throughout the 1820s and 1830s of the prevailing literary ideal of clarity of thought and experience,[55] Bancroft dismissed the sagas as 'mythological in form, and obscure in meaning' (I, 5) and the account in *Grœnlendinga saga* of Vínland's mild winter and fertile soil as 'fictitious or exaggerated' (I, 6).[56] He expressed his opinion of the alleged runic inscriptions on the Dighton Rock more colloquially in a communication to the ethnographer, Henry Schoolcraft: 'All they say about the Dighton Rock is, I think, the sublime of humbuggery'.[57] Rafn continued to hope that Bancroft would change his mind,[58] as a letter to Willard Fiske in 1853 indicates, but his 'thoroughly revised' six-volume 'Centenary Edition' of *History of the United States* (1876) simply removed all mention of the Vínland voyages.

Thanks to Rafn's vigorously pursued personal contacts, however, *Antiquitates Americanæ* was widely and favourably reviewed, and previewed, in America.[59] *The North American Review* eagerly anticipated the publication of this 'collection of Icelandic documents, consisting of ancient Sagas, and selections from geographical works, concerning the early voyages of the Northmen to North America'.[60] As early as 1833, Josiah Priest, an exponent of the discovery of America by the 'ancients' as ridiculed by Washington Irving in *Knickerbocker's History of New York*, says that he has heard of:

> A distinguished writer of Copenhagen . . . not long since engaged in the composition of a work on the early voyages of discovery to this continent, as undertaken by the inhabitants the north of Europe, more than eight hundred and thirty years ago.[61]

Lengthy, earnest, and laudatory review articles by eminent men of letters

---

55 See Charvat, *American Critical Thought*, pp. 188–90.

56 *History of the United States from the Discovery of the American Continent*, 5 vols (London, 1854).

57 Schoolcraft, *Memoirs*, p. 639.

58 'Det er da at vente at man i en ny Udgave af Bancrofts History of the United States ikke vil gjentage den utvivlsom feilagtige Notice betroffende somme i der stod i de tidligere Udgaver', Rafn to Fiske, 8 June 1853. Fiske Icelandic Collection, Cornell University. See Þórunn Sigurðardóttir, *Manuscript Material . . . in the Fiske Icelandic Collection*, Correspondence 1. 'Letters to Daniel Willard Fiske.'

59 For a comprehensive list of reviews of *Antiquitates Americanæ*, see Halldór Hermannsson, 'The Northmen in America', *Islandica* 2 (1909), 7.

60 *The North American Review* 43 (1836), 265.

61 Josiah Priest, *American Antiquities, and discoveries in the west: being an exhibition of the evidence that an ancient population of partially civilized nations, differing entirely from those of the present Indians, peopled America, many centuries before its discovery by Columbus*, etc. (Albany, NY, 1833), p. 233. Rafn was sent a copy of this book by John Bartlett, who says that 'in this there is much valuable Antiquarian matter, collected from a variety of sources (some of which cannot be depended upon). I trust, however, that you will find something interesting in it and can discriminate between the doubtful and authentic' (Bartlett to Rafn, 9 April 1838). Fiske Icelandic Collection, Cornell University. See Þórunn Sigurðardóttir, *Manuscript Material . . . in the Fiske Icelandic Collection*, Item 81.

appeared in *The North American Review* (Edward Everett), *The New York Review* (George Folsom), *The United States Magazine and Democratic Review* (Alexander Hill Everett), *The American Biblical Repository* (Henry Schoolcraft), and *The Western Messenger*, with shorter notices in *The Knickerbocker* and *The American Monthly Magazine*. All commented favourably on the high quality of the production of the book and its exciting revelations, although some frowned upon what appeared to be the appropriation of American history by non-Americans. *The Knickerbocker*, for instance, found it 'regrettable' that a lack of national interest in pre-Columbian culture meant that American history was being investigated by '*foreign* [sic] societies'.[62]

Prior to the publication of *Antiquitates Americanæ* accounts of the Vínland voyages had previously been available to American audiences only at second- or third-hand. In its size, splendour, confident assertions about actual Viking landing sites, and weighty scholarly apparatus, *Antiquitates Americanæ* gave them a substance and authority which, for some, constituted a potentially serious challenge, by a pack of barely Christian pirates, to Columbus and his divine purpose. Mindful of this possibility, Rafn took pains in the 'Prospectus' for *Antiquitates Americanæ* to counter any such impression by paying due homage to Columbus as the facilitator of the European colonization of America, 'whose glory cannot in any degree be impaired by the prior achievement', while claiming justifiable national pride in his Norse harbingers: 'Yet still we Northmen ought not to forget his meritorious predecessors, our own forefathers'.[63] A number of the reviewers of *Antiquitates Americanæ* made a qualitative contrast between the purposefulness of Columbus and the accidental nature of the Norse landfall. Wheaton anticipated the occasioning of 'no less chagrin than surprise' by the revelations of *Antiquitates Americanæ* in the opening sentence of his review in *The Foreign Quarterly Review*[64] and compared the purpose and grand design of Columbus, 'who with long premeditation, designing no less than to overleap the boundaries of the known world, succeeded in realizing so far the dreams of an enthusiastic imagination', with the chance discovery of the 'roving Scandinavians' (p. 90). This, he says, 'cannot emulate but rather serves by comparison to exalt the achievement of Columbus' (*ibid.*). Edward Everett prefaced his review in *The North American Review* with the statement quoted above concerning the quasi-divinity of Columbus. It was not until 1869 that an American critic, the anonymous *North American Review* reviewer of De Costa's *The Pre-Columbian Discovery of America*, discarded gravitas for irreverence on the subject of Leifr's and Karlsefni's alleged itinerary along the New England coast:

> In the same spirit [as Rafn], treating these Sagas precisely as though they were the log-book of Cunard steamer, he [De Costa] persists in following the Northmen up

---

62 *The Knickerbocker* 11 (1838), 289.
63 Charles C. Rafn, *America Discovered in the Tenth Century* (New York, 1838).
64 *The Foreign Quarterly Review* 21 (1831), 89.

the Seaconnet passage, and into Mount Hope Bay. To do this, he is obliged to transform this broad expanse of salt water into a lake, and gravely assures us that it not only has this appearance to the traveller passing it by rail, but is often called so, – a statement which, we venture to say, will astound those who have lived by it all their lives.[65]

In England, where the navigationally disoriented and unsuccessful colonists of *Grœnlendinga saga* and *Eiríks saga rauða* did not fit the Übermensch image of the heroes of Old Icelandic poetry and revelations of pre-Columbian voyages to America were of less national interest, *Antiquitates Americanæ* appeared to little fanfare and some condescension. Only *The Foreign Quarterly Review* accorded it a full-length article, by Henry Wheaton, and it attracted no more than brief citations in the reviews of Beamish's *Discovery of America by the Northmen* which appeared in *Tait's Edinburgh Magazine*, *The Monthly Review*, and *The Athenaeum*.[66] *The Athenaeum* patronizingly insinuated that *Antiquitates Americanæ* verged on the risible in its pretentiousness of size, cost, claims to new revelations, and statements of the obvious:

> Without wishing to depreciate M. Rafn's volume, or to deny its intrinsic importance, we confess that we cannot help smiling at the pomp and circumstance of its appearance. Statements, for the most part familiar to geographers, are produced as novelties; and being published in three languages, with summaries and prefaces in two languages, and critical accompaniments, they fill a very large and expensive quarto volume. (3 July 1841, p. 499)

Virtually all that *The Dublin Review*, which cast Columbus in the role of Copernicus or Newton to the Norsemen's 'ancient Syrian and Pythagorean system of astronomy . . . antique theories, that had been well-nigh consigned to oblivion',[67] had to say in a combined review of Rafn, Beamish, and Toulmin Smith was that the Homeric-style heroes of the Vínland voyages were likely to provide inspiration for novelists, which they did, although not for another thirty years:

> It will probably lead the way to many novels and romances, in which the bold heroism and gallantry of the Norse adventurers will be portrayed in their most dramatic and poetic light. They afford singularly striking specimens, scarcely less impressive than Homer's own delineations – of man in the might of manhood, – physical, animal manhood, – daring for the pleasure of daring, – fearing but the name of fear, – rejoicing in the arduous, – lured on by the perilous, – believing the almost incredible, – and achieving the almost impossible; they present us with a phase of human nature and human progress, admirably calculated for the boldest triumphs of fiction. (pp. 307–8)

I. A. Blackwell, who authored the chapter on *Grœnlendinga saga* and *Eiríks saga rauða* ('Colonization of Greenland, and Discovery of the American Continent

---

65 *The North American Review* 109 (1869), 268.
66 *Tait's Edinburgh Magazine* 8 (1841, 471); *The Monthly Review* 155 (1841), 337.
67 'The Successive Discoveries of America', *Dublin Review* 11 (1841), 305.

by the Scandinavians') in the 1847 edition of Percy's *Northern Antiquities*, simply dismissed the whole question of the engravings on the Dighton Rock and attempts to fix the latitude of Vínland as having occasioned an unnecessary amount of 'learned trifling'.[68] Samuel Laing was scathing in his *Heimskringla* translation about the embroidering of the simple fact of the Norse landing 'in vast and expensive publications, such as the "Antiquitates Americanæ"'[69] and hinted that a Yankee hoax was behind the discoveries of 'Viking' remains in Massachusetts:

> when the northern antiquaries proceed to prove the details, – to establish the exact points in the state of Massachusetts at which Leif put up his wooden booths . . . and to make imaginary discoveries of Runic inscriptions and buildings erected by Northmen in Rhode Island, – they are poets, not antiquaries . . . so much has been written in very expensive books to prove what is not susceptible of proof, and of no importance if proved . . . But those sly rogues of Americans dearly love a quiet hoax. (*The Heimskringla*, I, 160, 183)

Finally, and signalling the inconsequentiality of the matter with an air of weary disdain, Thomas Carlyle attributed the discovery of America to 'Eric the Red'[70] and glumly despatched the enterprise in a single sentence in his account of the events of the reign of Hákon jarl:

> It appears to be certain that, from the end of the tenth century to the early part of the fourteenth, there was a dim knowledge of those distant shores extant in the Norse mind, and even some straggling series of visits thither by roving Norsemen; though, as only danger, difficulty, and no profit resulted, the visits ceased, and the whole matter sank into oblivion, and, but for the Icelandic talent of writing in the long winter nights, would never have been heard of by posterity at all.[71]

Antiquitates Americanæ: *the scholarly legacy*

While Rafn was engaged in correspondence with Thomas Webb over the archaeological matters which were to taint the scholarly reputation of *Antiquitates Americanæ*, his contact with another New Englander, George Marsh, bore richer fruit. Marsh was one of a small group of New England intellectuals, of diverse talents and occupations but with a shared interest in European languages, who, in the 1830s, turned their attention to Scandinavia,[72] and, in

68 I. A. Blackwell, *Northern Antiquities . . . New edition, revised throughout and considerably enlarged* (London, 1847), p. 261.
69 *The Heimskringla*, I, 174.
70 'Early Kings of Norway', *Critical and Miscellaneous Essays*, Vol. 5 (London, 1899), p. 230.
71 *Ibid.* Karl Litzenberg calls this work 'a frightful hodgepodge of puritanism and Scotch patriotism interlarded with Norse tradition' (*The Victorians and the Vikings: A Bibliographical Essay on Anglo-Norse Literary Relations*, The University of Michigan Contributions in Modern Philology 3 [1947], 22). Edward J. Cowan labels it 'dismal' ('Icelandic Studies in Eighteenth and Nineteenth Century Scotland', *Studia Islandica* 31 [1972], 127).
72 See Benson, 'The Beginnings of American Interest in Scandinavian Literature', pp. 135–8.

the case of Marsh and Elihu Burritt, to Old Icelandic as well as Swedish and Danish. A fleeting visitor to this company was Washington Irving, who, in his review of Wheaton's *History of the Northmen*, produced one of the earliest appearances of Icelandic in an American publication when he cited a few lines of an Icelandic translation of Milton from Ebenezer Henderson's *Iceland* to illustrate the principles of alliterative verse.[73]

The autodidact Elihu Burritt, who had an extensive knowledge of European and Asian languages, added Old Icelandic to his repertoire during service from 1837 to 1839 as librarian of the American Antiquarian Society. Burritt's translation of portions of *Grœnlendinga saga* in *The American Eclectic* (1841), in an essay entitled 'Icelandic Literature: Translations, with Introductory Notes', is the first by an American of an extended piece of Old Norse narrative. 'Icelandic Literature' also contained extracts from *Njáls saga*, *Gunnlaugs saga*, and *Egils saga*, translated from the Danish of Erasmus Mueller, and a brief excursus on Icelandic history and culture. George Marsh contributed a translation of an article by Mueller, which had originally been published in the Danish periodical *Nordisk Tidsskrift*, on the 'Origin, Progress and decline of Icelandic Historical Literature' to the same issue.

Marsh admired Old Icelandic letters for their fulfilment of the very ideals of literature in which Bancroft found them deficient:

> in the opinion of those most competent to judge, it has never been surpassed, if equalled, in all that gives value to that portion of history which consists in spirited delineations of character, and faithful and lively pictures of events, among nations in a rude state of society.[74]

In the early 1830s Marsh began a correspondence with Rafn, who was no doubt already well known in New England circles through his correspondence with local historical societies, which continued, variously in English and Danish, for the rest of Rafn's life. In the first of these exchanges Marsh lamented the unavailability in America of books on Old Norse and, with a view to making purchases direct from Copenhagen, asked for bibliographical information about Scandinavian literary history and literature.[75] Rafn's enthusiastic response, which included a full account of the state of progress of the forthcoming *Antiquitates Americanæ* and the information that a copy of a volume by

---

73 *The North American Review* 35 (1832), 348; Ebenezer Henderson, *Iceland; or the journal of a residence in that island during the years 1814 and 1815*, 2nd edn (Edinburgh, 1819), p. 545. The first quotation from Old Icelandic literature in American print appears to be a strophe from *Bjarkamál*, cited from Rask's *A Grammar of the Anglo-Saxon Tongue*, in Henry Wheaton's article, 'Anglo-Saxon Language and Literature', *The North American Review* 33 (1831), 332.

74 George P. Marsh, *A Compendious Grammar of the Old-Northern or Icelandic Language, compiled and translated from the Grammars of Rask* (Burlington, 1838), p. ix.

75 Marsh to Rafn, 31 October 1833 (Grøndal, *Breve*, pp. 293–4). On Marsh's interest in Old Norse, see Richard Beck, 'George P. Marsh and Old Icelandic Studies', *Scandinavian Studies* 17 (1943), 195–203; David Lowenthal, 'G. P. Marsh and Scandinavian Studies', *Scandinavian Studies* 29 (1957), 41–52; *idem*, *George Perkins Marsh, Versatile Vermonter* (New York, 1959), pp. 52–5.

Erasmus Rask (*Kortfattet Vejledning til det oldnordiske eller gamle islandske Sprog*) was already in the mail, led to Marsh's compilation, supplemented by his own comments, of three of Rask's works, which he entitled *A compendious grammar of the Old-Northern or Icelandic language, compiled and translated from the grammars of Rask*.[76] The work was published in 1838, five years before the appearance of George Webbe Dasent's better known translation of Rask, *Grammar of the Icelanders or Old Norse Tongue*. Production difficulties, particularly in obtaining Icelandic characters, delayed printing, but Marsh was galvanized into action by the appearance of *Antiquitates Americanæ*, a work which, he says in his Preface, he expects 'to awaken the attention of American scholars to the remarkable language in which the ancient and curious memorials contained in that volume are embodied, and thereby to furnish a fit occasion for bringing out a manual designed to facilitate access to the literary treasures of which the Old-Northern tongue is the vehicle' (pp. iii–iv). He has himself, he says, made 'a copious collection' of syntatical rules and examples, with particular reference to comparisons between English and Iceland, which he intends to publish, 'if the subject shall be found to excite sufficient interest to warrant the undertaking' (p. vi). No such interest, as it happened, was awakened, and public access to the *Compendious Grammar* was limited. Three hundred copies were printed, but Marsh's absence from Burlington during the book's production resulted in so many proofreading errors that he circulated copies only privately.[77] The proposed comparative Icelandic-English grammar was never published.

One contemporary researcher, who was acquainted with Marsh and whose interest was piqued by the *Compendious Grammar*, was Henry Schoolcraft.[78] Although Schoolcraft does not appear to have been impressed by his election to the Royal Danish Society of Northern Antiquaries and, like George Bancroft, had no time for alleged Viking remains in Massachusetts and Rhode Island,

> I received a notice of my election as a member of the Royal Northern Antiquarian Society of Copenhagen . . . This Society . . . certainly undervalues American sagacity if it conjectures that such researches and speculations as those of Mr. Magnusen, on the Dighton Rock, and what it is fashionable now-a-Days to call the NEWPORT RUIN, can satisfy the purposes of a sound investigation of the Anti-[*sic*]Columbian period of American history.[79]

he considered Marsh's 'translation of *Rusk's* [sic] *Icelandic* Grammar . . . a

---

76 From, according to Marsh's Preface (p. iv), Rask's *Vejledning til det Islandske eller gamle Nordiske Sprog* (1811); *Anvising till Isländskan eller Nordiska Fornspråket* (1818); and *Kortfattet Vejledning til det oldnordiske eller gamle islandske Sprog* (1832).

77 See *Catalogue of the Library of George Perkins Marsh* (Burlington, 1892), p. 440.

78 Schoolcraft recalls a meeting with Marsh, who impressed him with his 'fine taste and acquirements'. See Henry R. Schoolcraft, *Personal Memoirs of a Residence of Thirty Years with the Indian Tribes on the American Frontiers: with brief notices of passing events, facts, and opinions, A.D. 1812 to A.D. 1842* (Philadelphia, 1851), p. 564.

79 Schoolcraft, *Personal Memoirs*, p. 630.

scholar-like performance'[80] and was intrigued by its demonstration of the survival of cognate forms in English and Old Icelandic and their implications for the history of language:

> It is curious to observe, in this language, the roots of many English words, and it denotes through what lengths of mutations of history the stock words of a generic language may be traced. Lond, skip, flaska, sumar, hamar, ketill, dal, are clearly the radices respectively of land, ship, flask, summer, hammer, kettle dale.[81]

A potentially serious student of the *Compendious Grammar*, whose desire to learn Old Icelandic may have been frustrated by its restricted publication, was James Bartlett, another of Rafn's Rhode Island Historical Society correspondents. Bartlett, who obtained a number of subscribers to *Antiquitates Americanæ* and engaged William Jackson as its American distributor, wrote to Rafn early in 1838 to say that he was 'Feeling desirous to become acquainted with the Danish and Icelandic Languages' and asked him to send him an Icelandic grammar in English. Rafn replied with the information that 'An Iceland Grammar in English will soon appear in America',[82] presumably Marsh's, although he does not say so, and the extent to which Bartlett managed to pursue his aim is not recorded.

Henry Longfellow proved a disappointing student of Old Norse. His life-long, although essentially diletantish, interest in things Scandinavian[83] resulted in a desultory attempt during a soggy and miserable summer in Stockholm in 1835, which was somewhat relieved by two livelier weeks in Copenhagen,[84] to learn some Old Icelandic from Rafn in return, the Danish scholar suggested, for information about Native Americans.[85] Longfellow was neither an apt nor interested pupil.[86] Icelandic, he wrote in his journal, is 'a tongue which has a harsh, sharp and disagreeable sound'.[87] Rafn also introduced Longfellow to 'Thorfinn Karlsefnes Saga' (*Eiríks saga rauða*) on the assumption that it would have particular interest for him as an American, and nominated him for

---

80 Schoolcraft, *Personal Memoirs*, p. 564

81 *Ibid.*

82 Bartlett to Rafn, 9 April 1838; Rafn to Bartlett, 1 June 1838. Fiske Icelandic Collection, Cornell University. See Þórunn Sigurðardóttir, *Manuscript Material . . . in the Fiske Icelandic Collection*, Item 81.

83 See Andrew Hilen, *Longfellow and Scandinavia. A Study of the Poet's Relationship with the Northern Languages and Literature*, Yale Studies in English 107 (New Haven, 1947), pp. 106–12.

84 . See Samuel Longfellow, ed., *Life of Henry Wadsworth Longfellow, with extracts from his journals and correspondence*, 3 vols (Boston and New York, 1891) 1: 209–16. [Vol. 12.i of *The Works of Henry Wadsworth Longfellow, with Bibliographical and Critical Notes and His Life, with extracts from his journals and correspondence*. Ed. Samuel Longfellow, 14 vols, 1891–2]; Hilen, *Longfellow and Scandinavia*, pp. 11–27, and Appendix A, 'Longfellow's Scandinavian Journal, June 16–September 24, 1835'.

85 Hilen, *Longfellow and Scandinavia*, p. 24.

86 Hilen, *Longfellow and Scandinavia*, pp. 89–90.

87 Hilen, *Longfellow and Scandinavia*, 'Longfellow's Journal' (September 15, 1835), p. 141.

membership in The Royal Danish Society of Northern Antiquaries.[88] Longfellow's extensive Scandinavian library does not contain a copy of the original edition of *Antiquitates Americanæ*.[89]

In the years following the publication of *Antiquitates Americanæ* Marsh and Burritt moved on to other things – Burritt to the work of international pacifism, Marsh to translations of Tegnér and other modern Scandinavian writers.[90] It was left to another of Rafn's correspondents, Daniel Willard Fiske, a scholar of a younger generation, to begin the institutionalized study of Old Icelandic in America on his appointment as Professor of North-European Languages at Cornell University in 1869.[91] Although Fiske's own Icelandic research interests lay outside the Vínland sagas,[92] early in his career and recently returned from Copenhagen where he had enjoyed the hospitality of Rafn and his family, he wrote to say that he had successfully placed a short article by his mentor on the Vínland voyages, intended to publicize the work of the Royal Society of Northern Antiquaries, 'in several of our leading journals'.[93] Despite Rafn's personal representations, however, the piece did not appear in the *Proceedings* of the Massachusetts Historical Society.[94]

Not long after Fiske took up his position at Cornell, the work of Rafn and his translators was appropriated entirely to entrepreneurial ends by Rasmus Anderson, Professor of Scandinavian Languages at the University of Wisconsin from 1875 to 1883. Anderson's *America Not Discovered by Columbus* (1874), 'a

88 Hilen, *Longfellow and Scandinavia*, pp. 24, 89–90.

89 It does, however, contain the shorter French edition, *Antiquites américaines* (1845), and J. T. Smith's *Northmen in New England* (Boston, 1839). See Hilen, *Longfellow and Scandinavia*, Appendix D ('A Bibliography of Longfellow's Scandinavian Library').

90 David Lowenthal, 'G. P. Marsh and Scandinavian Studies', *Scandinavian Studies* 29 (1957), 49–52.

91 According to Fiske's biographer and literary executor, Horatio S. White, in the decade of his teaching at Cornell (1869–79), 'instruction in Swedish was quite regularly given throughout the decade, and also occasionally in Icelandic'. See Horatio S. White, *Willard Fiske. Life and Correspondence. A Biographical Study* (New York, 1925), p. 60.

92 His best known published work on Iceland and the sagas is *Chess in Iceland and in Icelandic literature* (Florence, 1905). I have not been able to identify the article by Fiske on Vínland to which Guðbrandur Vigfússon refers in a letter to Fiske (17 November 1874) as 'a single column' which is 'clear and to the point'. Fiske Icelandic Collection, Cornell University. Þórunn Sigurðardóttir, *Manuscript Material . . . in the Fiske Icelandic Collection*, Correspondence 1. 'Letters to Daniel Willard Fiske.'

93 'Your interesting and compact little article on the early discovery of our country . . . has been extensively copied into our newspapers. I have myself caused its publication in several of our leading journals. So that your interesting disclosures concerning the Ante-Columbian history of this continent have almost become facts in the popular belief of America' (Fiske to Rafn, 23 April 1853). Fiske Icelandic Collection, Cornell University. Þórunn Sigurðardóttir, *Manuscript Material . . . in the Fiske Icelandic Collection*, Item 81. The article in question is a brief account of the Vínland voyages, which was published in, for example, *Proceedings of the New Jersey Historical Society* 6 (1851–53), 167–70; *The New England Historical and Genealogical Register* 7 (1853), 13–14; *Journal of the American Geographical and Statistical Society* 1 (1857), 178–9.

94 Rafn's article was referred to the Society's Committee of Publication for consideration (*Massachusetts Historical Society, Proceedings* 2 [1852, 504–5]) but not subsequently published.

pugnacious little book' as Einar Haugen called it,[95] had, according to Anderson's autobiography, a deliberately 'thoroughly sensational and defiant' title.[96] By his own admission to Willard Fiske, its contents were 'nothing specially original'.[97] Anderson's declared purpose, as stated in the book's Preface, was 'to create some interest in the people, the literature, and the early institutions of Norway, and especially in Iceland'. Although his knowledge of Icelandic was modest,[98] his promotional skills were considerable, and it was he who initiated the fundraising efforts that eventually resulted in the unveiling of the Leifr Eiríksson statue in Boston in 1887, perhaps the most significant act in what was to become the nineteenth-century 'theatre' of Vínland.[99]

The real legacy of *Antiquitates Americanæ* to Norse scholarship in America came two generations after its publication, in the form of Arthur M. Reeves's *The Finding of Wineland The Good. The History of the Icelandic Discovery of America* (London, 1890). This impressive work comprised editions of *Grænlendinga saga* and *Eiríks saga rauða*, the latter based on *Hauksbók* with occasional references to *Skálholtsbók*, facing-page facsimiles, full translations of both sagas, notes, and detailed commentary. Reeves, who was one of Willard Fiske's two outstanding students of Old Icelandic,[100] pays homage to Rafn's editorial expertise but criticizes the promotional zeal which clouded his judgment, noting with regret that Rafn's 'dubious theories and hazardous conjectures' rather than the original texts have preoccupied scholars over the fifty years since its publication.[101] When, two years after the publication of *The Finding of Wineland the Good*, Charles Sprague Smith, Guðbrandur Vigfússon's former student and Gebhard Professor of German at Columbia University from 1880 to 1891, published an article which defended the historicity of the Vínland sagas,[102] he gave approving acknowledgment of Reeves's contribution to Vínland scholarship (p. 530) but made no mention of either Rafn or *Antiquitates Americanæ*.

Although the contents of *Antiquitates Americanæ* engaged the interests of scholarly and popular historians and attracted extensive coverage in academic

95 'Wisconsin Pioneers in Scandinavian Studies: Anderson and Olson, 1875–1931', *Wisconsin Magazine of History*, Autumn 1950, p. 31.
96 *Life Story of Rasmus B. Anderson, written by himself*, 2nd edn (Madison, 1917), p. 210.
97 Anderson to Fiske, 25 July 1874. Fiske Icelandic Collection, Cornell University. Þórunn Sigurðardóttir, *Manuscript Material . . . in the Fiske Icelandic Collection*, Correspondence 1. 'Letters to Daniel Willard Fiske.'
98 Einar Haugen calls his training 'pitifully inadequate' ('Wisconsin Pioneers', p. 31). Anderson himself says that he was first taught Icelandic in 1871, by an Icelandic immigrant to Wisconsin (*Life Story of Rasmus B. Anderson*, p. 276).
99 See below, Ch. 3, pp. 65–67.
100 The other was W. H. Carpenter, who was appointed to an Instructorship at Columbia in 1884 and became Professor in Germanic Philology in 1895. See George T. Flom, *A History of Scandinavian Studies in American Universities, together with a bibliography*, Iowa Studies in Language and Literature 11 (Iowa City, 1907), 10, 13.
101 *The Finding of Wineland The Good. The History of the Icelandic Discovery of America* (London, 1890), p. 1.
102 'The Vinland Voyages', *Journal of the American Geographic Society* 24 (1892), 510–35.

journals and the wider press, they were marginal to the interests of the majority of the growing number of Old Norse scholars in the United States in the latter part of the nineteenth century.[103] Even had it not been blighted by production mishaps, Marsh's idealistic purpose for the *Compendious Grammar* is unlikely to have been realized. He bequeathed what was then the most extensive collection of Scandinavian literature in America to the University of Vermont, where Old Norse has never been taught. *The Finding of Wineland the Good*, a work of whose provenance the *Knickerbocker* reviewer of *Antiquitates Americanæ* would no doubt have approved, was widely ignored by prestigious periodicals like *The North American Review* and *The New York Review* which had devoted so much attention to *Antiquitates Americanæ*. Willard Fiske reviewed it for *The Nation*, and a short notice appeared in *The Saturday Review*, but the major focus of attention came from the prominent European philological journals *Zeitschrift für Deutsche Philologie* (Germany) and *Arkiv för nordisk filologi* (Sweden).[104] The work also received high praise from the *Proceedings of the Royal Geographical Society*, which called it 'on the whole, the most valuable contribution that has yet been published in the literature of the Norse discovery of America'.[105] Hugo Gering made detailed criticisms of Reeves's editorial procedure in *Zeitschrift für Deutsche Philologie* but concluded that the book was a fine accomplishment as an 'Erstlingsarbeit' and expressed regret at the premature death (Reeves was killed in a train accident at the age of thirty-five) of such a promising scholar.[106] On the other hand, George Flom lists neither *The Finding of Wineland the Good* nor Charles Sprague Smith's article on the Vínland sagas, *Íslendingabók*, and the *Íslendingasögur*, the latter inexplicably and the former presumably because it was published in England, in his bibliography of American Scandinavian scholarship to 1907.

According to Flom's survey of the curricula of Old Norse courses in American universities to that date, eddic poetry was popular, but the study of Old Icelandic prose was more or less limited to Snorri's *Edda*, *Laxdæla saga*, *Gunnlaugs saga*, and *Njála*.[107] If either *Grænlendinga saga* or *Eiríks saga rauða* was a set text for study, the edition is more likely to have been the long extract from *Eiríks saga rauða* in Vigfússon and Powell's *Icelandic Prose Reader* (1879),[108] which was used in Old Norse classes at the Universities of Wisconsin (in 1898–99), North Dakota, and Kansas,[109] than the expensive and cumber-

---

103 For an account of the development of institutionalized Old Norse studies in America to 1907 see Flom, *A History of Scandinavian Studies in American Universities*. See also Albert E. Egge, 'Scandinavian Studies in the United States', *Modern Language Notes* 3 (1888), 66–8.

104 For a full list of reviews of *The Finding of Wineland the Good* see Halldór Hermannsson, 'The Northmen in America', pp. 68–9.

105 Review by 'C.R.M.', *Proceedings of the Royal Geographical Society*, n.s. 13 (1891), 128.

106 *Zeitschrift für Deutsche Philologie* 7 (1892), 89.

107 Flom, *A History of Scandinavian Studies*, p. 40.

108 Gudbrand Vigfusson and F. York Powell, *An Icelandic Prose Reader* (Oxford, 1879), pp. 123–41.

109 Flom, *A History of Scandinavian Studies*, pp. 7, 25, 36.

some *Antiquitates Americanæ*. There appears to be only one surviving piece of evidence that *Eiríks saga rauða* ever featured in the nineteenth-century Norse curriculum: an exchange of letters between Smith and Guðbrandur Vigfússon mentions the despatch of several copies of the English translation of the extract in Vigfússon and Powell, by the Reverend John Sephton of Liverpool, for use in Smith's proposed Old Icelandic reading class on his appointment to Columbia University.[110] When, in 1887, a short anonymous contribution to *The Atlantic Monthly* entitled 'The Historical Value of the Vinland sagas' expressed the hope that 'the Icelandic literature will erelong be studied in this country as it is now at the two English universities',[111] Old Norse was, in fact, well established at Columbia, Johns Hopkins, and the University of Wisconsin.[112] Despite Rafn's declared hope and Marsh's expressed conviction, the publication of *Antiquitates Americanæ* did not stimulate wide interest in saga literature or in the study of Old Icelandic itself in the United States. By the end of the nineteenth century the subject was offered by at least twenty American universities,[113] but the contents of *Antiquitates Americanæ* had all but vanished into obscurity as an object of scholarly interest.[114]

*

The ultimate fate of *Grænlendinga saga* and *Eiríks saga rauða* at the hands of nineteenth-century American scholarship was to be read primarily as narratives which concerned the European 'discovery' of America. Just as Bjarni Herjólfsson and Leifr Eiríksson found themselves off course in territory west of Greenland in *Grænlendinga saga* and *Eiríks saga rauða*, so the Vínland sagas were removed from their Scandinavian provenance and stranded on the cultural map of America, on whose physical landscape Vínland was erratically positioned. John Fiske's argument that, since the Vínland sagas 'are closely intertwined with the authentic history of Norway and Iceland',[115] they are likely to be historical fact is a rare acknowledgment of their Scandinavian provenance. Despite George Bancroft's obdurateness, the Vínland voyages began to earn the seal of authenticity in some scholarly general histories of the United States published in the latter part of the century. Justin Winsor, who provided a

110 See Andrew Wawn, 'The Spirit of 1892: Sagas, saga-Steads and Victorian philology', *Saga-Book of the Viking Society*, 23 (1992), 217.

111 *The Atlantic Monthly* 60 (1887), 856.

112 See Flom, *A History of Scandinavian Studies*, pp. 6, 10–11, 17. There was a temporary interruption at Cornell between 1885 and 1891, where 'Instruction in Scandinavian was not offered . . . except in so far as Old Norse was studied in connection with the work in other old Germanic dialects' (Flom, *A History of Scandinavian Studies*, p. 9).

113 See Flom, *A History of Scandinavian Studies, passim*.

114 *AA* was reprinted in 1968 (Osnabrück: Otto Zeller). The 1895 edition of *The Finding of Wineland the Good, to which is added biography and correspondence of the author by W. D. Foulke* was reprinted in 1967 (New York: Burt Franklin).

115 John Fiske, *The Discovery of America, with some account of Ancient America and the Spanish Conquest*, 2 vols (Boston and New York, 1892), I, 151.

comprehensive account of Vínland scholarship in his eight-volume *Narrative and Critical History of America* (1889),[116] was prepared to accept the likelihood of a Norse landing in North America, although reluctant to accept *Grœnlendinga saga* and *Eiríks saga rauða* as credible evidence:

> We may consider, then, that the weight of probability is in favor of a Northman descent upon the coast of the American mainland at some point, or at several, somewhere to the south of Greenland; but the evidence is hardly that which attaches to well-established historical records. (I, 67–8)

Nevertheless, the inclusion of 'Extracts from the Sagas Describing the Voyages to Vinland' reprinted from Reeves's *Finding of Wineland the Good* in the educational series American History Leaflets (1892) – edited by two Harvard professors of American history, Albert Bushnell Hart and Edward Channing, and 'designed to promote the scientific method of studying history from its documents . . . that have become famous in our colonial and constitutional history' – gave the Vínland voyages the blessing of unimpeachable pedagogical authority.

On the other hand, public acknowledgment, or repudiation, of the Vínland voyages as part of the fabric of American history pushed the Vínland sagas to the fringes of the growing field of Old Norse studies. At the margins of scholarship, however, interest in the Vínland voyages rose steadily throughout the second half of the nineteenth century to reach the spectacular culmination of a process, which is charted in the following chapter, at around the time of the Columbus quatercentary.

---

116 (Boston and New York, 1889), I, 76–107.

CHAPTER THREE

The Popular Legacy:
Nineteenth-Century Theatre and Polemic

In the vanguard of American Scandinavian scholarship, Henry Wheaton and George Marsh revered the Icelandic Commonwealth as the embodiment of ancient traditions of liberty. At a more partisan level of engagement, however, Leifr Eiríksson emerged as a serious rival to Columbus; there were allegations that the Vínland colony had been the successful object of a Christian missionary expedition which took New England's episcopal pedigree back to medieval Rome; and proponents of racial Teutonism touted the Vínland voyages as evidence of Germanic supremacy. As the Leifr vs. Columbus debate and the notion of a centuries-long colony of Vínland gathered momentum in the popular imagination, the Vikings became the subject of strident rhetoric and the Vínland voyages the stuff of sensational claim and counterclaim. At times the shift from the scholarly quest of the 1830s for America's institutional 'gothic' origins to the construction of New England's Viking past reached a ludicrously literal level.

In a lecture delivered in 1843, entitled 'The Goths in New-England', George Marsh, whose knowledge of Old Norse was unequalled in nineteenth-century America, spoke of the Anglo-Saxon forefathers of the Pilgrims as 'Northern' in the most general terms:[1]

> our forefathers belonged to that grand era in British history, when the English mind, under the impulse of the Reformation, was striving to recover its Gothic tendencies, by the elimination of the Roman element . . . The founders of the first New England colony, and their brethren, who followed them to their new home in the course of the same century, belonged to the class most deeply tinctured with the moral and intellectual traits of their Northern ancestry.[2]

---

1 Despite Richard Beck's claim to the contrary, the lecture itself reveals nothing of Marsh's 'familiarity with Old Icelandic literature and his admiration for the Old Norse spirit' (Richard Beck, 'George P. Marsh and Old Icelandic Studies', *Scandinavian Studies* 17 [1943], 201).
2 *The Goths in New-England. A Discourse delivered at the anniversary of the Philomathesian Society of Middlebury College, August 15, 1843* (Middlebury, Vt., 1843), pp. 11, 19. On Marsh's brand of Teutonism, see Reginald Horsman, *Race and Manifest Destiny. The Origins of American Racial Anglo-Saxonism* (Cambridge, Mass., 1981) pp. 180–2.

Asahel Davis, an early and apparently tireless lecturer on the topic of the Norse Discovery of America, limited himself to a declaration that 'The present illustrious queen of England is a direct descendant of the Northmen'.[3] Some commentators insisted on making a distinction between Saxon and Scandinavian, bypassing America's English colonial legacy in favour of a direct line of inheritance by present-day New Englanders of the heroic past of Scandinavia. Whereas George Marsh had argued that the founders of New England embodied the spirit of the Reformation untainted by 'the atrocious tyranny of the bigoted Stuarts',[4] a few years later J. Elliot Cabot was claiming that, particularly in its maritime ability, 'we may confidently assert, that the modern New England character has in it much more of the Norse than of the Saxon'.[5] In the Preface to the second edition of his *The Pre-Columbian Discovery of America* (1890), Benjamin De Costa discarded the notion of ' "Saxon inheritance" ' in favour of a Scandinavian line of descent for American vigour, liberty, and, somewhat more cryptically, 'our strength of speech':

> In reality we fable in a great measure when we speak of our 'Saxon inheritance'. It is rather from the Northmen that we have derived our vital energy, our freedom of thought, and, in a measure that we do not yet suspect, our strength of speech.
>
> (p. 8)

On a speaking tour of America in 1874, Charles Kingsley went a step further. In a lecture entitled 'The First Discovery of America' he claimed the Pilgrims not only as the ethnic kin of the Norsemen but also, 'in many cases, their actual descendants'.[6] By the end of the century, Marie Shipley (née Brown) had taken ancestral hyperbole to its zenith: 'the entire North American continent has remained in the possession of the descendents [sic] of the ancient Scandinavians'.[7]

Nevertheless, although the notion of a Viking presence in New England was grist to the mill of the advocates of Teutonic racial supremacy, the image of the Vikings as the seafaring embodiment of the gothic ideal was not a unanimous one. In the broader context of nineteenth-century American medievalism, which, in the main, forged an idealized vision of the Middle Ages, the Vikings

---

3   Asahel Davis, *A Lecture on the Discovery of America by the Northmen, five hundred years before Columbus. Delivered in New York, New Haven, Philadelphia, Baltimore, Washington, and other cities: also in some of the first literary institutions of the Union*, 5th edn (New York and Boston, 1840), p. 18. Expanded and retitled *Antiquities of America, The First Inhabitants of Central America, and the Discovery of New-England, by the Northmen, Five Hundred Years Before Columbus*, Davis's lecture had gone through nineteen editions by 1847.

4   *The Goths in New-England*, p. 10.

5   'Discovery of America by the Norsemen', *Massachusetts Quarterly Review* 6 (1849), 189.

6   'The First Discovery of America', *The Works of Charles Kingsley* (London, 1885), p. 242.

7   Marie A. Shipley, *The Norse Colonization in America in the light of the Vatican finds* (Lucerne, 1899), p. 24. See also Marie A. Brown, 'The Norse Discovery of America', *Notes and Queries*, 7th ser. 2 (1886), 145–6; *idem, The Icelandic Discoveries of America; or, Honour to Whom Honour is Due* (London, 1887).

were problematic. In 'The American Scholar', an oration delivered to the Phi Beta Kappa Society in 1837, George Marsh's contemporary, Ralph Waldo Emerson (1803–82), expressed admiration for the elemental, generative vigour ('out of handselled savage nature, out of terrible Druids and Berserkirs, come at last Alfred and Shakspear')[8] of those he refers to elsewhere as 'these atrocious ancestors of Englishmen [–] the Briton, Saxon, Northman, Berserkir'.[9]

James Russell Lowell also admired Northern energy. After abandoning work on a Vínland poem originally begun in 1850, he derived the zest to complete it, as he explains in a letter to Charles Eliot Norton, from his reading of George Dasent's translation of *Njáls saga* (1861). Exhilarated and intrigued, he saw the axe-swinging but law-conscious 'old Icelanders' as the counterparts of the pro-slavery guerilla bands, the Border Ruffians, which created havoc on the Kansas-Missouri border from 1854 to 1859:

> It has revived my old desire to write the story of Leif's Voyage to Vinland, and I shouldn't wonder if something came of it. Ideal border-ruffians those old Icelanders seem to have been – such hacking and hewing and killing, and such respect for all the forms of law! (7 August 1861)[10]

Eben Norton Horsford, an active unearther of Viking New England,[11] who, like Charles Kingsley, associated the original settlers of Iceland with the Pilgrims, viewed them from a more idealized perspective. For Horsford, the Pilgrims and the first settlers of Iceland were refugees from tyranny. Leifr was to be distinguished from medieval Scandinavians of less savoury reputation:

> His ancestry were [*sic*] of the early pilgrims, or puritans who, to escape oppression, emigrated . . . from Norway to Iceland, as the early Pilgrims came to Plymouth. They were not of the Vikings, – the class that conducted predatory excursions over the then known seas.
>
> They established and maintained a republican form of government, which exists to this day, with nominal sovereignty in the King of Denmark.[12]

The pronouncements of the anti-Leifr forces were no less passionate. Whereas the reviewer of Wheaton's *History of the Northmen* in the *American*

---

8 *The Collected Works of Ralph Waldo Emerson*, I, *Nature, Addresses, and Lectures*, introd. Robert E. Spiller; text established by Alfred R. Ferguson (Cambridge, Mass., 1971), p. 61.

9 *The Journals and Miscellaneous Notebooks of Ralph Waldo Emerson*, ed. William Gilman *et al.* (Cambridge, Mass., 1960–82), V (1965), p. 100. On Emerson's ambivalent view of the Middle Ages, see Kathleen Verduin, 'Medievalism and the Mind of Emerson', in *Medievalism in American Culture. Papers of the Eighteenth Annual Conference of the Center for Medieval and Early Renaissance Studies*, eds Bernard Rosenthal and Paul E. Szarmach (Binghamton, NY, 1989), pp. 129–50.

10 *Letters of James Russell Lowell*, ed. Charles Eliot Norton (New York, 1893; rpr. 1977), 1, 312.

11 For discussions of Horsford's archaeological activities, see Williams, *Fantastic Archaeology*, pp. 206–9; Robin Fleming, 'Picturesque History and the Medieval in Nineteenth-Century America', *American Historical Review* 100 (1995), 1080–4.

12 Eben Norton Horsford, *Discovery of America by Northmen. Address at the Unveiling of the Statue of Leif Eriksen, delivered in Faneuil Hall, Oct. 29, 1887* (Boston and New York, 1888), pp. 54–5.

Quarterly Review (1831) spoke with mere condescension of medieval Scandinavia's 'singular state of society or barbarism',[13] and others continued simply to reiterate Bancroft's views concerning the unhistoricity of the sagas,[14] De Costa's reviewer in *The Nation* (1869) realized the worst fears of some medieval Icelanders – that foreigners would disparage them as the progeny of slaves and scoundrels.[15] Criminality and barbarism, the writer alleged, had put them beyond the pale of legitimate 'Northmen':

> The white inhabitants of the arctic circle had, for more than a century, ceased to be a part of the primitive nation, and should not be spoken of as Northmen. They were a branch broken off with violence from the parent tree; they had been driven forth as outlaws or expatriated as outcasts, and exiled beyond the northern line of the supposed habitable globe. . . . Ignorant, heathen, barbarous, brutal, when banished from Scandinavia, they were equally debased when, long afterward, venturing westward, they reached the shores of Greenland and Vinland.[16]

With even less foundation for its invective, the Celtophile J. P. MacLean's pseudo-scientifically titled *A Critical Examination of the Evidences Adduced to Establish the Theory of the Norse Discovery of America* (1892)[17] paints a grotesque picture of medieval Iceland:

> On the marriage day it was bad taste not to be drunk and find a bed on the rushes on the floor. Solid drinking continued from Wednesday until Saturday. Polygamy was also practiced. The Vikings were lawless in a bad sense . . . The women who accompanied these expeditions distinguished themselves by a fierce cruelty . . . The older the records the darker the picture. They ate nothing but raw cured meat and slept out of doors. (pp. 52–3)

Snorri Sturluson is subjected to personal excoriation:

> The prominent features of his character were cunning, ambition and avarice, combined with want of courage and aversion to effort. (p. 11)

---

13 *American Quarterly Review* 10 (1831), 318.

14 B. H. DuBois, for example, argues for the 'unreliable' nature of the sagas themselves, since: 'Even in the estimation of the Scandinavians themselves much of the saga record is indistinguishable from myth' ('Did the Norse Discover America?', *Magazine of American History* 27 [1892], 375).

15 As recorded in the *Þórðarbók* redaction of *Landnámabók*: 'En vér þykjumsk heldr svara kunna útlendum mǫnnum, þá er þeir bregða oss því, at vér séim komnir af þrælum eða illmennum, ef vér vitum víst várar kynferðir sannar' (*Íslenzk fornrit* I, ii, 336) ('but we think we can better meet the criticism of foreigners when they accuse us of being descended from slaves or scoundrels, if we know for certain the truth about our ancestry', Hermann Pálsson and Paul Edwards, trans., *The Book of Settlements. Landnámabók* [Winnipeg, 1972], p. 6).

16 'The Discovery of America by the Northmen', *The Nation* 8 (21 January 1869), 53.

17 The author is billed on the title page of *A Critical Examination* as 'Life Member of the Gaelic Society of Glasgow; Honorary Member of the Gaelic Society of Inverness; Corresponding Member of the Davenport Academy of Sciences; Corresponding Member of the Western Reserve Historical Society of Ohio; Author of a "History of Clan MacLean;" "The Mound Builders;" "Antiquity of Man;" "Mastodon, Mammoth and Man;" "Fingal's Cave;" "Jewish Nature Worship".'

Icelandic poetry compares unfavourably with Scottish,

> Notwithstanding its boasted literature, Iceland has never produced a poet of the highest order . . . Their poems lack the qualities of high imagination, deep pathos, fresh love of nature, passionate dramatic power and noble simplicity of language so characteristic of the Western Isles of Scotland. (p. 10)

and the sagas 'delight more or less in the improbable' (p. 12).

MacLean and Horsford share the more zealously eccentric fringes of Vínland scholarship with Aaron Goodrich and Marie and John Shipley. Horsford's interests were archaeological and egotistical rather than ideological,[18] but the agenda of MacLean and the Shipleys was driven by ethnic and religious bias: by a general aversion to Viking culture in the case of MacLean and an obsessive loathing for all things Roman on the part of Marie Shipley. Aaron Goodrich allegedly embraced the historian's 'higher moral duties' to champion the unjustly neglected heroes of the past,[19] but the principal purpose of his book, *A History of the Character and Achievements of the So-Called Christopher Columbus*, is the vituperation of its subject. With a different agenda – to promote the academic study of Scandinavian – Rasmus Anderson climbed onto the anti-Columbus bandwagon, declaring in the Preface to the third edition (1883) of his *America Not Discovered by Columbus* (first published in 1874) that Goodrich 'pronounces Columbus a fraud, and denounces him as mean, selfish, perfidious and cruel' and that he [Anderson] has 'looked in vain for a satisfactory refutation of his statements'.[20]

In a succession of exhortatory publications, and with increasing talk of plots, conspiracies, assaults upon her integrity, and an unjust lack of public recognition, Marie Shipley condemned Columbus as a charlatan, slave-hunter, and stealer of Norse information about voyages to America, who had never set foot on the continent itself:[21]

> I ask *why* there have been withheld from me all the honors and distinctions which are invariably accorded to one who has done the world such service, and which I have rightfully earned, – the broadening of my sphere of activity, the emoluments due to my long labors? I have the right to ask justice from the Government of every land whose historical prestige I have enhanced, notably England, the United

---

18 The statement that the Vikings will eventually be recognized as 'the greatest race in the history of mankind', which Fleming attributes to Horsford ('Picturesque History and the Medieval', p. 1081), was actually made by Judge Daly, President of the American Geographical Society. See Eben Norton Horsford, *The Discovery of the Ancient City of Norumbega* (Cambridge, Mass., n.d.), p. 7.
19 *A History of the Character and Achievements of the So-Called Christopher Columbus* (New York, 1874), p. vi.
20 Rasmus Anderson, *America Not Discovered by Columbus. An Historical Sketch of the Discovery of America by the Norsemen in the Tenth Century*, 3rd edn (Chicago, 1883), pp. 7–8.
21 *Ibid.* On suggestions that stories about Vínland may have been current in the seaports of Europe in the fifteenth century, see, for instance, Magnus Magnusson and Hermann Pálsson, trans., *The Vinland Sagas*, pp. 42–3; Fridtjof Nansen, trans. Arthur G. Chater, *In Northern Mists. Arctic Exploration in Early Times* (London, 1911), ii, 293.

States, Canada, Denmark, Norway and Sweden, and from my learned colleagues all over the world.[22]

In 1888, on behalf of the more than a thousand signed supporters, among them office-bearers of the historical societies of Maine, New Hampshire, Vermont, Wisconsin, and Virginia, Mrs Shipley pleaded the 'Leif Ericsson' cause before the Senate Committee in charge of the Columbus quatercentennial celebrations ('the contemplated Romish triumph')[23] and, unsuccessfully, asked for government support to search the records of the Vatican for documentary evidence of Norse America. The Shipleys' researches did, in fact, occasionally attract the kind of endorsement which Marie craved. Karl Blind, for example, made a foot-note reference, in an article published in 1892 in the *New Review*, to the 'useful writings published on the subject' by Marie and John Shipley to support his assertion that 'to a Northern Germanic race belongs the glory of having set foot upon the soil of America, and founded settlements there . . . five hundred years before Columbus'.[24]

Motivated by the desire to solve, and to be seen to have done so, one of the great geographical mysteries of history, the wealthy Horsford was the principal producer and director of the theatre of Vínland:

> As we all know, there have been before the world for many scores of years . . . certain grand geographical problems, challenging the spirit of research, the love of adventure, or the passion for discovery or conquest. They are such as these: Where was Atlantis? Where was the Ultima Thule? What is there at the North Pole? Was there a Northwest Passage? Where were the Seven Cities? Where were the El Dorado of Raleigh, and the Landfalls of Leif Erikson, of Columbus, of John Cabot, of Verrazano? And where were Vinland and Norumbega?[25]

'Norumbega' was the name variously given to a region or regions between the New Jersey coast and the Bay of Fundy on some sixteenth- and seventeenth-century maps of North America. The sixteenth-century cartographer, Abraham Ortelius, who considered it likely that 'some islanders of *Europe*, as namely of *Greenland*, *Island*, and *Frisland*', had set foot in the New World before Columbus, suggested that 'Norumbega' derived from 'Norway' and thus signi-fied 'a Northland, some Colony in times past . . . hither . . . transplanted'.[26] Norumbega, declared Horsford, was the Vínland of the sagas, and he had

---

22 'Mrs. Shipley's Claim to Historical Recognition', in *The Norse Colonization in America by the light of the Vatican Finds* (Lucerne, 1899).

23 *The English Rediscovery of America* (London, 1890). The full text of Marie Shipley's Plea is printed on pp. 30–61, and the 'memorial' on pp. 141–4.

24 *New Review* (1892), p. 356.

25 *The Discovery of the Ancient City of Norumbega*, p. 9.

26 Abraham Ortelius, introd. by R. A. Skelton, *The Theatre of the Whole World* (Amsterdam, 1968), Folio 5. On the appearance of the mythical island of 'Frisland' in Ortelius's map of Northern Europe, see C. Koeman, *The History of Abraham Ortelius and his Theatrum Orbis Terrarum* (Lausanne, 1964), p. 62.

unearthed the ruins of this city, which had traded with Europe for over three hundred years, on the Charles River, in Massachusetts.[27]

On 21 November 1889, Horsford staged a ceremony before office-bearers of the American Geographical Society to unveil a commemorative plaque on a tower which he had built on the alleged Norumbega site. The accompanying entertainment, as recorded in *The Discovery of the Ancient City of Norumbega*, included music by students from Wellesley College, of which Horsford was a benefactor, and a florid poetic recitation composed for the occasion by the journalist, E. H. Clement. Also printed in the volume (p. 10) is a letter from the then 82-year-old John Greenleaf Whittier, who had written a sonnet for the opening of Wellesley's Norumbega Hall,[28] named in Horsford's honour and opened three years earlier. Whittier sends his regrets and politely expresses his pleasure in hearing that the site of his poem 'Norembega' (1869),[29] which celebrates the 'Northern Eldorado' on the Penobscot River in Maine, has now been discovered on the Charles in Massachusetts.

Another piece of theatre in which Horsford played a prominent role was the erection and unveiling of the Leifr Eiríksson statue in Boston. De Costa's claim that 'the study of the Icelandic Sagas has resulted in the erection of a statue to Leif Ericson in the City of Boston'[30] had, in fact, nothing to do with it. The enterprise was conceived in the early 1870s as a purely promotional venture by Rasmus Anderson, with the support of the popular Norwegian violinist, Ole Bull, as part of Anderson's campaign 'to make the University of Wisconsin the chief center of Scandinavian study in the United States'.[31] This mission, he wrote to Willard Fiske, also included plans for a 'Leif Erikson Observatory' in Madison, 'especially as it was the stars, that guided Leif on his expedition to Vineland'.[32] The statue was originally intended to stand in the front of the main building of the Madison campus, but subscriptions from Norwegian communities in the Middle West, who showed considerably less interest in their gothic ancestry than some citizens of New England did in theirs, were not forthcoming. Having raised some $2500 from concerts in Wisconsin, Iowa, and Norway, Bull was successful in attracting interest for the project in Massachusetts.[33] A committee, which included Longfellow, Whittier, James Russell

27 Eben Norton Horsford, *The Defences of Norumbega: and a review of the reconaissances of Col. T. W. Higginson, et al.: A Letter to Judge Daly* (Boston and New York, 1891), pp. 20–5. See also Eben Norton Horsford and Cornelia Horsford, *Leif's House in Vineland; Graves of the Northmen* (Boston, 1893).

28 'Norumbega Hall', in *The Works of John Greenleaf Whittier*, 7 vols, IV (Boston and New York, 1892), 222–3.

29 *The Works of John Greenleaf Whittier*, I, 285.

30 *The Pre-Columbian Discovery of America by the Northmen*, 2nd edn (Albany, NY, 1890), p. 58.

31 *Life Story of Rasmus B. Anderson*, p. 190.

32 Anderson to Fiske, 22 May 1874. Fiske Icelandic Collection, Cornell University. See Þórunn Sigurðardóttir, *Manuscript Material . . . in the Fiske Icelandic Collection*, Correspondence 1. 'Letters to Daniel Willard Fiske.'

33 For Anderson's account of the enterprise see *Life Story of Rasmus B. Anderson*, pp. 190–1, 206–12. See also Julius E. Olson, 'The Leif Erikson Monument', *The Nation* 45 (1887), 395–6.

Lowell, and Horsford was formed, and the bronze statue, by Anne Whitney (this, according to Anderson, unfortunately ended up as 'a figure more or less resembling Ole Bull'[34]) was finally unveiled on Commonwealth Avenue, in the presence of the mayor of Boston and the governor of Massachusetts, on 29 October 1887. Edward Everett Hale was master of ceremonies, and the gathering was addressed by the indefatigable Horsford.[35] A replica of the statue, purchased by a wealthy resident of that city, was placed in Juneau Park, Milwaukee.[36]

Marie Shipley had even grander theatrical designs. In her plea to Congress prior to the Columbus quatercentennial she sketched a plan for a Viking exhibition, to be staged, essentially as a gesture of protest, at the Chicago Columbian Exposition of 1893. This was to consist of a model of the Gokstad ship and a replica of 'an ancient Icelandic Viking hall', replete with the figures of a Norse warrior and lady to serve as the evocation of Viking valour and as the audience for a skald who would recreate their bold exploits in song:

> the massive gold armlets and clasps, the ornate belt, worn by both, gleaming in the light of the central fires, which would also illumine the harp of the Icelandic skald, narrating to them some grand and heroic exploit of their renowned countrymen. Outside the hall could be a full-size reproduction of the famous Viking ship, exhumed at Gokstad, in Norway, in 1880.[37]

A replica of the Gokstad ship did sail from Norway to Chicago for the Exposition.[38] However, Shipley's proposal, as expressed in a letter seeking the support of Willard Fiske – whom she addressed as 'Prof. John Fiske'[39] – to have a 100 x 70ft model of the 'Viking-hall' placed behind the Leifr Eiríksson statue after it had served as the centrepiece of the exhibit[40] was, like the display itself, never realized.

A more elegant artistic tribute to the Vínland voyages had been initiated a decade earlier by the philanthropist, Catharine Lorillard Wolfe, who commissioned a stained glass mullioned window with Norse subjects for 'Vinland', her home in Newport, Rhode Island (now Salve Regina College) from (William)

---

34 *Life Story of Rasmus B. Anderson*, p. 207.

35 Horsford's address is printed in *The Boston Evening Transcript*, Saturday, October 29, 1887, p. 8.

36 A monument to Þorfinnr Karlsefni in Fairmont Park, Pennsylvania, was unveiled on 20 November 1920, and a painting of Leifr Eiríksson ('Leiv Eiriksson Discovers America A.D. 1000') was presented to the Statuary Hall in the U.S. Capitol on 23 March 1936.

37 *The English Rediscovery of America*, p. 49.

38 See Stanley Appelbaum, *The Chicago World's Fair of 1893. A Photographic Record* [New York, n.d.], pp. 51, 60, 86.

39 Presumably confusing him with the historian, John Fiske.

40 Shipley to Fiske, 12 January 1887. Fiske Icelandic Collection, Cornell University. See Þórunn Sigurðardóttir, *Manuscript Material . . . in the Fiske Icelandic Collection*, Correspondence 1. 'Letters to Daniel Willard Fiske.' In a publication some years later, Shipley accuses William Eleroy Curtis, of the U.S. State Department, and Professor Hjalmar Boyesen of Columbia University of 'making a rather too free application of my ideas and plan' for a 'Viking Exhibit' at the 1893 World's Fair. See *The Norse Colonization in America*, p. 13.

Morris & Co. 'I am sorry to say', Morris wrote to Jenny Morris in July 1883, 'that she is sadly stupid; and I believe monstrously rich.'[41] In a letter to an unknown recipient that same year, Morris suggested for the middle panel:

> a ship . . . & on each side a scroll, with the passages from Hávamál (Edda) about undying fame on it: proper enough on this occasion since the poor fisher men & sheep farmers of Greenland & Iceland have so curiously found a place among the worthies connected with the great Modern Commonwealth.[42]

Designed by Edward Burne-Jones, duly installed but since dismantled, the window survives in seven Burne-Jones cartoons. The one held by the Carlisle Art Gallery is entitled 'The Voyage to Vinland the Good'[43] and, less respectfully in Morris & Co.'s account book for January 1884, 'Norse heroes on the sea, making for other people's property'.[44]

Acknowledgment in print of the historicity of the Vínland voyages, with accompanying disclaimer of intent to diminish the stature of Columbus, was one thing; public, ceremonial affirmation of a style previously accorded only to the Admiral[45] was another. In 1880 William Everett addressed the Massachusetts Society to say that he considered that the matter of the proposed statue had assumed 'somewhat serious proportions' and that the Society might have a 'duty to protest' should they consider it not to be judicious.[46] A committee was appointed 'to consider the question of the alleged early discovery of America by the Norsemen'[47] and reached what looked like the perfect solution. With echoes of *The Dublin Review*'s Homeric comparisons of some forty years before, Leifr was to be ranked on a par with Agamemnon as a figure of mythological proportions, and thus implicitly endorsed as a fit subject for sculpture:

> there is the same sort of reason for believing in the existence of Leif Eireksson that there is for believing in the existence of Agamemnon; they are both traditions accepted by later writers, and there is no more reason for regarding as true the details related about the discoveries of the former, than there is for accepting as historic truth the narrative contained in the Homeric poems. Not only is it antecedently probable that the Norsemen discovered America in the early part of the eleventh century, but this is confirmed by the same sort of historical tradition, not

---

41 See *The Collected Letters of William Morris*, ed. Norman Kelvin, 4 vols (Princeton, 1987), II, 182–4.

42 *The Collected Letters of William Morris*, II, 182.

43 *Burne-Jones. The paintings, graphic and decorative work of Sir Edward Burne-Jones 1833–98* (The Arts Council of Great Britain, 1975), p. 70.

44 Georgiana Burne-Jones, introd. John Christian, *Memorials of Edward Burne-Jones* (London, 1993), II (1868–1898), p. 139.

45 On the construction of Columbus monuments in the United States in the eighteenth and nineteenth centuries, see Kirkpatrick Sale, *The Conquest of Paradise. Christopher Columbus and the Columbian Legacy* (London, 1991), pp. 339–40, 347–8.

46 *Proceedings of the Massachusetts Historical Society*, 18 (1880), 79.

47 *Proceedings of the Massachusetts Historical Society*, 2nd ser. 3 (1887), 42.

strong enough to be called evidence, upon which our belief in many of the facts of history rests.[48]

The elevation of Leifr to legendary status had the potential to satisfy everyone: it allowed his Vínland voyage the status of heroic achievement but not necessarily that of historicity.[49] Sara Bull, Ole Bull's American wife, was, however, so distressed at the Society's reluctance to acknowledge the authenticity of the sagas, for which she partly blamed Rafn's dubious claims for the Dighton Rock and the Newport Tower,[50] that both she and, on her behalf, Edwin Waters wrote to Willard Fiske to solicit his support for their case.[51] Fiske, by then resident in Florence, appears to have managed to keep his distance from the entire affair. Henry Haynes, one of the two original proposers of the motion, was so stung by De Costa's criticism of it that, some years later, he professed himself to have been a lifelong believer in Agamemnon but a disbeliever in the historicity of the sagas.[52] In a later communication to the Society, Haynes also took issue with the historian John Fiske's opinion that any comparison between Leifr and Agamemnon was 'inappropriate' on the grounds that, as Fiske had argued in *The Discovery of America*,[53] the sagas are historical and the *Iliad* is not.[54]

In a witty counter performance before the American Historical Association in 1893, James Phinney Baxter debunked the posturings of the 'Norsemaniacs' and consigned the 'ungodly Norumbegans' to the retribution of obscurity:

Of course we are all glad to learn that the location of Norumbega is at last settled, and that Massachusetts has it. It has been an insufferable nuisance to Maineacs with historical tendencies. We are glad to hear of its unexampled extent and the nature of its ancient traffic, themes which furnish the enterprising journals of the day with picturesque opportunities for description. We are glad to know that the pulpit has a new subject with which to attack sin; a great city right in Massachusetts, with its immense canals floating lumber from the interior to its splendid

---

48 *Proceedings of the Massachusetts Historical Society*, 2nd ser. 3 (1887), 44.

49 MacLean (*A Critical Examination*, p. 7) heartily endorsed the suggestion; B. H. DuBois, who considered the Vínland voyages probable but not provable, approved (*Magazine of American History* 27 [1892], 376), as did Justin Winsor (*Narrative and Critical History*, I, 98).

50 'Prof. Rafn's claims for the Newport Tower and the Dighton Rock have possibly prejudiced historians here as against his knowledge, inasmuch as his zeal unfortunately led him & Magnusen to give too much prominence to what really was unimportant.' Sara Bull to Fiske (18 June 1887). Fiske Icelandic Collection, Cornell University. See Þórunn Sigurðardóttir, *Manuscript Material . . . in the Fiske Icelandic Collection*, Correspondence 1. 'Letters to Daniel Willard Fiske'.

51 Sara Bull to Fiske (18 June 1887); Edwin F. Waters to Fiske (25 June 1889). Fiske Icelandic Collection, Cornell University. See Þórunn Sigurðardóttir, *Manuscript Material . . . in the Fiske Icelandic Collection*, Correspondence 1. 'Letters to Daniel Willard Fiske.'

52 Henry Haynes, 'The Historical Character of the Norse Sagas', *Proceedings of the Massachusetts Historical Society*, 5 (1890), 333, 334, 339–40; De Costa, *The Pre-Columbian Discovery of America*, 2nd edn (1890), pp. 58–9.

53 John Fiske, *The Discovery of America, with some account of Ancient America and the Spanish Conquest*, 2 vols (Boston and New York, 1892), I, 194–7.

54 Henry Haynes, 'A few Words more about Leif Ericson and the Norse Sagas', *Proceedings* of the *Massachusetts Historical Society*, 7 (1892), 349–54.

docks and wharves, whence it went on ships full laden to far outland havens; a city, in spite of its prosperity, which came to nought through ungodliness. The fate of these ungodly Norumbegans, who married and were given in marriage with the Canaanites about them, may prove a timely warning to bad Bostonians, while the good, it is to be hoped, may not vaunt themselves overmuch because they were especially raised up by Providence to succeed the wicked Norumbegans. Such is the story recently told to an approving audience, of 'The Norseman and the Puritan.'[55]

After Horsford's death that same year, his daughter Cornelia continued to fund excavations. A few years later she delivered a paper to the Viking Club in London on 'Vinland and its Ruins', which, according to the Club's journal, *Saga-Book*, was 'profusely illustrated by lantern slides'.[56] The audience appear to have received the paper politely, but their recorded comments are perhaps suggestive of an underlying scepticism: it was 'very interesting' and 'certainly interesting and stimulating to the imagination'; the appearance of brick in some of the alleged ruins was 'curious'.[57] By the end of the century, the theatre of Vínland – that post-medieval counterpart to the dramatic stagings of ritual in *Eiríks saga rauða* – had more or less played itself out, as had its companion in print, the story of the Lost Colony of Vínland.

The Lost Colony of Vínland

Although the French scholar Gabriel Gravier's picture of hordes of conquering Norsemen moving to the west of America and south to Brazil in his *Découverte de l'Amérique par les Normands au Xe siècle* (1874) was dismissed as laughable by *The North American Review*,[58] the notion of a lost colony of Vínland was seriously pursued in the nineteenth century by historians, enthusiastic amateurs, and out-and-out eccentrics. Beginning with the Danish poet Claus Lyschander in the early seventeenth century and reaching its apex at the end of the nineteenth, this is a triple-stranded story, according to which – and not every one of

---

55 Baxter, James Phinney Baxter, 'The Present Status of Pre-Columbian Discovery of America by the Norsemen', *Annual Report of the American Historical Association For the Year 1893* (Washington, DC, 1894), p. 105.

56 *Saga-Book of the Viking Society* 2 (1899), 134.

57 'In allowing that Miss Horsford had sent a very interesting paper, Mr. G. M. Atkinson said he feared no profitable discussion was possible, as very few had seen the Icelandic ruins . . . The walls found by Miss Horsford were certainly very primitive in character, but he thought the illustrations showed that they were built at different times, by people in different stages of culture . . . Mr. F. T. Norris said the meeting was indebted to Miss Cornelia Horsford for a very interesting and lucid paper . . . and, as far as her paper was concerned with tracing and identifying the localities of the events described in the Sagas, her work was excellent . . . When, however, the attempt was made to identify structural remains with buildings erected by the Norsemen, the evidence appeared less substantial.' *Saga-Book of the Viking Society*, 2 (1899), 134–5.

58 *The North American Review* 119 (1874), 181.

its proponents embraces all of the following components – a Norse colony was established in Vínland and survived for a number of centuries; its heathen members and large numbers of Native Americans were converted to Christianity by Bishop Eiríkr Gnúpsson in the first quarter of the twelfth century; the colonists mixed with the indigenous people to produce the light-skinned Beothuks of Newfoundland. The origins and inspiration of the lost Vínland colony are multiple: dreams of Nordic empire, scholarly error, nineteenth-century missionary fervour, Yankee ingenuity, and perhaps, Balkan fraud. As far back as *Grœnlendinga saga*, Eiríkr rauði's daughter, Freydís, sowed the seeds of the myth, by instructing her company to say that the slaughtered members of the Helgi and Finnbogi expedition have stayed behind in Vínland: *skulu vér þat segja, at þau búi hér eptir, þá er vér fórum í brott* (*GS* ch. 8: 267; 'we will say that those men and women stayed behind here, when we left'). Its sole vestige of possible historical credibility, the entry in the Icelandic annals for 1121 to the effect that Bishop Eiríkr Gnúpsson from Greenland went in search of Vínland',[59] bears only indirectly on the subject, although it has actively fuelled the myth. Why Bishop Eiríkr did so, and whether he succeeded in his quest or was ever seen again, medieval sources do not record.

Paucity of evidence has not, however, inhibited the post-medieval construction of a Christian colony of Vínland. In Lyschander's *Den Grønlandske Cronica* (1608) not only does Eiríkr Gnúpsson reach his destination, but he also founds a Christian colony which flourishes into Lyschander's own time:

> Oc Erich paa Grønland lagde haand oppaa
> Plandtet paa Vjnland baade Folck og Tro,
> Som er der end ved ljge.[60]

Or, as William Babcock translated it:

> Eric of Greenland did the deed;
> He carried to Wineland both folk and creed:
> Which are there e'en now surviving.[61]

On the face of it, Lyschander's image of Vínland is simply a wishful expression of pious enthusiasm, but it also projects a grander vision of Nordic empire inspired, perhaps, by chronological coincidence. *Den Grønlandske Cronica* was published in 1608. The English settlement of Jamestown, Virginia, was established in May, 1607. Rhetorically, at least, Lyschander may have merged Bishop Eiríkr's alleged Vínland settlement with the Virginia Company's much publicised enterprise.

A century later, in *Historia Vinlandiæ antiqva* (1705) Thormod Torfæus

---

59 See Introduction, above, p. xiii.
60 'Den Grønlandske Cronica', *C. C. Lyschander's Digtning 1579–1623*, ed. Flemming Lundgreen-Nielsen (Copenhagen, 1989), I, 658–60.
61 William H. Babcock, *Early Norse Visits to North America* (Washington DC, 1913), p. 55.

misread 'Vindland' ('Wendland' or Pomerania) for 'Vínland' in the report of the martyrdom of the Irish Bishop Jón, in the medieval Icelandic episcopal history *Hungrvaka*, and thereby set in train the notion of a Vínland in need of salvation. According to *Hungrvaka*:

> Jón byskup hinn írski . . . hafa þat sumir menn fyrir satt at hann fœri síðan *til Vindlands* [my italics] ok sneri þar mörgum mönnum til guðs, ok var síðan tekinn ok barðr, ok höggnar af bæði hendr ok fœtr, en höfuð síðast, ok fór með þeim píningum til guðs.[62]

> Jón the Irish bishop . . . some men believe it to be true that he then went to Vindland and converted many men there to Christianity, and was then captured and scourged, and both his arms and legs struck off, and finally his head, and with those tortures he went to God.

As Torfæus read it, however:

> Johannem Episopum Saxonicum (quem liber Hungrvaka . . . asseverat) primo in Islandia fidem Christianam . . . inde *in Vinlandiam* ad gentum illam convertendam profectum, prostremo supplicio ibi morteqve confessionem suam illustrasse.[63]

Later in the century, Mallet, who cites Torfæus as his chief source for the chapter on the Vínland voyages in *Histoire de Dannemarc*, also makes Jón and Eiríkr missionary emissaries to the Norwegian Vínland colony. Jón's voyage was unsuccessful, 'puisqu'il y fut condamné à mort'[64] and the fortunes of Eiríkr Gnúpsson, whose goal was the same as Jón's, are unknown ('s'y rendit aussi dans la même vue, mais on ignore avec quel succès' [*ibid.*]). Henry Wheaton also subscribes to the Vínland martyrdom of 'an Irish or Saxon priest, named Jon or John'.[65]

According to *Histoire de Dannemarc* it is likely that some in Helgi and Finn-bogi's company escaped death at the hands of Freydís, stayed in Vínland, and established a colony which was not actively abandoned but degenerated, for reasons that can only be guessed at.[66] Mallet goes on to cite the conjectures of Torfaeus and Pontoppidan that the descendants of the Norse settlers are to be found among the Beothuks of Newfoundland and Charlevoix's report that the Beothuks are fierce, eaters of raw meat, light-skinned and heavily bearded. These features, he concludes, are indicative of a degenerate colony of Euro-peans, brought low by want and ignorance.[67] In the 1763 edition of *Histoire de Dannemarc* Mallet removed his speculations concerning the Beothuks' ancestry

---

62 *Hungrvaka*, ed. Jón Helgason (Copenhagen 1938), p. 80.
63 *Historia Vinlandiæ antiqvæ*, p. 71.
64 Mallet, *Histoire de Dannemarc* (1755), p. 185.
65 *History of the Northmen*, p. 30. Wheaton's cited reference here is Frederik C. C. Münter, *Kirchengeschichte von Dænemark und Norwegen* I (Leipzig, 1823–33), p. 562.
66 'cessant d'avoir commerce avec l'Europe s'abatardissoit de son côté, par des causes qu'il est plus aisé d'imaginer que d'avancer avec certitude' (Mallet, *Histoire de Dannemarc* [1755], p. 185).
67 *Histoire de Dannemarc* (1755), pp. 187–8.

and suggested simply that, trade having ceased, the Norsemen either merged with their barbarous neighbours or were destroyed by them.[68]

Acknowledging Mallet as the source of his account of the Vínland voyages,[69] Crantz makes no mention of the martyred Bishop Jón, but speculates that an outlaw remnant from the Freydis expedition may have blended with the native population to produce the Beothuks:

> The rest of the colonists probably fled and dispersed in the country, for fear of punishment. At least from that time there are no more connected accounts to be found of this colony; except that in the year 1121 . . . bishop Eric from Greenland is said to have gone thither to convert his forlorn countrymen, who were mostly still heathens. 'Tis probable those Indians at present about Newfoundland, who are so very different in their shape and manner of living from the other Americans, may be descended from them.[70]

Vínland, he suggests,[71] might even have been a refuge for those resistant to the new faith. Deriving his account from Crantz, in *History of Discoveries and Voyages made in the North* (1786) Foerster postulated that Eiríkr Gnúpsson's mission in 1121 was to convert the descendants of these renegade 'Normans':

> The remaining Normans were dispersed; and it is probable, that their descendants were still in being for a long time after . . . and it is highly probable, that the tribe still existing in the interior parts of Newfoundland, which differs remarkably from all the American Savages as well as in shape as in their manner of living . . . are descended from those ancient Normans . . . it is supposed that, instead of going to Greenland, he [Eirik Upsi] went straight on to Winland, in order to convert the Normans, who were still heathens.[72]

Listing both Foerster and Crantz among his authorities in *American Biography* (1794),[73] Jeremy Belknap stated that 'a controversy arose in the colony, which induced them to return to Greenland. The others dispersed and mixed with the Skrælings'.[74] He adds a further twist to the story by suggesting that Eiríkr Gnúpsson's mission was one of rehabilitation as well as conversion:

> Eric, Bishop of Greenland, went to Winland, with a benevolent design to recover and convert his countrymen who had degenerated into savages.[75]

---

68 'les Norvégiens de *Vinlande* eux-mêmes, n'ayant plus de commerce avec l'Europe, se mêloient avec les barbares leurs voisins, ou étoient détruits par eux' (*Histoire de Dannemarc* [1763], pp. 271–2).

69 *The History of Greenland: containing a description of the country, – and its inhabitants*, 2 vols (London, 1767), I, 254.

70 Crantz, *The History of Greenland*, I, 257.

71 Crantz, *The History of Greenland*, I, 256n.

72 *History of Discoveries and Voyages made in the North*, translated from the German of John Reinhold Forster (London, 1786), pp. 86–7.

73 *American Biography* I (1794), 56.

74 *American Biography* I (1794), 51.

75 *Ibid.*

Belknap was prepared to follow up in the scientific spirit. In a footnote to this episode he announced that:

> At my request, Governor Wentworth, of Nova Scotia, has employed a proper person, to make inquiry into any vestiges of this ancient colony, which *may* yet be subsisting. I am sorry that the result could not be had, before the publication of this volume; but when it comes to hand, it shall be communicated.[76]

but the record of the investigation ends here.

Although the Beothuks were all but extinct by 1828,[77] Washington Irving repeats virtually verbatim Foerster's comments on the likelihood that the natives of Newfoundland trace their origins to a Norse colony:

> there is every appearance that the tribe which still exists in the interior of Newfoundland, and which is so different from the other savages of North America both in their appearance and mode of living, and always in a state of warfare with the Esquimaux of the northern coast, are descendants of the ancient Normans.[78]

Rafn had himself noted Torfæus's 'Vínland/Vindland' error,[79] a misreading which persists into twentieth-century scholarship.[80] Nevertheless, his ready identification of the 'Newport Tower' – a structure which, even in the mid-nineteenth century, was generally assumed to have been built as a windmill in the late seventeenth – as an eleventh-century round church[81] spawned a more successful missionary discourse of its own. The Newport Tower became Rafn's inspiration for the following tale: reports that, separated from Mother Church, the Christian colony of Vínland is in a pitiful condition prompt Eiríkr Gnúpsson, bishop-elect of Greenland, to tender support and encouragement to the Vínland settlers and to convert the heathen; the Vínland mission of 1121 becomes his inaugural episcopal act; once there, he decides to stay and to abandon the Greenland diocese of Garðar. Rafn's missionary narrative ends here in the absence, he reluctantly and somewhat belatedly concedes, of documentary evidence.[82] Athough he does not go so far as to credit Eiríkr with a

---

76 *American Biography* I (1794), 56n.

77 The last Beothuk died in 1829. See Peter Such, *Vanished Peoples. The Archaic Dorset & Beothuk People of Newfoundland* (Toronto, 1978), pp. 80–4.

78 *The Life and Voyages of Christopher Columbus*, ed. John McElroy, The Complete Works of Washington Irving, 9 (Boston, 1981), 842.

79 *AA*, pp. 461–2.

80 Sayers, for example, points to the *Hungrvaka* incident as evidence which 'seems to symbolize that some responsibility had been borne to take Christianity to the New World' ('Vinland, the Irish', p. 14, n. 14).

81 'Bemærkninger om en gammel bygning i Newport', *Annaler for nordisk Oldkyndighed* (1840–41), 37–51.

82 'Mais pour les actes d'Éric dans le Vinland les anciens manuscrits ne nous en racontent rien. Il dépendra ainsi des recherches ultérieures si nous serons à même de lever un joure voile qui nous cache pour le moment cette partie ténébreuse de l'ancienne histoire de l'Amérique' (p. 52). The quotation is from the French translation of this article in C. C. Rafn, *Mémoire sur la découverte de l'Amérique au dixième siècle*, 2nd edn (Copenhagen, 1843).

successful colonial enterprise, Rafn spins an imperial fantasy in the concluding sentence of the piece, in which he speculates that 'our ancestors' might have listened in the Newport Tower to Latin masses and 'the Old Danish tongue':

> Ces recherches nous conduiront peut-être en même temps à determiner si l'ancien édifice de Newport, dont la construction paraît coïncider avec le séjour de l'evêque E:ric dans le pays, a appartenu à l'ancien culte des Scandinaves, à une église ou à couvent, où nos aïeux auraient alternativement fait retentir les messes latines et l'ancienne langue danoise. (p. 52)

Heirs to Rafn's 'missionary discourse' of Vínland, their imperial interests religious rather than nationalistic, are a number of nineteenth-century church historians. Johan Adam Möhler, for example, suggested that Christians and heathens lived side by side in Vínland from 1000 to 1121, that there were multiple Christian missions, and that Bishop Eiríkr worked there for three years around 1120.[83] The likely contents of certain alleged Vatican records, which many thought would provide fully documented evidence of the Christian Vínland colony, became the focus of fervent interest.

Ecclesiastical rewriting of the Vínland voyages seems to have taken place as early as the late twelfth century, by the Icelandic monk, Gunnlaugr Leifsson, who may have inserted the historically doubtful information that Leifr Eiríksson was Óláfr Tryggvason's agent in the Christianizing of Greenland (*ES* ch.5) into his lost saga of that king. Luka Jelič, Yugoslavian priest and church historian, whose knowledge of the Vínland voyages was derived entirely from secondary sources, is Gunnlaugr's nineteenth-century counterpart. In two papers delivered to the Congrès scientifique des Catholiques (Paris, 1891; Brussels, 1894), both of them entitled 'L'Évangélisation de l'Amérique avant Christophe Colomb', Jelič claimed Eirík Gnúpsson as the successful evangelizer of native Americans.[84] His apostolate, reports Jelič, 'produisit des fruits abondants' (1891, 172). Like Torfaeus, Mallet, and Wheaton, Jelič relates that a Saxon bishop named Jonus went on a missionary expedition to Vínland (in 1050) to convert the natives and was martyred there. His assertion that relations between natives and Norsemen had by this time been formalized in marriages[85] implies that a mixed race had established itself in the colony.

One of the seven Latin legends on the 'Vínland Map' indicates that the Vínland colony continued at least into the early twelfth century:

---

83 See Richard Hennig 'Die Vinlandreise des Grönland-Bischofs Eirik Gnupson', in *Terrae Incognitae. Eine Zusammenstellung und kritische Bewertung der wichtigsten vorcolumbischen Entdeckungsreisen an Hand der darüber vorliegenden Originalberichte*, II (Leiden, 1950), 393.
84 *Compte rendu du Congrès scientifique international des Catholiques tenu à Paris 1891*, V (Paris 1891), 170–84; *Compte rendu du troisième congrès scientifique international des Catholiques tenu à Bruxelles 1894*, V (Brussels 1895), 3–7. The article of the same name which appeared in *Le Missioni francescane* 8 (1897), 556–60, is a reprint of the 1894 paper.
85 'les indigènes . . . avaient déjà d'étroites relations avec les colons normands, jusqu'au point de contracter avec eux des mariages.' 'L'Évangélisation de l'Amérique avant Christophe Colomb' (1891), p. 172.

Henricus Gronelande regionumq finitimaru sedis apostolicae episcopus legatus in hac terra spaciosa vero et opulentissima in postmo anno p. ss. nrj. Pascali accessit in nomine dei omnipotetis longo tempore mansit estiuo et brumali postea versus Gronelanda redit ad orientam hiemalem deinde humillima obediencia superiori voluntati processit.

Eric, legate of the Apostolic See and bishop of Greenland and the neighbouring regions, arrived in this truly vast and very rich land, in the name of Almighty God, in the last year of our most blessed father Pascal [d.1118], remained a long time in both summer and winter, and later returned northeastward toward Greenland and then proceeded [home to Europe?] in most humble obedience to the will of his superiors.[86]

This narrative bears a strong resemblance to a statement in Jelič's paper of 1891, according to which Eiríkr did not, as Rafn told it, wilfully abandon the episcopal seat of Greenland but, after a long time in Vínland, obeyed the call to return.[87]

The chief American proponents of the 'missionary discourse' of Vínland were Richard Clark, author of a sequence of articles in *The American Catholic Quarterly Review*, and Marie Shipley. Despite the somewhat misleading titles of his articles – 'America Discovered and Christianized in the Tenth and Eleventh Centuries' (1888), 'The First Christian Northmen in America' (1889), 'The Norse Hierarchy of America' (1890) – Clark, who draws upon, among others, Rafn and Gravier, makes no case for a continuous Christian settlement of Vínland from the eleventh century. He does, though, claim Greenland for the New World, and 'The Norse Hierarchy of America' is simply a list and commentary concerning its bishops. In 'America Discovered and Christianized in the Tenth and Eleventh Centuries' Eiríkr Gnúpsson is 'the apostle of Vinland', and his presence there indicative of 'a permanent settlement of Northmen in Rhode Island' (p. 231). Whereas Foerster had characterized Leifr first and foremost as an ambitious founder of colonies,[88] in this article Clark emphasizes his role as the evangelist of Greenland:

> Leif, with a brave soul and Christian faith, rejecting the pagan superstitions in which he had been educated, and which he had now abjured, joyously sailed in his stout ship with his thirty-five sailors and the Christian missionaries sent to evangelize the pagan Greenlanders . . . His was a veritable voyage of discovery. It was more – it was a mission of Christianity.   (p. 220)

Clark voices regret at the failure of the exemplary pioneering couple, Guðríðr and Karlsefni, to become founders of a colony of Vínland and does not seem to be entirely convinced that a permanent Norse settlement was ever established there:

---

86 Ed. and trans. R. A. Skelton, in *The Vinland Map and the Tartar Relation* (New Haven and London 1965), p. 140.
87 'L'Évangélisation de l'Amérique avant Christophe Colomb' (1891), p. 173.
88 *History of Discoveries and Voyages made in the North*, p. 82.

> If any permanent colony was ever established in Vinland by the Northmen, as some suppose, and cite the old tower at Newport as proof of this fact, or if even occasional intercourse was maintained between Greenland and Vinland . . .
>
> (p. 232)

Marie Shipley dismissed Clark as the servant of 'superstition and mediævalism',[89] but she had no doubts about the existence of the Vatican Vínland records and the nature of their contents, or reservations about the duration of the colony. Having declared that she was 'not in the slightest sympathy'[90] with Catholic theologians and historians, she conceded that only they and she were in command of the facts concerning the Christian colony of Vínland, in which Eiríkr's apostolate was not only successful but also tolled the death knell of Viking culture:

> the very date that might have made them the supreme race on earth, the year 1000, marked their subjugation under the only master to which they had ever succumbed, the Roman Catholic Church. Consequently it was not the Vikings, the proud, defiant, independent, freedom-loving Norsemen, who planted those colonies in Greenland and Vinland, but the submissive vassals of the Pope, whose spirits were completely broken.[91]

Leifr, as missionary, was 'on a par with the meanest and most ignorant drudges who force distasteful doctrines upon the helpless',[92] and the 'Greenland colonies' were condemned to servitude under the rapacious dominion of Rome. Untroubled by the absence of the presumed Vatican records ('The only mystery, as yet unsolved, is, what became of these records? Are they still in existence?'[93]), Shipley constructs an unbroken Vínland history to the early fifteenth century, when Greenland and Vínland were abandoned by 'the then Catholic mother country, Norway'.[94]

Confirmation, established through an investigation initiated by William Eleroy Curtis of the U.S. State Department, a man high on Shipley's list of enemies,[95] of the non-existence of the Vatican Vínland records[96] did not deter her from publishing *The Norse Colonization in America by the Light of the Vatican*

---

89 'The Missing Records of the Norse Discovery of America', *Congrès international des Américanistes, huitième session (Paris 1890)* (Paris, 1892), p. 196.
90 'The Missing Records', p. 190.
91 'The Missing Records', p. 197.
92 *Ibid.*
93 *Ibid.*, p. 194
94 *Ibid.*, p. 199.
95 *The Norse Colonization in America*, p. 13.
96 See his 'Recent Disclosures Concerning Pre-Columbian Voyages to America in the Archives of the Vatican', *National Geographic Magazine* 5 (1893–94), 197–234.

Finds (1899). Privately printed in Switzerland after its rejection by *The Fort-nightly Review* on the grounds that it had nothing new to say,[97] this piece displays a marked modification of Shipley's previous anti-Catholic bias, which is explained by the information that she and her husband have made a pact with Luka Jelić 'to devote our three lives to these great researches' (p. 22). Jelić, she says, has been occupied in unearthing from the recesses of the Vatican 'some old maps, pre-Columbian ones'.[98] There are hints of forthcoming stunning (but never delivered) revelations by Jelić, who is said to have found records 'in several of the capitals and other archive-centres of Europe, to which he holds the clues'.[99] Among Jelić's reported Vatican finds, and allegedly photographed by him, is a 'Map of the World containing America, drawn probably in the time of Leo X [1513–21]'.[100] The article ends with another tantalizing reference to maps: 'The appetite for old maps . . . can never become sated, and here is the enticing prospect of several'.[101] Jelić's cartographic credentials are emphasized by both the Shipleys, who credit him with having discovered 'the original maps of Ptolemy'. Marie Shipley adds that his findings, recently published by the Bosnian government, have been verified by Austrian, German, and English experts.[102] The Shipleys' collaboration with Jelić and Marie Shipley's allegations that maps are among other documents relating to the Vínland voyages which he has discovered provide further reason to believe that Jelić may have played some role in the production of the Vínland Map.[103]

Mythical Vatican records aside, Horsford shows how it takes only a little tinkering with the textual machinery of the Vínland sagas themselves to produce the Christian settlement of Vínland. According to *Grœnlendinga saga*:

> Ok er Karlsefni var andaðr, tók Guðríðr við búsvarðveizlu ok Snorri, sonr hennar, er fœddr var á Vínlandi. Ok er Snorri var kvángaðr, þá fór Guðríðr útan ok gekk suðr ok kom út aptr til bús Snorra, sonar síns, ok hafði hann látit gera kirju í Glaumbœ. Síðan varð Guðríðr nunna ok einsetukona ok var þar, meðan hon lifði.
>
> (*GS* ch. 9: 269)

97 The initial letters of acceptance and subsequent rejection by *The Fortnightly Review* are printed, with bitter commentary, at the beginning of this piece.

98 *The Norse Colonization in America*, p. 12.

99 *Ibid.*, p. 23.

100 *Ibid.*, p. 24.

101 *Ibid.*, p. 25.

102 John Shipley, 'Addendum', *The Norse Colonization in America*; Marie Shipley, 'Some More Dis-coverers of their Predecessors' Discoveries! An Exposé of the Plot', *op. cit.* (insertion), p. 6. The publication by Jelić referred to here appears to be *Najstariji kartografski spomenik o rimskoj pokrajini Dalmaciji* (with MS notes by John Shipley) (Sarajevo, 1898). A German version, *Das älteste karto-graphische Denkmal über die römanische Provinz Dalmatien*, appeared in the series *Wiss. Mitth. Bosnien* 8 (1900).

103 See Erik Wahlgren, 'Vinland Map', in *Medieval Scandinavia: An Encyclopedia*, p. 703. Most recently, Kirsten Seaver has proposed a German Jesuit priest, Josef Fischer (1858–1944), as the author of the Map and suggested that he may have drawn upon Jelić's work. See 'The "Vinland Map": who made it, and why? New light on an old controversy', *The Map Collector* 70 (1995), 32–40.

After Karlsefni had died, Guðríðr and Snorri, her son who had been born in Vínland, took over the farm. And when Snorri was married, Guðríðr travelled abroad and went south [i.e. on a pilgrimage to Rome] and returned to her son Snorri's farm, and he had a church built at Glaumbœr. Then Guðríðr became a nun and anchoress and remained there for as long as she lived.

As rejigged by Horsford:

Gudrid was the lady who, after the death of her husband, made a pious pilgrimage to Rome, where she was received with much distinction, and where she told the Pope of the beautiful new country in the far west, of 'Vinland the Good', and about the Christian settlements made there by Scandinavians.[104]

Horsford attributes the disappearance of the Greenland settlements to emigration and miscegenation in the Vínland colony, a practice which is also said to explain the disappearance of any evidence of a pre-modern Scandinavian culture in North America:

That most who came to Vineland remained, and ultimately became merged in the native race, might naturally have been expected. That this emigration of Northmen (an estimated one of ten thousand) continued, to the ultimate depopulation of Greenland, – a hitherto unsolved problem; – suggests itself as not improbable. As evidences of it, there are found, it is believed, traces of Norse life, habits, ethnological features, and language among the Indian tribes once here at the East, as well as among those now at the West, and not less at the South and North.[105]

It is, perhaps, one of history's ironies that the first Icelander known to have settled permanently in America should have come in the missionary spirit. Thordur Thidriksson, a Mormon from the Vestmannaeyjar, arrived in New York in 1856 and went on to found an Icelandic settlement at Spanish Fork, Utah,[106] whence, presumably, he fulfilled his proselytizing obligations to the Mormon faith. Some 750 years after Bishop Eiríkr's departure for Vínland, his spiritual descendant had, as Claus Lyschander put it, 'plantet derpå både Folk og Tro'.

---

104 *The Problem of the Northmen. A Letter to Judge Daly, The President of the American Geographical Society* (Cambridge, Mass., 1889), p. 13.
105 Eben Norton Horsford, *The Defences of Norumbega*, p. 83.
106 Vilhjalmur Stefansson, *Iceland: The First American Republic* (New York, 1939), p. 238.

Vikings and natives: eighteenth- and nineteenth-century perceptions

The saga-writer's lack of comment on the unprovoked massacre of native Vínlanders by Þorvaldr and his company (*GS* ch. 5) is typical of Old Icelandic saga style, but many nineteenth-century readers, particularly those who were unfamiliar with Old Icelandic narrative conventions, passed judgments upon the incident which reflect the ambivalence of contemporary attitudes towards both Vikings and Native Americans. For some commentators, the Norsemen's conduct posed a moral problem. Richard Clark, for instance, was clearly deeply troubled by it, whereas others simply state the facts as the saga relates them.[107] In a number of the summaries of Þorvaldr's expedition which appear in reviews of *Antiquitates Americanæ* and historical commentaries, the Norsemen are absolved from censure by the omission of any reference to the bloody events which precede his death. The natives, implicitly, assume the role of aggressors: 'they passed along the coast . . . where Thorwald was killed by the Indians' (George Folsom);[108] '[t]he Northmen found three canoes, each having on board three of the natives . . . A skirmish ensued, in which eight of the natives were killed' (Alexander Hill Everett);[109] 'they came in contact with the native Skraelings, and Thoroald [sic] was mortally wounded' (L. H. Barnum);[110] 'in a battle with the Skrællings an arrow from one of the natives of America pierced his side, causing death' (Rasmus Anderson);[111] '[w]ith these natives they came into hostile conflict, in which Thorvald received a wound of which he subsequently died' (Rev. Edmund F. Slafter);[112] '[a] hostile conflict arose, however, with the natives' (Karl Blind);[113] '[a] contest ensued, and eight of the nine Skrællings were killed' (Edward Everett; John Frost);[114] 'une querelle . . . s'engagea avec eux' (C. C. Rafn);[115] '[o]n this voyage Thorwald was killed by the

107 For example: 'they discovered canoes and men, all of whom they caught, except one. They killed the eight they caught. Then came out from the inside of the frith [sic] an innumerable crowd of skin-boats, filled with Skrælings (Indians), and Thorvald said, "We must put out the battle-screen, but fight little"' (Charles W. Elliot, *The New England History, from the discovery of the continent by the Northmen, A.D. 986* [New York, 1857], p. 27; cf. Thomas Wentworth Higginson, *A Book of American Explorers* (Boston and New York, 1877), p. 11; Samuel Laing, 'Preliminary Dissertation' to *The Heimskringla; or, Chronicle of the Kings of Norway* (London, 1844), III, 163; I. A. Blackwell, *Northern Antiquities* (London, 1847), p. 54.
108 Review of *AA*, *The New York Review* 2 (1838), 355.
109 'The Discovery of America by the Northmen', *United States Magazine and Democratic Review* 2 (1838), 91.
110 'The Discovery of America by the Northmen', *The Cornell Review* 1 (1874), 255.
111 *America Not Discovered by Columbus* (1874), p. 75.
112 *The Discovery of America by the Northmen 985–1015* (Concord, NH, 1891), p. 8.
113 'The Forerunners of Columbus', *New Review* 7 (1892), 353.
114 Review of *AA*, *The North American Review* 46 (1838), 174; John Frost, *The Pictorial History of the United States of America* (London, 1843), p. 4.
115 *Mémoire sur la découverte de l'Amérique au dixième siècle*, 2nd edn (Copenhagen, 1843), p. 8.

natives' (Hubert Howe Bancroft).[116] Some American commentators of the 1870s and 1880s make the natives the assailants: 'This expedition was here attacked by the natives, who, in skin boats, placed themselves beside the ship and made their assault' (E. S. Riley, Jr.);[117] 'they were attacked by hostile Skræl-lings (*natives*)' (Aaron Goodrich).[118]

Expressed opinion about the episode falls into three broad categories: it is either a gratuitous act of violence on the part of the Norsemen; an incident unfortunately typical of European–native encounters; or a demonstration, for good or ill, of Viking mores. There is a discernible shift in opinion between late eighteenth- and early nineteenth-century commentators, who, in the main, derive their knowledge of the Vínland voyages from Mallet, and reviewers of *Antiquitates Americanæ* and its adaptations from 1838 to the end of the century. The former tend to condemn the killings as a barbarous crime; the latter are more likely to reflect the diminution of sympathy for Native Americans which accompanied the mid-century beginning of westward expansion and burgeoning of racial Teutonism.[119] Mallet's judgment (1755) was that the assault upon nine peaceful people, 'tranquilles & à moitié endormies',[120] was perpetrated 'par une férocité aussi imprudente que barbare' (*ibid.*) and that Þorvaldr 'porta les justes peines de son inhumanité'.[121] Percy (1770) remains faithful to his source here:

Thorvald and his companions . . . by a ferocity as imprudent as it was cruel, put them to death the same day . . . Thorvald . . . paid the penalty that was justly due for his inhuman conduct.[122]

Crantz (1767) remarks that the Norsemen 'killed them out of mere cruelty' and that Thorwald 'alone was obliged to suffer for his barbarity'.[123] Foerster (1786) calls it a wanton and cruel attack: 'they discovered three boats covered with leather, in each of which there were three men; these they seized: but one man found the means to get off, the others were all wantonly and cruelly attacked by the Normans'.[124] Jeremy Belknap (1794) was wholehearted in his condemna-tion of the massacre: they 'inhumanly killed them all but one; who escaped and

---

116 *The Works of Hubert Howe Bancroft* (San Francisco, 1882), V, 107.
117 'Pre-Columbian Discovery of America by the Northmen', *Southern Magazine* 13 (1873), 707.
118 *A History of the Character and Achievements of the so-called Christopher Columbus* (New York, 1874), p. 78.
119 For a comprehensive analysis of the shifting and sometimes contradictory attitudes towards the Native American in nineteenth-century America, see Helen Carr, *Inventing the American Primitive. Politics, Gender and the Representation of Native American Literary Traditions, 1789–1936* (New York, 1996).
120 *Histoire de Dannemarc* (1755), p. 180.
121 *Ibid.*, p. 181.
122 *Northern Antiquities*, I, 286, 287.
123 *The History of Greenland*, pp. 255–6.
124 *History of Discoveries and Voyages made in the North*, p. 84.

collected a larger number of his countrymen, to make an attack on their invaders'.[125] Henry Holland (1812) attributed Þorvaldr's death to retaliation for his 'act of barbarous cruelty'.[126] Joseph Moulton (1824) speaks of 'Thorwald's . . . furious attack' as an 'inglorious adventure'.[127] Hugh Murray (1829) also sees the action as savage and wanton, and the slaying of Þorvaldr as a justifiable act of retaliation:

> Sorry I am to say, that the Norse adventurers, in the most savage and wanton manner, attacked these poor creatures, and killed them all except one, who contrived to escape. They were not long, however, of reaping the fruits of this crime . . . Thorstein . . . not discouraged by the too-merited fate of his kinsman, fitted out another expedition, composed of twenty-five followers.[128]

Henry Wheaton commented twice on the episode, in *History of the Northmen* (1831) and in his review of *Antiquitates Americanæ* for *The Foreign Quarterly Review* (1838). In the former he subscribes to the late eighteenth- and early nineteenth-century view that Þorvaldr was guilty of an act of 'wanton cruelty', for which the natives exacted due vengeance:

> the adventurers descried on the shore three small batteaux made of hides, under each of which was a band of three natives. These they took prisoners, except one, who made his escape to the mountains, and inhumanly put them to death the same day. A little while after, their wanton cruelty was avenged by the natives.[129]

In an interesting change of attitude, Wheaton assumes a more objective stance a few years later in the *Antiquitates Americanæ* review. Only his use of the term 'murdered' implies disapproval of Þorvaldr's actions:

> Of the nine natives they murdered eight, but found themselves in a short time surrounded by a great multitude, hastening from all sides to avenge the death of their fellows. The Northmen beat them off, but Thorwald received a mortal wound in the combat.[130]

English and American reviewers of *Antiquitates Americanæ* and its adaptations offer a wide range of opinion on the incident. Among those who relate it to post-Columbian history, Beamish's reviewer in *The Monthly Review* makes specific comparison with the Spanish ('He and his companions seem to have been not less cruel towards the aborigines than their Spanish successors centuries later').[131] Henry Brownell remarks in *Pioneer Heroes of the New World* that

125 *American Biography* (1794), I, 51.
126 'Preliminary Dissertation', in Mackenzie, *Travels in the Island of Iceland*, p. 44.
127 *History of the State of New York* (1924), p. 117.
128 *Historical Account of Discoveries and Travels in North America* (London, 1829), I, 16. Murray cites Peringskiöld and Torfaeus as his sources.
129 *History of the Northmen*, p. 25.
130 *The Foreign Quarterly Review* 21 (1831), 97.
131 *The Monthly Review* 155 (1841), 339.

the Northmen's conduct is characteristic of Europeans in the New World: 'Here they met with several of the *Skrœllings* or natives, whom, after the usual fashion of European discoverers, they killed'.[132] Similarly, William Cullen Bryant and Howard Gay note that this is the first of many such European-Amerindian encounters and decry the cold-blooded cruelty of the Norsemen. They interpret Þorvaldr's injunction to *vega lítt í mót* (*GS* ch. 5: 256) ('fight little against them'), when a retaliatory party appears, as a tacit admission of his earlier ruthlessness:

> For the first time the Northmen here met with the natives – met them as Europeans so often did in subsequent centuries . . . they saw . . . nine Skrællings, on whom they stole unawares and captured eight of them. The ninth escaped; the eight they immediately killed in cold blood. This cruel deed done, they lay down to sleep upon the grass under the trees; but it was not to pleasant dreams. 'Fight little against them,' was Thorvald's order, mindful now of the mercy he should have shown before.[133]

The liveliest discussion of the incident is by the English writer, Joshua Toulmin Smith, whose *The Discovery of America by the Northmen* (1839), an adaptation of *Antiquitates Americanæ*, takes the form of a dialogue between a certain Dr Dubital and Messrs Cassall and Norset. Smith, a constitutional lawyer, social reformer, and amateur geologist, lived in the United States from 1837 to 1842, where he lectured on phrenology and philosophy.[134] *The Discovery of America by the Northmen* was not, it seems, a popular success. *The North American Review* attributed its alleged rapid relegation to obscurity to the 'oppressive' nature of its Socratic design.[135] In Smith's account of the Þorvaldr incident, Dr Dubital declares the killings unjustified and the natives' vengeance just:

> Well, I think it served them right. I don't see what business they had to put the natives to death, whether they found them under canoes or any thing else.
>
> (p. 114)

His interlocutor suggests that the Norsemen may have responded to unreported signs of provocation and that, in any case, their actions pale into insignificance in comparison with the infinitely worse treatment meted out to Native Americans by the Spanish, English, and present government of America:

> I would by no means defend any cruelty of the Northmen, yet no treatment that the natives received at their hands can exceed, in cruelty, that which they have since received at the hands of European nations boasting a higher degree of refinement and civilization. You will especially remember the treatment inflicted upon

---

132 'The Northmen in America', *The Pioneer Heroes of the New World* (Cincinnati, 1857), p. 24.
133 *A Popular History of the United States* (London, 1876), p. 44.
134 See *The Dictionary of National Biography*, XVIII, 502–3.
135 The comment is made in a review of De Costa's *The Pre-Columbian Discovery of America* in *The North American Review* 109 (1869), 266.

them by your worthy friends, the Spanish colonists, though I don't know that they are receiving much better treatment at the present day, at the hands of a government which boasts much of its preëminent liberality. (*ibid.*)

Dubital having conceded that the speaker has a point,

I cannot pretend to defend the treatment the Indians have received from the early settlers, whether Spanish or English, or which they are receiving at this day from our own government. I believe, indeed, it is indefensible. (p. 115)

the dialogue progresses to a passionate condemnation of the dispossession of the Cherokees.

Despite such expressions of distaste for Þorvaldr's brutality, nineteenth-century English and American writers alike take an insouciant view of the ethics of trading furs for milk (*Grænlendinga saga*) or pieces of red cloth (*Eiríks saga rauða*). Moving from outrage at Þorvaldr's actions to approval of Karlsefni's, Hugh Murray turns the scene in *GS* (ch. 7) from one of bartering to gift-giving. Karlsefni's company are represented as enlightened philanthropists who, 'wiser and more humane', bestow milk and other articles upon the 'simple' natives:

These simple people were affrighted beyond measure by the lowing of the bull . . . the present visitors, wiser and more humane, invited them back, presented various articles to them unknown, and milk, which extremely delighted their palates.[136]

When Smith has Dr. Dubital remark that the exchange of furs for shrinking pieces of red cloth indicates that the natives 'were generous of their goods',[137] Mr. Norset's rejoinder is that the exchange was a fair one according to the principles of supply and demand, and the dialogue continues without further comment:

No particular generosity; the bargain was equally advantageous on both sides. The Skrælings could get red cloth nowhere else, while the skins were of little value to them, being the fruits of their hunting expeditions, and capable, therefore, of being easily replaced. The red cloth, on the contrary, was of little value to the Northmen, while they valued the skins highly. It was a good bargain on each side, according to the most approved doctrines of the "*demand and supply*" system of political economy.[138]

Confident that the Skrælings are 'of the Esquimaux race', Henry Wheaton makes no secret of his distaste for their appearance and commercial practices in his review of *Antiquitates Americanæ*. They are, he claims, eager traders, avid for weapons and red cloth and stupidly unaware of the value of their merchandise. Karlsefni is applauded for his good sense in declining to deal in arms. When supplies of the cloth shrink, native greed does not:

136 *Historical Account of Discoveries and Travels in North America*, I, 17.
137 *The Discovery of America by the Northmen*, p. 177.
138 *Ibid.*, p. 178.

They readily entered into barter, coveting above all things swords and spears, which Karlsefne, on the other hand, prudently declined to sell them. They were obliged to content themselves, therefore, with red cloth, and for a piece large enough to tie round the head, gave a whole skin of fine grey fur. As the cloth grew scarce it was dealt out by the Northmen in smaller portions, but without any abatement of mercantile eagerness on the part of the natives.[139]

Those who comment on the Þorvaldr incident as characteristically Viking are either censorious, indulgent, or overtly approving. John S. C. Abbot, for instance, who looks upon it as typical both of European–native encounter and Viking conduct, condemns the Norsemen as worse than savages and their actions as diabolical. Þorvald's death is an act of divine retribution:

These barbarian Northmen, with cruelty which would have disgraced savages, pursued the harmless natives, and killed eight of them. One only escaped. The fiend-like deed roused the tribe . . . The Northmen, sheltered by planks, could bid defiance to the assaults of these justly exasperated natives . . . They knew not that one barbed arrow, God-directed, had entered the vitals of Thorwald . . . In this encounter the Europeans were palpably and outrageously in the wrong.[140]

Less passionately, P. De Roo sees the Norsemen as the true sons of their blood-thirsty forbears:

The Northmen had not yet lost the spirit and habits of their piratical ancestors. A battle ensued, if so it can be called, in which eight of the Skraelings were put to death, while the ninth succeeded in fleeing to the ocean with his canoe . . . Tired after their long search and bloody crime . . .[141]

Among those reluctant to condemn the killings outright, John R. Baldwin sees the episode simply as characteristic of the warrior ethos:

They seized all the men but one, who was so nimble as to escape with his boat . . . *they killed all those whom they had taken.* The doctrine of 'natural enemies' was more current among the old Northmen than that of human brotherhood.[142]

For the Aryan supremacist, Charles Morris, the Norsemen's only error was not to have slaughtered the entire company:

The blood-loving instinct of the Norsemen was never at fault in a case like this. Drawing their swords, they assailed the hidden men, and of the nine only one escaped, the others being stretched in death upon the beach.

139 *The Foreign Quarterly Review* 21 (1838), 103.
140 *The History of Maine* (Augusta, Maine, 1882), p. 15.
141 *History of America Before Columbus*, II, *European Immigrants* (Philadelphia and London, 1900), pp. 224–5.
142 *Ancient America, in notes on American archæology* (New York, 1872), p. 282.

The mariners had made a fatal mistake. To kill none, unless they could kill all, should have been their rule, a lesson in practical wisdom which they were soon to learn.[143]

The reviewer of Gabriel Gravier's *Découverte de l'Amérique par les Normands* in *The North American Review* makes light of the incident by treating the Viking stereotype with heavy-handed jocularity:

> In the evening a party of nine natives, or Skrellings, as the Norsemen called indifferently all inhabitants of America, came off [sic] in their canoes. Eight of these Skrellings were seized by the Norsemen, and as life had been comparatively tame of late, apparently for sheer amusement they cut the throats of the unfortunate savages.[144]

These eighteenth- and nineteenth-century assessments of the first Euro-Amerindian encounter reflect contemporary debate, in history, literature, political thought, and journals like *The North American Review*, about the evolutionary and social status of Native Americans and Vikings.[145] Were the former noble savages or barbarous and hostile ones, whose extinction was an inevitable part of and indeed a benefit to Christian progress? Did the latter rival them in barbarity or were they prototypical Pilgrims? Longfellow and artists like George Catlin and Seth Eastman subscribed to an idealized image of the Native American.[146] The eminent historian, Francis Parkman, thought otherwise.[147] The reviewer of Thomas McKenney and Hames Hall's *History of the Indian Tribes of North America* in *The North American Review* (1838) reflected a widespread viewpoint in condemning as 'utterly false' the idealized representation of the 'low, gross, sensual' Native American by poets and novelists.[148]

Even among those eighteenth- and nineteenth-century readers who condemn the unprovoked slaughter of the *skrælingar* in *Grænlendinga saga*, only two, Jeremy Belknap and Joshua Toulmin Smith, imply that the indigenes have a

---

143 'Vineland and the Vikings', *Historical Tales. The Romance of Reality*, I (New York and Los Angeles, 1893), p. 21. For Morris's views on Teutonic superiority, see his *The Aryan Race, its origin and its achievements* (Chicago, 1892).

144 *The North American Review* 119 (1874), 170.

145 For a survey of the debate from the 1820s to the early 1850s, see Lucy Maddox, *Removals. Nineteenth-Century American Literature and the Politics of Indian Affairs* (New York and Oxford, 1991), Chapter 1.

146 See, for example, Rena Coen, 'Longfellow, Hiawatha, and American Nineteenth Century Painters', in *Papers Presented at the Longfellow Commemorative Conference, April 1–3, 1982* (Longfellow National Historical Site, 1982), pp. 69–91.

147 For an illuminating analysis of the views of Bancroft, Parkman, and Prescott on this issue, see David Levin, *History as Romantic Art* (New York and Burlingame, 1959), Chapter 6.

148 *The North American Review* 47 (1838), 138, 139. On this essay, see Maddox, *Removals*, pp. 42–3.

superior claim to the land. Smith was an active public reformer, and Belknap, whose *American Biography* appeared at the time when Henry Knox was raising the question of land entitlement before Congress,[149] offers implicit recognition of native territorial rights by referring to the Norsemen as 'invaders'. By the time of the publication of *Antiquitates Americanæ*, however, the fact of prior occupancy had been abandoned as a criterion for the right of ownership. As Helen Carr comments, with a quotation from Alexis de Tocqueville:

> By 1830 the principle of natural rights could be ignored. By then the Committee of Indian Affairs would maintain: 'The fundamental principle, that the Indians had no rights by virtue of their ancient possession either of soil or sovereignty, has never been abandoned either expressly or by implication.' For Knox, in 1789 and the years immediately following, it was still not so easy to argue away 'rights of soil' for the Indian.[150]

*

In general, nineteenth-century American commentary on the Vínland voyages reflects an ambivalence of attitude towards the settlers of medieval Iceland and Greenland which the flawed characters of *Grœnlendinga saga* and *Eiríks saga rauða* – only recently Christian or recalcitrantly pagan; brutal but enterprising; discoverers of new lands but failed pioneers – do little to dispel. For De Costa's reviewer in *The Nation* (1869), who had declared them ostracized Northmen no longer worthy of the name, they were, in any case, 'but little superior to the aborigines', who, '[w]hen the grandson of Rollo the Marcher was ruling a kingdom carved out of France . . . were bartering strips of red cloth with the Esquimaux and the naked Indian for whalebone, seal-skins, and blubber' (p. 53). Charles Kingsley might declare that, of the Vikings in general, 'one loves them, blood-stained as they are',[151] Charles Morris attribute their brutality to the innate nature of the master race,[152] and Morris & Co.'s bookkeeper express a less reverent opinion ('Norse heroes, making for other people's property') in his caption for the Burne-Jones cartoon of Catharine Wolfe's stained glass window, but, for a number of American commentators, they remained irretrievably barbarian and therefore ineligible for a legitimate place in the European history of the nation.

Whereas the Vínland sagas remained largely on the periphery of Old Norse scholarship and mainstream American history and the Vikings teetered at best on the margins of respectability, the Norse 'discovery' of America was wholeheartedly embraced by some of the more eccentric proponents of that form of nineteenth-century medievalism which strove to link America with an idealized

---

149 See Carr, *Inventing the American Primitive*, pp. 39–51.
150 *Inventing the American Primitive*, p. 51.
151 'The First Discovery of America', p. 259.
152 See *The Aryan Race. Its Origins and Achievements, passim.*

'gothic' past in architecture, the decorative arts, and political institutions.[153] The notional colony of Vínland provided a bridge across five hundred years of pre-Columbian history which linked the New World directly to a tradition of Northern and, moreover, Christian republicanism. As William Clark, Richard Clark's brother, put it:

> the form of government in Iceland, Greenland and Vinland was republican . . . from the foundation of the respective colonies till the year 1261 . . . There was, therefore, a little Catholic republic on this continent seven hundred, perhaps eight hundred years ago.[154]

For a small but voluble group among those who believed in their authenticity, the sagas became the substance of a personal political crusade in the cause of what Henry Schoolcraft once called the 'anti-Columbian'[155] history of America. Passionately argued around the time of the Columbus quatercentenary, the Leifr vs. Columbus debate had more or less played itself out by the end of the century. It erupted only briefly when the 'Vínland Map' was unveiled in the mid-1960s and exerted virtually no impact on the politics of the quincentenary in 1992. The Vínland sagas were, however, as the following chapters argue, to secure a more substantial niche in the literary imagination of England and America.

---

153 For a comprehensive discussion of nineteenth-century American medievalism, see Robin Fleming's 'Picturesque History and the Medieval in Nineteenth-Century America', *American Historical Review* 100 (1995), 1061–94.

154 'Extracts from Centennial Discourse delivered by Rev. Wm. F. Clark, S.J., at St. Joseph's Church, Philadelphia, July 4, 1876', cited John B. and Marie A. Shipley, *The English Rediscovery and Colonization of America* (London, 1890), p. 69.

155 *Personal Memoirs*, p. 630.

CHAPTER FOUR

Vínland in British Literature to 1946[1]

British Vínland literature begins in 1819 with the publication of the Scottish poet James Montgomery's *Greenland*, a five-canto narrative inspired by Crantz's *History of Greenland*,[2] in which the Vínland voyages are only one episode in the poem's overarching concern with the Christian history of Greenland and the Moravian mission there in 1733. Canto IV traces the discovery of Iceland, Greenland, and *Wineland*, the establishment of the medieval Greenland settlements, and the beginning of their decline. Wineland is a verdant paradise, untouched by humankind and teeming with flora and fauna from the breadth of North America:

> Regions of beauty there these rovers found;
> The flowery hills with emerald woods were crown'd;
> Spread o'er the vast savannahs, buffalo herds
> Ranged without master; and the bright-wing'd birds
> Made gay the sunshine as they glanced along,
> Or turn'd the air to music with their song.
>
> Here from his mates a German youth had stray'd,
> Where the broad river cleft the forest glade;
> Swarming with alligator-shoals, the flood
> Blazed in the sun, or moved in clouds of blood;
> The wild boar rustled headlong through the brake;
> Like a live arrow leap'd the rattle snake;
> The uncouth shadow of the climbing bear
> Crawl'd on the grass, while he aspired in air;
> Anon with hoofs, like hail, the greenwood rang,
> Among the scattering deer a panther sprang:
> The stripling fear'd not, – yet he trod with awe,

---

1   An earlier, shorter version of some sections of this chapter appears in 'The Fireside Vikings and the "Boy's Own" Vinland: Vinland in Popular English and American Literature (1841–1926)', in *Reinventing the Middle Ages and the Renaissance: Constructions of the Medieval and Early Modern Periods*, ed. William F. Gentrup (Turnhout, Belgium, 1998), pp. 147–65.
2   David Crantz, *The History of Greenland: Containing a Description of the Country and its Inhabitants: and Particularly, a Relation of the Mission, carried on for above these Thirty Years by the Unitas Fratrum, at New Herrnhuth and Lichtenfels, in that Country*, 2 vols (London, 1767).

89

> As if enchantment breathed o'er all the saw,
> Till in his path uprose a wilding vine;
> – Then o'er his memory rush'd the noble Rhine.   (p. 89)[3]

'Greenland's bold sons', collectively and anonymously (the Rhinelander, Tyrker, is the only named individual in the episode), make their landfall on the American continent by instinct rather than accident:

> – Greenland's bold sons, by instinct, sallied forth
> On barks, like icebergs drifting from the north,
> Cross'd without magnet undiscover'd seas,
> And, all surrendering to the stream and breeze,
> Touched on the line of that twin-bodied land
> That stretches forth to either pole a hand.   (p. 89)

They colonize America from coast to coast ('where they fixed their foot they reign'd./ Both coasts they long inherited' p. 90), but war and natural disaster subsume their prize into the sorry fate of the medieval colony of Greenland:

> – Yet was their Paradise for ever lost:
> War, famine, pestilence, the power of frost,
> Their woes combining, wither'd from the earth
> This late creation . . . (*ibid.*)

The Norse interests of Montgomery's better known compatriot, Walter Scott, did not extend to the Vínland voyages.[4] His 'abstract of the more interesting parts' of *Eyrbyggja saga* in *Illustrations of Northern Antiquities* (1814)[5] relegates an episode at the end of that saga which takes place in a mysterious foreign-speaking land west of Iceland (*Eyrbyggja saga* ch. 64) to a footnote comment that: 'the whole story serves to show that the Icelanders had some obscure tradition, either founded on conjecture, or accidental intercourse, concerning the existence of a continent to the westward of the Atlantic'.[6] Scott's antiquarian interest in the North, not in West Atlantic voyages, prompts him to draw upon the Latin extract from *Eiríks saga rauða* by Thomas Bartholin in order to make Þorbjǫrg, the seeress of that saga, the model for the soothsayer Norna in *The Pirate* (1822).[7]

Some years later, in a 'review' of *Antiquitates Americanæ* and its derivatives by Beamish and Toulmin Smith, *The Dublin Review* expressed the opinion that the publication of Beamish's *Discovery of America by the Northmen* would inspire the writers of novels and romances:

3   *The Poetical Works of James Montgomery, collected by himself* (London, 1851).
4   See, for example, Paul Robert Lieder, 'Scott and Scandinavian Literature. The Influence of Bartholin and Others', *Smith College Studies* 2 (1920), 8–57.
5   H. Weber and R. Jamieson, *Illustrations of Northern Antiquities* (Edinburgh, 1814), p. 478.
6   Weber and Jamieson, *Illustrations of Northern Antiquities*, p. 503.
7   *The Pirate, with introductory Essay and Notes by Andrew Lang* (London, 1893), II, 579. See Lieder, 'Scott and Scandinavian Literature', pp. 15–16.

It will probably lead the way to many novels and romances, in which the bold heroism and gallantry of the Norse adventurers will be portrayed in their most dramatic and poetic light. They afford singularly striking specimens, scarcely less impressive than Homer's own delineations – of man in the might of manhood, – physical, animal manhood, – daring for the pleasure of daring, – fearing but the name of fear, – rejoicing in the arduous, – lured on by the perilous, – believing the almost incredible, – and achieving the almost impossible; they present us with a phase of human nature and human progress, admirably calculated for the boldest triumphs of fiction.[8]

It was nevertheless not until the last third of the nineteenth century that the story was given independent literary form in English, when a combination of growing interest on the part of scholars and amateurs in all things Icelandic and the beginning of a popular culture of imperialism introduced the Vínland voyages to the wider English-reading public.

Imperial Vínland: from R. M. Ballantyne to Nevil Shute

The publication of R. M. Ballantyne's *The Norsemen in the West or America Before Columbus* (1872) coincides with the rise of competition from the European powers and the first stirrings of British anxiety after the unswerving confidence which had characterized colonial activity from the 1830s. The invasion of Egypt in 1882 provoked divisions at home, and General Gordon's death at Khartoum in 1885 left the nation aghast. There were fears about national productivity and, with the decrease in the birth rate among the middle classes at home from the 1870s and the worrying prospect of miscegenation in the colonies, degeneration of the race and cultural decline.[9] The authorized imperial female role was, as *The Heart of Empire* (1901) puts it, to produce 'the future colonizers and soldiers, not to mention the traders, who hold the Empire together'.[10] The alleged 'feminisation' of literature – as demonstrated by the popularity of women writers in the 1880s and 1890s – and the rise of the women's suffrage movement in the early 1900s were regarded by some as

---

8 'The Successive Discoveries of America', *Dublin Review* 11 (1841), 307–8. The article is, in the main, a rambling discussion of the location of Plato's Atlantis and Celtic traditions of voyages to West Atlantic lands.

9 Robert Dixon, *Writing the Colonial Adventure. Race, gender and nation in Anglo-Australian popular fiction, 1875–1914* (Cambridge and Melbourne, 1995), p. 2. The 1870s were, as Dixon sums it up here, 'a time of doubt about the civilising mission of British commerce, worries about national efficiency, and fears of racial decline and cultural decadence'.

10 C. E. G. Masterman, *The Heart of Empire* (1901), p. viii, cited Anna Davin, 'Imperialism and motherhood', in Raphael Samuel, ed., *Patriotism: The Making and Unmaking of British National Identity*, I: *History and Politics* (London and New York, 1989), p. 217.

serious threats to British manhood.[11] The time was ripe for the bolstering of national identity through the mass marketing of an imperial ideal based on underlying assumptions about the superiority of British institutions, morality, efficiency, race, and masculinity. Thus was born the 'masculine romance' or 'ripping yarn'.[12]

On the face of it, the tale of the Norse 'discovery' of America is the archetypal ripping yarn, in which the ethnic kin of the English demonstrate vigour, intrepidity, and resourcefulness in an exotic locale inhabited by unpredictable and irrational people of colour. The bonds of race and seamanship between England and Scandinavia were widely promoted by nineteenth-century Northern enthusiasts who saw England as the legitimate heir to the Viking virtues of boldness and initiative.[13] As Ballantyne expressed it in *The Norsemen in the West*:

> there can be no question that much of the ultimate success of Britain on the sea is due not only to our insular position but also to the not-sufficiently-appreciated fact that the blood of the hardy and adventurous vikings of Norway still flows in our veins.[14]

The trouble was that, as told in its primary sources, the discovery and attempted settlement of Vínland is ultimately a story of frustration, failure, and unmanning at the hands of its natives (*Grœnlendinga saga* and *Eiríks saga rauða*) and a woman (*Grœnlendinga saga*). The challenge for late nineteenth- and early twentieth-century writers of British Vínland narrative was to devise strategies to contend with the historical fact of the failure of the enterprise in a time beset with anxieties about the imperial mission, race, and gender.

The first two tellings of the story in English fiction, Ballantyne's *The Norsemen in the West* and J. F. Hodgetts's *Edric the Norseman: A Tale of Adventure and Discovery*, are, in their different ways, representative of the juvenile literature which occupied a significant place among the many vehicles of popular imperial propaganda generated from the 1870s to World War I. The most popular and long-lived (to 1967) of the many late nineteenth- and early twentieth-century

11 See Elaine Showalter, ed., *Daughters of Decadence. Women Writers of the Fin-de-Siècle* (New Brunswick, NJ, 1993), pp. vii–xx; *idem*, *Sexual Anarchy: Gender and Culture at the Fin de Siècle* (London, 1991), pp. 79–81; Dixon, *Writing the Colonial Adventure*, pp. 4–5.

12 See Dixon, *Writing the Colonial Adventure*, pp. 1–4; John M. MacKenzie, *Propaganda and Empire. The Manipulation of British Public Opinion, 1880–1960* (Manchester, 1984), pp. 1–14. For a comprehensive and succinct account of the late nineteenth-century imperial ethos and its expression in English literature, see Elleke Boehmer, *Colonial & Postcolonial Literature* (Oxford and New York, 1995).

13 For a brilliantly entertaining account of late Victorian perceptions of England's Viking interests and connections, see Andrew Wawn, 'The Spirit of 1892: Sagas, Saga-steads and Victorian Philology', *Saga-Book of the Viking Society* 23 (1992), 213–52; *idem*, *The Vikings and the Victorians, Inventing The Old North in 19th-Century Britain* (Cambridge, 2000).

14 R. M. Ballantyne, *The Norsemen in the West, or America before Columbus. A Tale* (Toronto, 1872). p. 52. All quotations and page references are from this edition.

boys' story papers which catered for a readership between the ages of ten and eighteen and promoted the virtues of courage, patriotism, intrepidity, and unwavering and well-bred masculinity[15] was the Religious Tract Society's *The Boy's Own Paper*, whose first issue appeared in 1879. *Edric the Norseman* was serialized in the *BOP*, in eighteen weekly instalments between October 1887 and January 1888.[16]

Ballantyne inclines to the jocular, often patronizingly so, in *The Norsemen in the West*, and embellishes his version of the story with history and geography lessons on such topics as the settlement of Iceland and the topography of Greenland. Hodgetts favours an often morally didactic register. The Vínland narratives of both authors foreground the hostile confrontation of prospective colonists with indigenous people, but, in each case, the decision to withdraw is immediately attributable either to the failure of the natives to live up to the terms of their 'partnership' with the Norsemen (Ballantyne) or to female criminality (Hodgetts).

Ballantyne's acknowledged source is the 'Icelandic Saga' – the reader is referred to Laing's *Grœnlendinga saga* chapters in his translation of *Heimskringla* for full information in regard to it – which he claims to have followed closely 'in all matters of importance' (p. iv). The overriding concern in *The Norsemen in the West*, however, is the establishment of the colonial ground rules, whereby the Norsemen demonstrate their physical and mental superiority over, first, the natives of Greenland ('Skrælingers') and, second, the native Vinlanders.

The Norsemen in the West begins in Greenland, whose Scandinavian settlers are paragons of blonde Teutonic good looks. The women are 'fresh-looking', the children 'rosy', the men 'ruddy'. Gudrid, for example, is 'a fair comely young woman, with exceedingly deep blue eyes, and a bright colour in her cheeks' (p. 7). The only intruder into the Teutonic homogeneity of Leif's circle is Tyrker, called a *suðrmaðr* ('Southerner' or 'German') in *Grœnlendinga saga* where he is said to be short, shifty-eyed, and diminutive (*Hann var brattleitr ok lauseygr, smáskitligr í andliti*, ch. 4: 252). Ballantyne's simple solution to this apparent eugenic aberration is ethnic reclassification. Leif, he says, is mistaken in calling Tyrker a German, for:

---

15   See for example, Louis James, 'Tom Brown's Imperialist Sons', *Victorian Studies* 17 (1973–74), 89–99; Philip Warner, *The Best of British Pluck: The Boy's Own Paper* (London, 1976); Patrick A. Dunae, 'Boys' Literature and the Idea of Empire, 1870–1914', *Victorian Studies* 24 (1980), 105–21; *idem*, 'New Grub Street for boys', in Jeffrey Richards, ed., *Imperialism and juvenile literature* (Manchester and New York, 1989), pp. 12–33; Stuart Hannabuss, 'Ballantyne's message of empire', in Richards, ed., *Imperialism and juvenile literature*, pp. 53–71; Joseph Bristow, *Empire Boys: Adventures in a Man's World* (London, 1991), pp. 37–48; Kelly Boyd, 'Exemplars and Ingrates: Imperialism and the Boys' Story Paper, 1880–1930', *Historical Research* 67 (1994), 143–53. Surprisingly, there is no Vínland work by G. A. Henty, who published a number of novels of Anglo-Saxon and later medieval times and was particularly popular in America. See Guy Arnold, *Held Fast for England. G. A. Henty, Imperialist Boys' Writer* (London, 1980), pp. 130–45.

16   *Edric the Norseman* was translated into Danish as *Nordmændenes Opdagelse af Amerika* (Kristiania, 1891).

It is much more probable that he was a Turk, for, whereas the Germans are known to be a well-sized handsome race of fair men, this Tyrker was an ugly little dark wiry fellow, with a high forehead, sharp eyes, and a small face.   (p. 30)

The nobly-born Celts, Hake and Heika, are fine figures of men, but less endowed with physical beauty: 'tall, strong-boned, and thin, but with broad shoulders, and grave, earnest, though not exactly handsome countenances' (p. 36).

Clad in seal-skins and usually referred to simply as 'hairy creatures', the 'Skrælingers', are grotesque, ursine, infantile figures. Their leader, his face 'quite as round and nearly as flat as a frying-pan' (p. 4), speaks a language 'unintelligible to civilized ears' (p. 4) and lumbers along 'like a good-natured polar bear' (p. 203). They might wish to rob the Norse settlers of home and family, but the capacity to plan, let alone execute this desire is beyond their capacity. After a rowdy 'parliament' they disburse, 'doubtless with the intent to gorge themselves with raw blubber, prepare their weapons, and snatch a little repose' before their attack upon the 'innocent heads' (p. 6) of the Norsemen collapses at the sound of a sneeze.

Ballantyne's Inuit in *The Norsemen in the West* are essentially caricatures of his portrait of the Hudson Straits Inuit in *Ungava* (1858), a novel of Arctic life which followed his six years of employment in the 1840s as a clerk at the Hudson's Bay Company.[17] The *Ungava* Inuit are honest, industrious, and friendly, round and oily of face, cheerful of disposition, and exuberant in social intercourse. One is said to look, 'in his hairy garments, like a shaggy polar bear' (p. 140),[18] a simile which reappears in *The Norsemen in the West*. Although he finds them slovenly housekeepers – their camp is 'a scene of the utmost confusion and filth' (*Ungava*, p. 225)[19] – Ballantyne credits the Labrador Inuit with patience, providence, and honesty. He saw in the men a degree of natural nobility, although he found the women irredeemably repellent.[20]

Ballantyne's representation of Native Americans in *The Norsemen in the West*

---

17 See Eric Quayle, *Ballantyne the Brave. A Victorian Writer and his Family* (London, 1967), pp. 29–78.

18 References are to *Ungava. A Tale of Esquimau Land*, new edn (London, Edinburgh, New York, 1894).

19 W. G. H. Kingston's Inuit are similarly poor housekeepers: 'Their heads were large, with a narrow, retreating forehead; strong, coarse, black hair, flat nose, full lips, almost beardless chin, and full, lustrous black eyes – not beauties, certainly, but their expression was very amiable, and so was their conduct . . . I . . . saw their huts . . . There were heaps of filth in front . . . I saw some of their women, the elder ones being the most hideous-looking of the human race I ever beheld' (*Peter the Whaler* [London, 1930], pp. 216–17).

20 Aneetka, the betrothed of Maximus in *Ungava*, would not, Ballantyne says, '[a]mong civilized folk probably . . . have been deemed even pretty' (p. 129), although, when she is abducted, Maximus's pursuit is likened to a chivalric quest: 'No puissant knight of old ever buckled on his panoply of mail, seized his sword and lance, mounted his charger, and sallied forth single-handed to deliver his mistress from enchanted castle, in the face of appalling perils, with hotter haste or a more thorough contempt of danger than did our Esquimau giant pursue the Indians who had captured his bride' (p. 141).

is indicative of the general perception in nineteenth-century England that they were superior to Africans, inferior to Asian Indians, but otherwise difficult to evaluate in terms of character and culture.[21] Predictably, the natives of Vinland are more capable and attractive than Greenland's 'Skraelingers'. They are 'taller, though not stouter, and clothed in well-dressed skins of animals, with many bright colours about them' (p. 169) and less given to the collectivized infantilism endemic among indigenous peoples in popular imperial narrative.[22] Their chief, Whitepow, who appears to be modelled on Powhatan, the name given by the English to the leader of the natives of Tidewater, Virginia, in the early seventeenth century, is 'an aged and white-haired though vigorous and strong-boned savage' (p. 280). But, like the Skraelingers, the native Vinlanders lack any sense of civic pride: their wigwams are 'pitched without any regard to order' (p. 280). The birth of Gudrid and Karlsefin's son, Snorro, provides occasion for a bald statement of Northern European superiority. The child is, Leif laughingly reminds his companions, 'the dearest, sweetest, and in every way the most delightful Vinlander that had ever been born', because 'he is the only white Vinlander that ever *was* born' (p. 370).

In the classic ritual of empire, Karlsefin appropriates Vinland by running up the flag: 'Karlsefin then set up a pole with a flag on it and took formal possession of this new land' (p. 117). Leif and Karlsefin are natural managers, who prefer negotiation to armed confrontation: 'I do not love the bloody game of war' (p. 14), says Leif. Ill-treatment of the natives, even under provocation, is discouraged. Leif, who takes one of his company to task for not recognizing the bond of humanity which they share with the natives ('Is not his flesh and blood the same as thine, his body as well knit together as thine, and as well suited to its purposes?'), to which the grudging reply is 'Doubtless it is, though somewhat uglier' (p. 205), wishes only to give them 'a good fright', if necessary. Karlsefin counsels against killing them but urges his men to 'give as many of them the toothache if you can' (p. 171) for entirely practical reasons: 'We must be friends with these people if we are to live in peace here, and that won't be possible if we kill many of them . . . when we have them in our power we will treat them well', says Karlsefin (pp. 171, 180). Even when the Vinlanders make a direct attack, Leif is mindful of future relations and acts with restraint:

21 'Although the Amerindian was seen as inferior to white Anglo-Saxons he was not universally regarded as barbarous or indolent. Indeed if there were the slightest vestiges of the Rousseauian noble savage to be attributed to any race, they were usually reserved for the North American Indian . . . Notwithstanding the sometime romantic edification of the braves, the Amerindian was still regarded as "uncivilized," and to the Victorian this was an emotive word with a whole range of denigrating associations. The term easily inspired disparaging reports of the Indians and inevitably these appeared in the juvenile press.' Patrick Dunae, 'Boys' Literature and the Idea of Race: 1870–1900', *Wascana Review* (Spring 1977), p. 98.
22 See Dunae, 'Boys' Literature and the Idea of Race: 1870–1900', pp. 84–107.

Leif's desire to spare life, with a view to future proposals of peace, was exemplified in his ordering the men to draw their bows slightly, so as to wound without killing, as much as possible, and to aim as well as they could at the legs of the foe! (p. 305)

The Norsemen demonstrate moral superiority in their conduct towards defeated aggressors. When one of the Vinland natives is wounded and taken prisoner by the Norsemen, his captors show themselves to be benign jailers:

It is probable that the poor wretch expected to be taken off summarily to have his eyes punched out, or to be roasted alive, – for the natives of Vinland, no doubt, expected from their foes, in those days, the same treatment that they accorded to them – although the Saga says nothing to that effect. (p. 176)

Under Karlsefin's leadership, Leifsgaard, the Vinland settlement, develops into a thriving model of administrative organization and industrial productivity – with house building, hay-making, fishing, salmon smoking, egg and feather collecting, and timber-cutting by day, and songs around the campfire by night – in which Vinland's natural resources are harnessed and supported by an efficient infrastructure of houses, dams, provisioning, and a successful commercial arrangement with the volatile natives. In so doing, the Norsemen have, it is implied, staked a legitimate territorial claim, not only by virtue of natural superiority but also because, in failing to develop its resources in any systematic way, the natives cannot be seriously considered as Vinland's 'owners'. The Vinlanders' perception of the Norsemen as the 'white invaders' of their land, which motivates their resolution to attack, kill, and rob them, is, the reader is encouraged to infer, erroneous and absurd. The notion of 'invasion' assumes the overthrow of a pre-existing order, which, the novel indicates, does not exist. Whereas the development of fertile land implicitly authorizes the European appropriation of Vinland, the glacial landscape of Greenland and the physical unattractiveness of its natives are patronizingly dismissed as obvious reasons for the groundlessness of Inuit fears that 'the white men had come there to wrest from him his native hills and glaciers, and rob him of his wife and children' (p. 5).

Ballantyne confronts the issue of the questionable ethics of Norse commercial practice ('the savages possessed a large quantity of beautiful furs, with which, of course, they were willing to part for the merest trifle, in the shape of a shred of brilliant cloth or an ornamental bauble' [p. 355]) with assurances to the reader that the desire to barter furs for milk, cream, and sparkling trinkets comes naturally to the unsophisticated natives. He shores up his position on the moral high ground with a sententious claim about the civilizing and improving mission of hard work:

This was not only fortunate, as affording an opportunity for the Norsemen to procure full and valuable cargoes for both their ships, but as creating a busy and interesting occupation, which would prevent the natives from growing weary of inaction, and, perhaps, falling into those forms of mischief which proverbially lie ready to idle hands.   (p. 355)[23]

The work ethic serves both as a means of defining virtue and of exercising and containing the dangerous energies of women. Karlsefin recognizes the need for more women in the colony, but as the solution to the servant problem rather than to the sexual frustration which breaks out amongst Karlsefni's company in *Eiríks saga rauða* (ch. 12: 432).[24] Whereas the natives profit morally from manual labour, women enjoy its physical benefits. It is housework, for example, which is said to have honed Gudrid, who enters the narrative 'drying her hands and arms on a towel, – for she had been washing dishes' (p. 7), into an elegantly muscular model of female virtue:

> women of the richer class were remarkably healthy and well made in those days. They did a great deal of hard work with their hands, hence their arms were strong and well developed without losing anything of their elegance.   (p. 7)

Married men should, says Karlsefin, be encouraged to settle in Vinland, 'especially those men who chance to have a good many daughters, for we would be the better of a few more busy little hands, fair faces, and silvery tones in this beautiful Vinland of ours' (p. 190). Ballantyne's reviewer in *The Athenæum* approvingly commented that 'girls who read the book will be pleased that women were amongst the adventurers, and were a most important help in the labours of the colony'.[25]

The homicidal Freydís of *Grænlendinga saga* is disempowered by domestication and ridiculed by her failure to conform to an acceptable female stereotype. As Freydissa, she is reduced to a bit of a nag and a scold, who is at the centre of various domestic squabbles in Vinland but guilty of transgressing the bounds of gender rather than law:

> Freydissa was one of those women who appear to have been born women by mistake – who are always chafing at their unfortunate fate, and endeavouring to emulate – even to overwhelm – men; in which latter effort they are too frequently successful. She was a tall elegant woman of about thirty years of age with a decidedly handsome face, though somewhat sharp of feature. She possessed a powerful will, a shrill voice and a vigorous frame, and was afflicted with a short, violent temper. She was decidedly a masculine woman. We know not which is the more disagreeable of the two – a masculine woman or an effeminate man.   (pp. 53–4)

Her weaponry limited to a piece of wrung-out washing, she misses her target, a servant named Bertha, and hits a hen instead:

---

23   On the expression of the work ethic in colonial writing, see Boehmer, *Colonial and Postcolonial Literature*, pp. 38–9.
24   'Gengu menn þá mjǫk sleitum; sóttu þeir er kvánlausir váru í hendr þeim er kvángaðir váru.' (Then there was a lot of backsliding; those who were wifeless annoyed those who were married.)
25   November 16, 1872, p. 633.

Freydissa enforced her command by sending a mass of soapy cloth which she had just wrung out after the retreating Bertha. The missile flew past its intended object, and, hitting a hen, which had ventured to intrude, on the legs, swept it with a terrific cackle into the road, to the amazement, not to say horror, of the cock and chickens. (p. 291)

Marriage itself proves a salutary experience for Freydissa. 'Thorward will kill or cure her', says Karlefin (p. 132), and, by the end of the novel, Karlsefin is moved to declare that she has 'improved vastly of late' (p. 387).

Matters of heterosexual affection are briskly relegated to the margins of the narrative, in which the only mouth-to-mouth embrace is a robust display of affection between Leif and Karlsefin:

> they seized each other in an embrace, and their bearded mouths met with a hearty masculine smack that did credit to their hearts and which it might have gratified the feelings of an affectionate walrus to behold. (p. 13)[26]

Although it may be love at first sight between Gudrid and Karlsefin, Ballantyne assures his audience that the matter will be dealt with quickly and priority given to the more manly concerns of the novel:

> Now, good reader, pray do not run away with the notion that this love affair is the plot on which the story is to hinge! Nothing of the kind! (p. 17)

What his readers would probably have called the 'soppy bits' are supplied by members of the lower orders: the Scottish thrall, Hake, who eventually turns out to be the son of an earl, falls in love with Bertha, and eventually marries her. Leif's Christian principles eventually make him free Hake and Heika, who are not, as in all other modern versions of the story,[27] a male–female couple, but brothers.

Peaceful relations having been successfully established after a skirmish earlier in the novel, Ballantyne comments ruefully on the sadly fleeting nature of the unequal 'friendship' between Norsemen and Vinlanders:

> Thus was established a warm friendship between the natives of Vinland and the Norsemen; a friendship which might have lasted forever – to the great modification, no doubt, of American history – had not unfortunate circumstances intervened to break it up. (p. 185)

The 'unfortunate circumstances' which put an end to the Vinland idyll are, the novel implies, largely the fault of the natives. Like ungrateful children – unreasonably and unaccountably it is suggested – they grow greedy and discontented with their uneven trade in furs for pieces of cloth and milk: 'the natives had become a little more exacting in their demands while engaged in barter, and

---

26 On homosocial bonding in colonial writing, see Boehmer, *Colonial & Postcolonial Literature*, pp. 74–9.
27 The *Skálhóltsbók* text of *ES* makes Haki male and Hekja female (p. 424); according to *Hauksbók*, they are both male (p. 223).

were, on the whole, rather more pugnacious and less easily pleased' (p. 226). Irrationally fearful of the prospect of white invasion, they abduct young Olaf and Snorro, and eventually attack Leifsgaard.

Karlsefin successfully acts as mediator in the first instance, and the children are returned unharmed. The kidnappers are pacified with more cloth and ornaments, and a convivial evening around the campfire. The rest of the Vinlanders, however, hold a council of war and resolve 'to attack the white invaders of their land, kill them all, and appropriate their property' (p. 296). Leifsgaard is stormed and burnt, and the natives begin to divide into 'hostile' and 'friendly' groups (pp. 343–4).

Ballantyne rewrites the failure of the Vínland enterprise as the native Vinlanders' loss by making the Norsemen's subsequent withdrawal an implicit punishment for their bad behaviour. Without a trace of authorial irony, Karlsefin comforts them with the suggestion that, one day some of their European friends might return, and that they should be well prepared for future business transactions:

> perhaps some of them might return again with large supplies of the gay cloth and ornaments they were so fond of, and he recommended them in the meantime to make as large a collection of furs as they could, in order to be ready to trade when the white men returned.   (p. 368)

After the Norsemen entertain them at a farewell feast, the only reported reaction by the Vinlanders to the departure of their Norse friends is a lacklustre attempt at reciprocal valediction:

> they gave vent to one vigorous parting cheer, which was replied to by the savages with a feeble imitation and a waving of arms.   (p. 369)

Ballantyne does, however, face up to the course of history and indirectly charges the Norsemen with a slippage of masculine nerve. In a chapter entitled 'The First Congress and the Last Farewell' it is agreed that the fledgling colony should be abandoned. Thorward, Freydissa's husband, is the lone dissenter who gives prescient voice to Vinland's potentially vast rewards for pioneering fortitude. He predicts that the land will eventually be settled by 'a bolder race' of men, unafraid of hard work and noisy savages:

> It seems to me that we might, if we chose, lay the foundation of a new nation that would rival Iceland, perchance equal old Norway itself, if we take advantage of the great opportunities that have fallen to our hands. But if we get frightened of the yell of every savage that makes his appearance or grow weary of good, vigorous, hard work, and begin to sigh like children for home, then there is small chance of doing anything, and it will doubtless be the fate of a bolder race of men to people this land at some future time.   (p. 360)

Instead of opportunity missed, labour shirked, and masculinity unnerved, J. F. Hodgetts gives his readers a more positive interpretation of events which suggests that the Norsemen can, in fact, lay valid claim to a stake in the history of post-Columbian America, since their trading 'partnership' with the natives foreshadows the present-day commercial might of the site of their transactions:

> The Skrællings liked the cloth, however, and gave piles of fur for half a dozen yards of this material, so that the Northmen's stock began to get quite low; they therefore dealt out smaller quantities, claiming more furs in pay; and on the river's bank a market seemed to grow that faintly shadowed forth the vast emporium that now is flourishing upon the spot where these old sagas say that full eight hundred years ago the Northmen made their winter settlement. (p. 214)

Hodgetts's imposing pedagogical credentials are announced in the first instalment of *Edric the Norseman* as 'Late Professor and Crown Examiner at Moscow, Author of "Harold the Boy-Earl," "Ivan Dobroff," "Kormak the Viking," etc. etc.'[28] The narrative contains little intentional levity or campfire camaraderie. Ballantyne's 'Cowboys and Indians' war games are replaced by bloody skirmishes with fatalities on both sides. Hodgetts's overt didacticism is spiced with occasional touches of Conradian 'unspeakable rites' and other pagan excesses. Tyrker, for example, narrowly escapes being the last human sacrifice to Thor (pp. 150–1). Explicitly articulated in its closing paragraphs, the underlying message of the work is the fundamental importance of duty and Christian values. Edric Sigvaldson, 'a little chap of some ten years old or less' (p. 9) at the beginning of the narrative and only three years older at its end, becomes a role model for English schoolboys:

> for though he had not, like the fabled heroes of romance, overcome armies with his boyish arm, or shown experienced warriors how to war, he had been known to do his duty upon all occasions bravely and well . . . For him Icelandic had no holier word than "mother." And in those days honour to parents was a sacred duty.
>
> (p. 228)

Edric and his friend Nils 'the Fleet-footed', who, in the absence of counterparts to Haki and Hekja, serve as scouts, are exemplars of industry and good manners in the establishment of the Wineland settlement: '[t]hey worked as hard as any of the warriors, and always had a courteous word for all' (p. 133). In the course of the story, in which the voyage to Wineland is only one of many episodes, Edric demonstrates the stuff of leadership by seizing a poisoned drinking horn intended for Leif Erikson. Having chosen to sail with Leif from Iceland to Greenland as his reward for this action, Edric is the first to spot the new land. Nils is equally resourceful. He comes up with a practical solution, although it is never put to the test, to the problem of verbal communication with the Wineland natives, with the suggestion that he and Edric should learn their language by taking prisoners and forcing them to become language instructors.

Instead of functioning as the vehicle for whimsy and comedy which it

---

28 *The Boy's Own Paper* 10 (1887–88), 9. Subsequent page references are to this volume.

becomes in *The Norsemen in the West*, family life in *Edric the Norsemen* becomes a focus for the narrative's moral message. Leif, for example, shares Edric's filial piety in his conduct towards his eccentric, staunchly pagan father:

> His conduct to his father was respectful in the extreme and almost childish in the touching way in which he humoured all the old man's whims. (p. 53)

Hodgetts does, though, share Ballantyne's views on the proper place for women in the masculine enterprise of adventuring and empire-building: the kitchen. Although Hodgetts finds it necessary to explain the presence of Leif and Thorfinn's wives on the voyage to Wineland by an imagined Norse convention, perhaps inspired by Lady Baker's accompaniment of Sir Samuel on his Nile explorations of 1861–65 ('It was the custom of the North for the married warriors to take their wives with them on distant expeditions' [p. 118]), on the second Wineland expedition, led by Freydisa and Thorward, women are relegated to service in the galley:

> There were so many ladies down below that the stout champions were well waited on, and served with ale, and mead, and wine, while regularly at the midday meal, huge portions of smoked and salted flesh of goats, of elks, of boars, and bears were served with as much parade as was observed in any wealthy hall on land.
>
> (p. 181)

Whereas Leif's family life is quietly regularized in *The Norsemen in the West* – Ballantyne intimates that he is a widower by replacing Þorgils, his out-of-wedlock son in *Eiríks saga rauða*, with a child called Olaf, whose mother is said to be dead – Hodgetts undertakes a more extensive reorganization of the Eirikssons' domestic life. Leif is provided with a wife, a Christian missionary named Hallfrida, whom he marries in a double wedding with Thorfinn the Accomplished and Hallfrida's sister, Guthrida. His absence from the company of Thorfinn, Thorward, Freydisa, Helgi, and Finnbogi on the second expedition to the land which Edric has discovered, and which Tyrker has named Wineland, is explained by his dutiful reluctance to abandon the mission of Christian conversion ('he thought his duties in promoting Christianity in Greenland claimed all his time and energy' [p. 180]) and the care of his ageing father.

The Wineland natives in *Edric the Norsemen* are formidable opponents. With their 'sallow faces, high cheek-bones, long, strange, curious hair, large eyes, and swarthy appearance' (p. 199), they closely resemble the *skrælingar* of *Eiríks saga rauða*. These 'Skrællings', explains a character introduced as Tostig Arvidson, the leader of an independent exploration party, are blots on the landscape of an otherwise paradisial land through which he has recently travelled. They are, he says, hostile, impossible to trade with, and 'treacherous and warlike' (p. 19). In an incident which parallels events in *Grænlendinga saga* (*GS* ch. 5) but runs counter to the colonial ethos articulated in *The Norsemen in the West*, Tostig initiates a fatal attack on a group of them. There is no overt criticism of his action, but, when an avenging party arrives, Tostig and many other Norsemen are killed.

101

Given the natives' greater numbers, common sense dictates to Thorfinn that peace should be the Norsemen's goal. On his first encounter with them, he sends Edric out with a white shield and then makes a speech which, without any discernible irony, projects the sense of occasion which Samuel Baker might have reserved for his first encounter with an African tribe:

> Brave men, we have arrived from distant lands, to barter with you very useful things, of which ye stand in need. If there be one amongst you knowing our Northern speech, I would advise him to approach and act as our interpreter. We mean you well. (p. 199)

When Thorfinn hears of the arrival of a large party of Skrællings, he is, with gratifying results, prepared to treat them as honourable men who will continue to respond to the display of a white shield as a signal of peaceful intent:

> But still they recollected how these Skrællings had recognised and honoured the peaceful emblem of the shield. So Edric was again sent forth to meet them as before, and then the Skrællings laid aside their poles and came ashore in number.
> (p. 214)

At the same time, he has reservations about trading in weapons: 'Thorfinn saw that putting arms like theirs into strangers' hands would inevitably lead to trouble' (*ibid.*).

Hodgetts pursues the darker side of the Vínland story through the crimes of Freydisa. Laughably 'mannish' in *The Norsemen in the West*, she develops into a fiendish criminal in *Edric the Norseman*. There are ominous hints earlier in the narrative that she and Thorward are no more than nominal Christians:

> Her education by her mother and grandmother, both exercising the profession of witchcraft, was not a good preparation, nor were the convictions of her new husband very firm. (p. 36)

'Her Christianity did not appear very deeply rooted' (p. 108), Hodgetts remarks of her display of pique when Leif's nuptials eclipse the splendour of her own. That underlying paganism transforms Freydisa into a 'warrior maiden',[29] when, after a shameful lapse of masculinity on the part of Thorfinn's company during an attack by the Skraellings, and supported by Edric and Nils, she rallies the wavering troops:

> she . . . cried, 'Follow me, Edric! Lo! our champions run, and women and unbearded lads take up their arms!'
> And this, however humiliating to the Northern name, was true, for Nils had joined his 'foster-brother', and Freydisa, who now had turned her wrath upon the Skraellings, and in a sort of maniac-like excitement raved at them, furiously brandishing the sword, which glittered gloriously in the sun.

---

29 For a recent discussion of this figure, see Jenny Jochens, *Old Norse Images of Women* (Philadelphia, 1996), pp. 97–112.

> Our two young friends rushed forward, each holding in his left hand his shield, with which he kept the missiles from Freydisa, who . . . was certainly more like a fiend that moment than a woman.   (p. 214)

But when she next transgresses the boundaries of gender, Freydisa also crosses the line between heroism and savagery. After Thorfinn considers withdrawing his company from Wineland in the face of external opposition and internal ructions,

> Thorfinn now clearly saw that though this coast might be a very heaven as far as climate was concerned, and though it was rich in many things, yet it would take a larger force than he had at command to occupy it, for the natives were so hostile and so numerous that now there was no chance of living there in peace. Then in their little band there were continual quarrelings.   (p. 214)

their departure is directly precipitated by Freydisa's slaughter of the women in Helgi and Finnbogi's party:

> Freydisa, as the chronicle informs us . . . seized an axe, and with her own infuriate hands butchered the women as they lay.   (p. 215)

She and Thorward are immediately ordered by Leif to be taken back to Greenland as prisoners, and the story ends with the parcelling out of retribution back in Iceland. Brought to judgment at the 'All-Ting' (ON *Alþing*), Thorward is banished from the Scandinavian world and Freydisa sentenced to exile on her trollish grandmother's estate near Mount Hecla. The abandonment of Wineland is thus eclipsed by the imprisonment, trial, and spectacularly ghastly end of this demonic embodiment of feminine menace who perishes, fittingly, in a volcanic eruption.

Even more terrifying than Freydisa is Freydize, the tyrannical 'Queen of Vinland' in *Tamers of the Sea* (1897),[30] the English rendition, by Frances Cashel Hoey,[31] of Edmond Neukomm's *Les Dompteurs de la mer* (1895). Having despatched the grotesquely alluring 'Queen of the *Skrellings*' at a single stroke,

> Freydize was fascinated, rooted to the spot by the magnetic gaze of her adversary . . . she recovered herself, her spirit rose, she fell like a thunderbolt upon the Queen of the *Skrellings*, and cleft her head from crown to chin with one stroke of her sword.   (p. 95)

Neukomm's Freydize evolves into a Nordic version of Rider Haggard's 'She',

---

30 *Tamers of the Sea. The Northmen in America from the Tenth to the Fifteenth Century* (London, 1897). *Tamers of the Sea* was published in America as *The Rulers of the Sea* (1896), without reference to the translator's name, in a 'Boys' Own Author Series' by Dana Estes & Company.

31 Frances Cashel Hoey was herself the author of a number of sensational novels of romance, violence, mystery, and religion. For a study of her life and works, see P. D. Edwards, *Frances Cashel Hoey*, Victorian Fiction Research Guides 8 (Department of English, University of Queensland, 1982).

imposing a reign of terror over the remnant of Thorfinn's abandoned settlement:

> Freydize . . . then appeared to them, and her flashing eyes and trembling lips appealed to the men's hearts irresistibly. She was beautiful thus, with a murderous beauty, her hair was loosened in the wind, a corslet of steel and a dark blue chamys clasped upon the shoulder set off the figure of the fierce Amazon . . . They were all subjugated by this woman, the lads of the Stranm-Fjord and the colonists of Vinland.   (pp. 118–19)

'[L]ike the goddess of crime' (pp. 120–1), she frenziedly hacks the five women in Helge and Finn's company to a bloody pulp of carrion for interested predators:

> she sprang upon the women who were rooted to the ground by terror, whirled her axe, which seemed to revolve in a mist of blood, round her head, and soon hacked the group into a heap of mashed flesh, at which the long-haired dogs, scenting strange game, sniffed inquisitively.   (p. 120)

Neukomm's inspiration, according to his introductory 'A Short History of this Book', was a conversation with the French scholar, Gabriel Gravier, a leading proponent of the notion of the Lost Colony of Vínland.[32] This exchange led, he says, to his reading of, among others, the works of Rafn, Torfæus, Wheaton, and Horsford (pp. xii–xvii). The result is an historical fantasy which draws upon the material of *Grœnlendinga saga* and *Eiríks saga rauða* but extends the alleged history of Norse settlement in America to the late fourteenth century. Gudrid's pilgrimage to Rome leads to the despatch of Bishop Jonus to the New World, where he is sacrificed to the gods by the recidivist pagans of Vinland in 1059. A century later, Erik Gnúpsson, who takes up his episcopal residence in the Newport Tower, succeeds as a 'prelate-pirate' (p. 171) in re-establishing the faith. Vinland is eventually destroyed in the fourteenth century by the Black Death, depredations of pirates, and the internal politics of mainland Scandinavia.

An instant convert to Christianity after he witnesses Olaf Tryggvason shatter a statue of Thor with his spear, Leif Erikson becomes renowned for the exemplary piety which earns him the mission of converting the Greenlanders:

> Not only was he converted, but he soon became remarkable for edifying piety. The king himself was sponsor at his baptism; and in order to utilise his 'first fervours,' Olaf entrusted the distinguished neophyte with the missionary enterprise of converting the Greenlanders to Christianity.   (p. 22)

He sets out for Greenland in a ship with a golden cross at its prow and extracts a pledge from Erik to accept baptism if he succeeds in finding the land previously sighted by Bjorn Herwolfson. Erik is duly converted and delivers a lengthy

---

32 See Chapter 3, above, pp. 70–79.

lesson in pagan mythology and its decline to mark the event. Vinland's grapes directly serve Leif's missionary zeal by providing the means through which he can insult Odin, by usurping his role as the sole drinker of wine at the banquet of the gods. After her murderous rampage, Leif consigns Freydize's ill-gotten gains to the Church, and she and Thorward end their days as outcasts back in Greenland:

> Then, utterly beaten and miserable, spurned by all, and pointed at as noisome beasts, the former sovereign of Vinland and her craven husband betook them to the solitudes, where they ended their desolate days amid the rocks and the eternal snows. (p. 122)

Imperialism in *The Tamers of the Sea* is not the essentially secular enterprise of English Vínland narrative but a question of extending the empire of Christ and wresting Vinland from occupancy by satanic natives 'who have . . . invaded the American coast' (p. 56). Its demonization of Vinland's indigenes gives *The Tamers of the Sea* an affinity with the mode of late Victorian and Edwardian fiction which Patrick Brantlinger calls 'imperial Gothic',[33] in which fiendish invasion is a principal theme. The diabolical intruders into Edenic Vinland are the '*Skrellings*, or Eskimo' (p. 56), and as the wine flows at Leifs-Budir, Thor-wald Erikson and his company drink to genocide as the only remedy against this 'traditional enemy, the foul-smelling beast, the gnome abhorred of their race' (*ibid.*).

The *Skrellings* pose no further threat, but Thorfinn abandons Vinland for two reasons: the drying up of the settlers' source of furs, occasioned by the enemy's withdrawal after their queen is killed, and open quarrelling between Gudrid and Freydize. Acknowledged as 'the undisputed Queen of Vinland' (p. 111) after Thorfinn's departure and vainly aspiring to the role of despot ('Freydize still indulged in the baseless dream of reigning over Vinland, and imposing her laws, her power, and her whims upon the people' [pp. 109–10]), Freydize's killing spree finally awakens the slumbering consciences of the remaining colonists and her Vinland reign comes to an end. Events of the following chapter, in which a Vinland colonist named Hervador and his wife, Syasi, found a prosperous colony south of Vinland in the mid-eleventh century are derived from a nineteenth-century hoax, the alleged discovery near Skálholt in 1862 of a medi-eval Latin manuscript relating a Vínland expedition led by an Icelander named Hervador.[34] Neukomm makes the local populace, who appear to be Amerindian ('These people had light blue eyes . . . They wore feathers in their hair, necklaces of shells, and on their arms and legs shell bracelets and anklets' [p. 123]) rather than *Skrelling*, rapidly and harmoniously assimilate Scandinavian culture and live happily with 'their brethren of the North' (p. 142). But Hervador and

---

33 See Patrick Brantlinger, *Rule of Darkness. British Literature and Imperialism, 1830–1914* (Ithaca and London, 1988), Chapter 8.
34 For a detailed account, see the review of Gabriel Gravier, *Découverte de l'Amérique par les Normands au Xe siècle* in *The North American Review* 119 (1874), 170–1.

Syasi's productive idyll is short-lived. Brutish *Skrelling* invaders attack and destroy the settlement. Syasi is killed, but Hervador makes it back to Iceland, where he retires to a monastery. Vinland and its offshoots remain resistant to colonization, whether benign or malign.

Its theme of reincarnation also lends a touch of imperial gothic to Rudyard Kipling's 'The Finest Story in the World'. Published in the collection *Many Inventions* (1893), this short story provides another perspective on the deleterious effect of female trespass upon the masculine province of lived and literary adventure by attributing authorial failure to complete the Vínland story itself to a woman. A young aspiring author named Charlie regales the story's first-person narrator with bad poetry, but also with uncannily accurate accounts of what appear to be his previous incarnations as a Greek galley slave and Norse sailor. In the latter persona he voyages to lands west of Greenland under the ruthless leadership of a red-haired man. Appalled by his poetry but enthralled by his personal story, which seems to offer a first-hand insight into all of human history, the narrator gives Charlie five pounds for the 'notion', which he sees as a potential source of fame and riches under his own name:

> I might rewrite the Saga of Thorfin Karlsefne as it had never been written before, might tell the story of the first discovery of America, myself the discoverer.
>
> (p. 110)[35]

This classic piece of unequal exchange casts the narrator as would-be colonizer of Charlie's narrative and Charlie as the native eager to trade pearls for beads. The narrator sees the story as a 'jewel' for himself: 'I – I alone held this jewel to my hand for the cutting and polishing' (p. 101). He is, however, warned by an Indian acquaintance that the power to recall previous incarnations can be undermined by feminine allure. Charlie is duly smitten by an unnamed 'tobacconist's assistant with a weakness for pretty dress', and the 'finest story in the world' goes up in smoke.

Maurice Hewlett, by contrast, offers an explicitly positive 'feminization' of the Vínland story in *Gudrid the Fair* (1918), its first telling in an adult English novel. Writing during World War I, Hewlett attributes 'our soldiers' crude jesting at death to their Scandinavian blood' (Preface, pp. xi–xii).[36] At the same time he implicitly rejects the eighteenth-century English image of the death-defying Viking of Old Icelandic poetry and the nineteenth-century inclination to transplant it to the Icelandic sagas, as exemplified by Andrew Lang, who characterizes the medieval Icelanders as 'no less cruel than brave; the best of soldiers, laughing at death and torture' and the sagas as 'tales of enterprise, of fighting by land and sea, fighting with men and beasts, with storms and ghosts and fiends'.[37] Although Hewlett acknowledges his debt to *Grœnlendinga saga*

---

35 Rudyard Kipling, *Many Inventions* (London, 1893), p. 110.
36 References are to Maurice Hewlett, *Gudrid the Fair* (London, 1924).
37 Andrew Lang, *Essays in Little*, new and revised edn (London, 1892), pp. 142, 144.

and *Eiríks saga rauða*,[38] his mission as a novelist is, he says, to remedy what he sees as a general deficiency of human emotion in the Icelandic sagas ('Their frugality freezes the soul; they are laconic to baldness . . . the starkness of the sagas shocks me' [Preface, p. x])[39] and to 'humanize' the Vínland story. The Preface to *Gudrid the Fair* declares the author's indifference to the story as an account of the early exploration of America. The novel is designed instead as a counter to masculine romance. Heroic exploits are eschewed in favour of a telling of the story from the viewpoint of Gudrid, wife of Thorfinn Karlsefne:

> while I have shown, I hope, due respect to the exploration of America, I admit that my tale turns essentially upon the explorers of it. My business as a writer of tales has been to explore them rather than Wineland the Good . . . Wineland does not fail of getting discovered, but meantime some new people have been born into the world who do the business of discovering while doing their own human business of love and marriage and childbirth . . . I confess that to me Gudrid, the many times a wife and the always sweet and reserved, is more absorbing a tale than the discovery of Wineland. (pp. vi–vii)

Motherhood, the imperial female virtue *par excellence*, is the enabling force. Gudrid's son, Snorre, is the instrument whereby liking turns to love in her union with Karlsefne

> 'Tell me, Gudrid, why you love me.' She touched her child's head. 'Because you are strong, and good, and brave. And because you gave me this. A woman must love her child's father.' (p. 247)

and the means of facilitating their first contact with the natives of Wineland. 'Bring your baby with you', Karlsefne tells her, rightly optimistic that their visit will be a friendly one, as a flotilla of boats advances upon their lakeside settlement, 'I don't think they mean us any harm' (p. 241). Fascinated by the sight of mother and child, the native Winelanders push forward one of their number, who is also nursing an infant. Gudrid holds out her hand, the woman stares at her white breast, displays her own, suckles her baby, 'and grinned community of nature in Gudrid's face' (p. 243). Maternality signals the common bond of humanity to the men in the visiting party as well ('presently they pushed one of their own men forward, and joined his hand with that of the mother', *ibid.*).

Motherhood also brings out the best in Freydis, who is neither Ballantyne's figure of fun, Hodgetts's villain, nor Neukomm's dominatrix, but, says Hewlett, a *femme incomprise* (Preface, p. x). Unlike Gudrid, she finds no satisfaction in pregnancy, but, after the birth of the child who, somewhat to her chagrin, is a girl, loves her 'more than life itself' (p. 255). Later she confesses to Gudrid that

---

38   Hewlett names his sources as Samuel Laing's *Heimskringla* and the lengthy portions of 'two sagas' (Preface, p. v) in Gudbrand Vigfusson and F. York Powell, eds and trans., *Origines Islandicae. A Collection of the more important sagas and other native writings relating to the settlement and early history of Iceland* (Millwood, NY; Kraus Reprints, 1976), pp. 2, 598–625.
39   Cf. *The Light Heart* (London, 1920), pp. xi–xii.

she was happiest in her tomboy childhood, that she loathes the embrace of men, and that, although she is jealous of her goodness and superior maternal status ('you have had yours first, and it is a boy. So you are better than me still' [p. 257]), Gudrid is her role model. The difference between Gudrid's idealized, passive model of maternal woman and the unorthodox Freydis is underlined by the contrast between the soothing effect of Gudrid's breast upon in the native Winelanders in their first encounter and the terror which the sight of the half-naked Freydis induces in their last:

> so far on with child that she could scarcely walk . . . She had the long sword in one hand, but needed two to swing it. Her shift incommoded her, so she ripped it open and let it fall behind her. Then bare-breasted she whirled the great sword over her head and began to lay about her like a man. Her yellow hair flew out behind her like a flag; her face was flame-red, and her eyes glittering like ice. The savages fell back before her.   (p. 252)

The discourse of motherhood in *Gudrid the Fair* articulates the late nineteenth and early twentieth-century imperial concern to maintain and increase the race. A number of official and voluntary societies for the care and education of mothers and the health of their children were instituted in the early years of the 20th century. The middle and upper classes were encouraged not to limit the size of their families, the size of which had been declining since the 1870s. Babies were frequently collectively denoted as male in the educational literature of the period. Although condensed milk was becoming popular, mortality, it was confirmed, was lower in breast-fed infants.[40] By these standards, Gudrid is the ideal mother. She gives birth to a male child and 'did not fail of milk' (p. 237). 'Can you have too many children?' Karlsefne asks, when he brings home the two children he has captured in Markland. 'I don't think so' (p. 260) is her exemplary reply.

Despite the goodwill generated by their mutual appreciation of motherhood, Hewlett's natives soon prove to be childishly and dangerously irrational. Moved to hospitality at their first encounter, Karlsefni sends out for milk and fish. In the scene which follows, the Winelanders abruptly revert to oral fixation and infantile whim:

> milk he offered, and that they drank greedily and on the spot . . . Red cloth took their fancy most; they seemed as if they must have it, it was a kind of lust.
>
> (p. 245)

This is less a case of unequal exchange than of frenzied suckling at the European breast. Karlsefne tries first to appease and then to rein in their feverish desires:

> The breadths he could spare them grew narrower and narrower; they pushed out their furs for it with no consideration of what they got in exchange. At last it became a kind of madness, and Karlsefne said it had better stop.   (pp. 245–6)

40 See Davin, 'Imperialism and motherhood', pp. 203–35.

When supplies are finally exhausted, 'they howled and chattered and looked dangerous' (p. 246).

The Winelanders become progressively uglier in appearance and dehumanized in speech and gesture. Whereas the men whom Thorwald kills early in the novel are said to be 'short and very dark, with black hair, in which were feathers' (p. 145), those whom Karlsefne first encounters are downright ugly:

> Small people they were, very dark brown, very ugly, with flat faces, coarse black hair twisted and tortured into peaks and knots. They had broad fat cheeks and enormous eyes. (p. 242)

They seem less than human in language ('Their talk was like the chattering of birds', p. 242) and demeanour ('they . . . were out in the water like a horde of rats' [p. 245]). The 'men' and 'Winelanders' of the peaceful encounter in which Gudrid and her baby are the focus of attention become 'savages' (pp. 246, 249, 250, 252) after the excitement of the trading episode. Karlsefne regards their flotilla as sinister. He puts himself on alert but is reluctant to alarm his wife:

> In a few moments the lake was black with canoes; it was . . . as though the water was covered with floating charcoal. Karlsefne did not like the look of things at all. He doubled the watch on the ship and strengthened the stockade; but he did not wish to frighten Gudrid, who was so happy with her child, and beginning, as he could see, to love himself. (pp. 246–7)

Karlsefne decides that the hostility of the Winelanders makes permanent settlement for the Norsemen an impractical proposition. Wineland itself ultimately turns out to be a sinister place. Evil portent, in the shape of a fetch-like figure who frightens Gudrid, rather than overwhelming numbers of hostile natives indicates that this a land to be shunned rather than settled. The desire to reach familiar shores for the sake of his family is at the forefront of Karlsefne's mind as they prepare for departure:

> Gudrid's boy Snorre was just two years old, and Karlsefne was anxious to be safe at home before he had a brother or sister. (p. 259)

Paternal responsibility thus overrides any suggestion of a lapse of masculine nerve, and the withdrawal from Wineland becomes a matter of successful escape rather than failed colonization.

Another imperial anxiety addressed in Vínland literature is, to borrow a phrase from Andrew Wawn, that late Victorian 'sense of potential splendour unachieved and actual splendour undermined by ultimately unappeasable forces of destruction'[41] in the face of looming imperial decline. Like Kipling, Ernest Edward Kellett tells the story as a case of fame unrealized in his poem 'Bjarni', published in a collection on Norse and classical themes – predominantly the

---

41 'The Spirit of 1892', p. 242.

former – entitled *The Passing of Scyld and Other Poems* (1902).[42] The volume celebrates the heroic virtues of the North but also mourns the passing of its heroes.
The subject of Kellet's poem is not Leifr Eiríksson or Þorfinnr Karlsefni but the
tragedy of Bjarni Grímólfsson, that member of Karlsefni's company in *Eiríks
saga rauða* who, when his ship is eaten through by worms in the 'Maggot Sea'
on the return trip to Greenland, heroically surrenders his place in the lifeboat to
a young Icelander (*ES* ch. 13).[43] In 'Bjarni' the exultation of Bjarni's crew at
their anticipated telling of their discovery of a paradisial new land and the prospect of lasting renown

> 'Then', said they, 'we will tell the wondrous tale
> Of the strange land which lately we have found,
> Of vine-clad slopes, and many a sunny dale
> Where corn and wine and pleasant fruits abound,
> And other wonders of that fairy ground;
> So shall we be, in ages yet unborn,
> Glorious as he who sighted first the Horn.'   (p. 29)

turns to horror as they contemplate their doom in the Maggot Sea – 'that fatal
ocean of the west/ Where lurks unseen a ship-destroying pest' (p. 30) – and
witness Bjarni's action. 'Joyful, his face with godlike frenzy lit', he gives his life
not for the anonymous young Icelander of *Eiríks saga rauða* but for his foster-
brother, Thorkell. Overcome with remorse, Thorkell plunges into the sea to join
him and the survivors head for Greenland, 'In Eric's ears to pour the mournful
tale' (p. 35). Mournful though it may be, this is not a story of individual or
collective failure but of heroic self-sacrifice.

Like Kipling, John Buchan and Nevil Shute incorporate the Vínland story
into narratives of contemporary life. In his novel *John Macnab* (1925) Buchan
ties the story to a plan to catch a cheeky poacher, who goes by the name of John
Macnab, on the ancestral land of a certain Colonel Raden, the patriarch of an
ancient Highland family of mixed Norse-Celtic ancestry. When an American
archaeologist coincidentally unearths the tomb of a Viking called Harald Blacktooth on the Raden estate and identifies artefacts in it as Native American, the
Raden genealogy is linked to the presumed discoverer of America. Local and
national interest in the find, however, focuses not on this startling revelation but
upon the true identity of John Macnab, who is believed by many to be the reincarnation of Harald Blacktooth. The ideological issue which underlies this often
very funny story is the cultural imperialism of wealthy outsiders from the South
who cultivate a phoney Scottish identity:

---

42 For Kellett's views on Old Norse literature, see his *Ex Libris: Confessions of a Constant Reader*
(London, 1940), pp. 231–6.
43 On the treatment of Germanic fate in nineteenth-century English literature see Russell Poole,
'Constructions of Fate in Victorian Philology and Literature', in *Old Norse Studies in the New World*,
eds Geraldine Barnes, Margaret Clunies Ross, and Judy Quinn (Sydney, 1994), pp. 110–19.

> Janet found Lady Claybody in a Tudor hall which had as much connection with a Scots castle as with a Kaffir kraal . . . tapestries which included priceless sixteenth-century Flemish pieces, and French fakes of last year; Ming treasures and Munich atrocities; armour of which about a third was genuine; furniture indiscriminately Queen Anne, Sheraton, Jacobean, and Tottenham Court Road.   (p. 215)[44]

and threaten to transform (or 'feminize') the Highlands from 'the home of men to the mere raw material of picture post cards' (*ibid.*).

Nevil Shute, a writer ideologically situated in the imperial tradition but historically positioned at the point of transition from Empire to Commonwealth, told the Vínland story twice; first in the form of a novel, *An Old Captivity* (1940), and second as a film script, *Vinland the Good* (1946). The central characters of *An Old Captivity* are two figures who occupy marginal positions in *Eiríks saga rauða*, the Celtic thralls Haki and Hekja. In a strategy which may owe something to Kipling's 'Finest Story in the World', the Vínland story is enacted in a dream sequence in the latter part of the book by Donald Ross, an aviator of Scottish–Irish ancestry who appears to be the reincarnation of Haki. Seeking reassurance about his mental health from a psychiatrist he meets on a train, Ross, now a corporate executive with Imperial Airways, asks if he will listen to his account of an intensely vivid dream which he had five years before. The narrative backtracks to the circumstances which led to the dream and never returns to the issue of Ross's sanity or delivers him to his unnamed destination.

Taking over as narrator, Ross tells his travelling companion how, during the Depression, he was forced to take a summer job as pilot and photographer on an archaeological expedition to Greenland led by an Oxford don named Cyril Lockwood. Lockwood's daughter, Alix, is a member of the party. The exploits of medieval Scandinavian seafarers and modern aviators are a natural equation for Shute, who spent many years in the aircraft industry,[45] and Lockwood's expedition to Greenland becomes the twentieth-century version of Leifr's. Ross, who has fallen in love with the standoffish Alix, relives the Vínland voyage, playing Haki to Lockwood's Leifr in a dream induced by a self-ministered, accidental overdose of sleeping pills.

The dream begins with the capture of Haki and Hekja by a Norwegian raiding party and their enslavement to a tall man with yellow hair named Leif. Their growing reputation as sprinters makes Olaf Tryggvason assign the captives as explorers to the first colonizing expedition from Norway to Greenland. When Leif decides to go on a timber-gathering mission to the lands which Bjarni has sighted west of Greenland, Haki and Hekja are promised their freedom if they accompany him. On board ship, Tyrker carves Haki's name in runes on a stone, and Leif adds Hekja's to the inscription. When they reach a

---

44 References are to John Buchan, *John Macnab* (London and Aylesbury, 1935).
45 See Donald Lammers, 'Nevil Shute and the Decline of the "Imperial Idea" in Literature', *Journal of British Studies* 16 (1977), 123–4.

land of honey-sweet dew and balmy climate, Haki and Hekja, now betrothed to each other, set up the stone above a lagoon at which Leif makes camp and are despatched on a three-day mission of exploration.

They find themselves in a paradisial world, empty of human inhabitants and filled with berries, grapes, wild wheat, and exotic bird life. Haki and Hekja have free rein over its abundant resources and end a glorious day with a dinner of roast venison, the consummation of their union, and an expressed desire by Hekja to seize this opportunity for independence: 'Haki, don't let's go back to the ship. We can stay here, in this good land . . . We can stay here and be our own masters' (p. 245).[46] Haki insists on remaining loyal to the deal he has struck with Leif, but Hekja eventually succeeds in persuading him of the rightness of her cause, and Ross's dream ends with Haki's resolution that they will establish their family there: 'This is a good country . . . better than Greenland. I will ask Leif to let us stay here when the ship goes back, and you shall have your children here' (p. 211). At this point Ross wakes up, and the story of Haki and Hekja remains unfinished. Their Greenland mission accomplished, Ross flies Lockwood and his party to Cape Cod. Landing on its south side at a place which Ross recognizes from his dream, he and Alix find a stone carved in runic script with the names Haki and Hekja. The sight triggers a primeval sense of *déjà vu* in Alix in the closing lines of the story: 'I know these marks', she said at last. 'I've done this before, some time' (p. 276). The reader is left with the assumption that Ross's talents will bridge the social gap between them, and that he and Alix will replay their former lives and share a happy future beyond the pages of the novel.

An Old Captivity's Wineland is Edenic. Leif's crew suspect that they have reached the Islands of the Blest: 'And, if so, what would they meet next? Would earthly weapons be of any use to them?' (p. 239). As it happens, the land offers neither human nor supernatural challenge. The dream ends at the point at which Haki and Hekja, in a demonstration of British resourcefulness and enterprise,

> They found no difficulty at all in living in this fertile country. They could throw a stone with quite extraordinary accuracy and force, born of long practice at the quarters of the cattle that they herded. They gathered a few pebbles from a brook and wandered about until they saw a little deer; they stalked it carefully up-wind till they were close enough, and threw their stones together. At twenty-five yards range both hit it on the head. It staggered and fell down; they rushed up and despatched it with a knife. Very pleased with themselves, they carried it in turn till they reached a woody glade beside a stream, here they made a fire in a spot where bushes kept the draught from their backs.
>
> As night fell, they cooked the meat on wooden skewers over a fire, and ate it with a quantity of the big purple berries.   (p. 245)

determine to ask Leif for permission to remain in this land. British canniness is

46 References are to *An Old Captivity* (London, 1940).

shown to be equal to Norse might in exploiting its riches, and Haki and Hekja are in a better position than the Norsemen to reap its benefits. Whereas, as Hekja points out, he and she are able to penetrate the land's interior, the Norsemen must remain restricted to its coastal fringes, since they will be reluctant to go far from their ship.

An Old Captivity entertains no prospect of Wineland the Good's loss, present or foreshadowed. Imperial failure is explicitly addressed, but only in relation to Greenland's history as a medieval Norwegian colony. Lockwood fixes the blame for its 'going native' on the mother country's dereliction of duty. He gives Ross and Alix a brief lecture on the subject:

> The don said: 'This colony was Norwegian. Norse settlers from Iceland started it, about the year 980. It died out in the fourteenth century.'
> Alix said: 'Is this the place that went native, Daddy?'
> Lockwood nodded. 'The colony that died of neglect.'
> 'How did that happen?' asked the pilot.
> 'The Norwegians used to send a ship here every year, to trade, to sell the colonists axes, weapons, things of that sort in exchange for their furs. I don't suppose the trade was worth much to Norway. Under the Hanseatic League they began to send the ships less frequently. In the end, there was an interval of eighty years when no ship came here. When they did come at the end of that, there were no Norsemen here at all. Only Eskimos.' (p. 190)

> The pilot said: 'I suppose all they needed was a square deal from the mother country, and they didn't get it.'
> The don said: 'But for that, they might have been here still.' (p. 196)

The European–native encounter common to most versions of the Vínland story is also played out in Greenland, where the twentieth-century Inuit are represented in patronizing terms, not dissimilar to those in Ballantyne's *Ungava*, as cheerful, fat, dirty, and naive. Dehumanized by synecdoche, they become body parts, and dirty ones at that. Luki, the expedition's host at an Inuit settlement, where the company are granted permission to land in bad weather provided they do not supply the natives with weapons or drink, is, for example, primarily a 'copper-coloured face'. When Ross introduces himself, '[t]he dirty, copper-coloured face beamed with pleasure (p. 150); and when he communicates a question in sign language, '[t]he copper-coloured face brightened with intelligence' (p. 151). The English syntax of the Inuit is of the 'me Tarzan' variety, and their pronunciation equally inept. The local Shell representative introduces himself to Ross as 'Me Thomas. Me Shell representative' (p. 139) and, to an enquiry about the expedition's petrol supplies, replies, 'Plenty petrol. Plenty gasoline. Plenty oil. Plenty in store' (p. 139). Luki attempts to say Ross's name after their introduction: ' "Rogg," he repeated' (p. 150). Further evidence of Inuit backwardness is a childish gusto for unappetizing food combinations. At the Inuit settlement, Ross's offerings of pemmican, oatmeal, and margarine are thrown together in a communal stew, and cocoa powder is 'poured into each grubby palm, and sucked off it' (p. 156). The hitherto reserved Alix happily joins in what she remembers as a gooey childhood indulgence: ' "I haven't done this since I was ten years old," she said' (p. 156). The message is that, although the Inuit have a sense of community spirit, they are childish, dirty, superstitious, and live like animals in squalid conditions: they 'twitched and whimpered in their sleep to chorus with the dogs upon the lower part of the floor' (p. 157).

Nevertheless, in an unexpected divergence from the accepted values of High Imperialism, later in the novel Lockwood asserts that racial superiority is a matter of relativity. Whereas, he says, the Norse settlers of Greenland were superior to the natives for as long as they were able to import the comforts of mainland Scandinavia, when trade with the homeland ceased, the colonists became the inferiors of the Inuit, who knew how to exploit the natural resources of the land:

> while the ships kept coming here, and they had iron weapons, timber, corn, and all the culture of their homeland, the colonists were better men than the Eskimos. When the ships stopped coming, the Eskimos became the better men, because they could live on the country. The colonists would have had to take lessons from the Eskimos in hunting, building houses, making clothes . . . All their superiority must have vanished very soon. (p. 190)

Framed as a lesson in American history given just after World War II to the Lower Fifth of an English public school, Shute's *Vinland the Good* is a self-conscious 'deheroicization' of the story. Its narrator, the recently demobbed Major Callender – whose resumé includes a Second from Oxford, a reputation for eccentricity, service at Tobruk and Anzio, and a stint as a POW in Pisa – has turned down a job as a razor salesman to return to the teaching profession. Having begun with Callender's categorical statement that 'America was first discovered by a bloody fool called Bjarni about the year one thousand and two' (p. 13),[47] the lesson proceeds, in flashback, to the careers of Eiríkr and Leifr. Guðríðr and Freydís are absent, but Þorgunna, Leifr's Hebridean lover in *Eiríks saga rauða*, is central to the plot.

The message of *Vinland the Good* is as down to earth as its narrator: happiness and success are the products of hard work and initiative, not gifts waiting at the end of the rainbow. If the paradise to the west of Ireland, about which the Hebridean princess, Thorgunna, has heard from an Irish monk, exists, it would, she tells Leif, 'be worth while to spend one's whole life looking for it' (p. 58). Thorgunna visualizes this Happy Land as a world of peace, security, eternal spring, joy, love, and perpetual youth:

> No thief, no robber, and no enemy pursues one there; there is no violence, and no winter snow. In that place it is always spring. No flower or lily is wanting, no rose or violet but you will find them there. There apple trees bear flowers and fruit on the same branch, all the year round. There young men live in quiet happiness with

---

47 References are to *Vinland the Good* (London and Toronto, 1946).

their girls; there is no old age, and no sickness, and no sorrow there. All is full of joy . . . (*Her voice dies away.*)   (p. 58)

Leif, 'gently' according to the stage direction, denies the existence of such an earthly paradise. Later, the spirit of Thorgunna's mother gives her a vision of the future in which modern America appears as an industrial society, grown mighty and prosperous through the harnessing of its great natural resources. Niagara Falls ('a waterfall, but so enormous that it never could have been . . . Then there was a sort of whirling thing, in a house. It might have been a temple' [p. 79]) is dominated by a power station; Manhattan ('an island with stone houses like tall cliffs, taller than any house could ever be, all white and shining in the sun' [p. 79]) by its skyscrapers; and the wheatfields of the Midwest ('it was all wheat as far as one could see, more wheat than all the people in the world could eat. And then there was a dragon' [p. 79]) by combine harvesters.

In the service of Olaf Tryggvason but a reluctant convert to Christianity himself – 'I was never a religious man, King, and these things don't mean a great deal to me, personally', he says (p. 90) – Leif undertakes a mission for the king. His brief is not to bring Christianity to Greenland, as in *Eiríks saga rauða* (*ES* ch. 5), but, in return for the regularizing of that settlement's 'outlaw' status as a legitimate Norwegian colony, to search for land west of Greenland. The glories of empire-building, however, take second place to the virtue of the work ethic, which is reinforced in Callender's concluding tribute to the common man's role in the forging of nations: kings and princes are, he muses, merely 'the froth upon the surface' of history. Its substance is the hard work of ordinary folk:

> History is made by plain and simple people like ourselves, doing the best we can with each job as it comes along. Leif, went out to get timber to build cow-houses, and found America. That's how real people make real history.   (p. 142)

In the final scene, 'somewhere on the south coast of Cape Cod' (p. 131), Leif finds a land of honey-sweet dew and many of the properties – flowers, fruit, youthful love in the mutual devotion of Haki and Haekia – of Thorgunna's Happy Land, which make him wonder if he has, indeed, found her place of eternal contentment. Haki and Haekia reconnoitre and, as in *An Old Captivity*, frolic in an idyllic landscape. This time, though, they also sight snakes and buzzards, creatures absent from the Wineland of that novel and from Thorgunna's vision of the Happy Land.

The parallel with *An Old Captivity* is maintained for as long as Haki and Haekia explore what appears to be virgin territory, but diverges when they sight evidence of prior and current occupation in the form of snakes, buzzards and an old Indian camp site. At this point, as none of his predecessors has done, Shute confronts head on the question of why the Norsemen failed to establish themselves in the New World. Back in the Lower Fifth, Major Callender tells the class that the nascent Norse settlement of America failed. What it took, he says at the narrative's conclusion, to achieve the European colonization of the New World was the invention of guns:

> each time they tried to make a settlement the Indians came down on them and beat them in a battle. It wasn't until five hundred years later, when men came with the new weapons they called guns, that Europeans settled in America.   (p. 141)

Shute's brutally succinct demystification of the European conquest of the New World constitutes a valediction to imperial Vínland narrative. The story continues to inspire novelistic retellings in England and America, but postcolonial Vínland literature is less concerned with Leifr's 'discovery' for its own sake than with its consequences for the New World. Whereas imperial Vínland narrative must come to terms with the ultimate failure of the enterprise, postcolonial Vínland literature rewrites the story to reflect late twentieth-century reservations about settlement and development as laudable and desirable ends in themselves.

CHAPTER FIVE

Vínland in American Literature to 1926[1]

American literary circles in the nineteenth century were more hospitable than the historical establishment to the Norse 'discovery' of America. The shifting of the geographical genesis of the New World from the Caribbean to the northeast seaboard had undeniable regional appeal, and the publication of *Antiquitates Americanæ* made an immediate impact upon the New England poetic consciousness. The American reading public had, moreover, been more or less simultaneously introduced to a seductively romanticized view of ancient Scandinavia by the Swedish poet, Esaias Tegnér (1782–1847),[2] who, as Andrew Hilen puts it, 'embraced the freedom of the past and the law of love while eschewing the "deeds of blood" that had characterized his Viking ancestors'.[3] Hugely popular in Germany, England, and America, Tegnér's best-known work, *Frithiofs saga* (1831),[4] is a stanzaic retelling of the late medieval Icelandic romance *Friðþjófs saga*. Longfellow's celebrated essay on *Frithiofs saga* in the *The North American Review* (1837)[5] influentially articulated the literary attraction of medieval Scandinavia.[6] He and others among the New England 'Fireside Poets' – James Russell Lowell (1819–91) and John Greenleaf Whittier (1807–92) – found the Vínland voyages a fertile source of inspiration; and, in the Centennial year of 1876, Sidney Lanier (1842–81) validated the Viking landfall in America as an

---

1   An earlier, shorter version of some sections of this chapter appears in 'The Fireside Vikings and the "Boy's Own" Vinland: Vinland in Popular English and American Literature (1841–1926)', in *Reinventing the Middle Ages and the Renaissance: Constructions of the Medieval and Early Modern Periods*, ed. William F. Gentrup (Turnhout, Belgium, 1998), pp. 147–65.
2   See Adolph B. Benson, 'The Beginning of American Interest in Scandinavian Literature', *Scandinavian Studies and Notes* 8 (1924–25), 133–41.
3   Andrew Hilen, 'Longfellow and Scandinavia Revisited', *Papers Presented at the Longfellow Commemorative Conference April 1–3, 1982* (1982), p. 6.
4   On the popularity of the saga in England and the reception of Tegnér's *Frithiofs saga* there, see Andrew Wawn, 'The Cult of "Stalwart Frith-thjof" in Victorian Britain', *Northern Antiquity. The Post-Medieval Reception of Edda and Saga*, ed. Andrew Wawn (Enfield Lock, 1994), pp. 211–54.
5   'A review of the fifth edition of Tegnér's poem, and a German and English translation', *The North American Review* 45 (1837), 149–83.
6   See Andrew Hilen, *Longfellow and Scandinavia* (1947); *idem*, 'Longfellow and Scandinavia Revisited', pp. 1–11.

integral part of the poetic history of the nation in his Centennial Ode, 'Psalm of the West'.

The attention of American novelists was slower in forthcoming. Ralph Bergen Allen comments on the likelihood of the Vínland voyages taking novelistic form, 'whenever huge skeletons or suspicious scratchings are found upon the mainland',[7] in *Old Icelandic Sources in the English Novel* (1933), but although Viking 'finds' proliferated in New England from the 1830s, American novelists ignored and American publishers displayed no great enthusiasm for the subject.[8] Ballantyne's *The Norsemen in the West* (1872) had gone through six printings in England by 1880 but did not appear in an American edition until 1878.[9] William Morris's characterization of the Norse-speaking resident of the mysterious West Atlantic land in *Eyrbyggja saga* (ch. 64) as a 'real ruler of men, an American goði' ('chieftain'),[10] and Edmund Gosse's reference in an 1880 article on *Eyrbyggja saga* to the inhabitants of that land, which he identifies with either Vínland or Hvítramannaland, as 'Americans'[11] appear to have made no impact on American writers of creative prose until the early twentieth century.

The prose fictional impulse was channelled instead, in the latter part of the nineteenth century, into popular history of various kinds. William Cullen Bryant and Sydney Howard Gay's *A Popular History of the United States, From the first discovery of the western hemisphere by the Northmen, to the end of the first century of the Union of the States* (1876) devotes a full chapter to 'The Northmen in America'. Derived from the accounts of Beamish and De Costa, the Vínland voyages are narrated in novelistic style with omniscient authorial commentary. Against a backdrop rich with narratorially imagined luxuriance, Leif's veneration for Vínland's grapes is attributed to the pagan significance of wine, which, he anticipates, will impress the value of the land upon his hard-drinking compatriots:

> Then, no doubt, he led them to the woods, that they might see with their own eyes the climbing vines and the clustering fruit, and it may well have seemed to them that in a country where these grew wild there could be no real winter. So precious were they to Leif. . . . What better evidence could he bring of the value of the land to a people whose greatest delight, next to fighting, was drinking? They had not yet forgotten, notwithstanding their new religion, that the chief of their old Pagan gods, Odin, had no need of food only because wine was to him both

7   Ralph Bergen Allen, *Old Icelandic Sources in the English Novel* (Philadelphia, 1933), p. 68.
8   Joseph J. Moldenhauer has recently argued that the account of the Dighton Rock in *AA* was among Edgar Allen Poe's sources for *The Narrative of Arthur Gordon Pym* (1838). See his 'Pym, the Dighton Rock, and the Matter of Vinland', in Richard Kopley, ed., *Poe's Pym: Critical Explorations* (Durham and London, 1992), pp. 75–94.
9   See Allen, *Old Icelandic Sources in the English Novel*, p. 69n.
10 William Morris and Eiríkr Magnússon, trans. *The Story of the Ere-Dwellers (Eyrbyggja Saga)* (London, 1892), p. xxix.
11 *The Cornhill Magazine* (1880), 720–1.

meat and drink; that all the heroes of Valhalla drank daily of the wonderful flow of milk from the she-goat Heidrun, and that the milk was mead.   (p. 42)

Later, Thorvald and his company take a summer cruise along the New England coast in the 'Cunard log-book' style which had amused De Costa's *North American Review* reviewer a few years earlier:[12]

They spent the summer in this pleasant excursion, coasting along the shores of Rhode Island, Connecticut, and Long Island, the whole length of the Sound, penetrating, probably, to New York . . . The next spring (1004), Thorvald sailed northward along the sea-coast of Cape Cod, where a heavy storm caught him off a ness (cape), and drove his ship ashore, perhaps at Race Point.   (p. 43)

Conversely, Richard Clark makes Leifr the evangelist of Greenland in his article, 'America Discovered and Christianized in the Tenth and Eleventh Centuries' (1888). For him, the 'discovery' of America plays a subsidiary role to Leifr's conversion of the Greenlanders:

Leif, with a brave soul and Christian faith, rejecting the pagan superstitions in which he had been educated, and which he had now abjured, joyously sailed in his stout ship with his thirty-five sailors and the Christian missionaries sent to evangelize the pagan Greenlanders . . . His was a veritable voyage of discovery. It was more – it was a mission of Christianity.[13]

The Norsemen themselves are less the heirs of 'gothic' traditions of freedom than perpetuators of the savage ethos of paganism:

The Northmen were by education and national tradition adventurers, pirates and murderers, looking upon piracy and murder not as crimes, but as so many claims to distinction and honor in this world and in the Valhalla of the future life.

(p. 223)

Fictional embellishment of the unprovoked slaughter of a group of natives by Þorvaldr Eiríksson in *Grœnlendinga saga* (*GS* ch. 5) serves as an illustration of Viking barbarity. As *Grœnlendinga saga* tells it:

Þá skiptu þeir liði sínu ok hǫfðu hendr á þeim ǫllum, nema einn komsk í burt með keip sinn. Þeir drepa hina átta.   (*GS* ch. 5: 256)

They divided their forces and seized all of them, except one who escaped in his boat. They killed those eight.

In Clark's retelling:

Their first impulse was to seize and slaughter the natives found concealed under the carabos, an impulse no sooner felt than executed. One only escaped, and he

12 See Chapter 2, above, pp. 49–50.
13 Richard H. Clark, 'America Discovered and Christianized in the Tenth and Eleventh Centuries', *The American Catholic Quarterly Review* 13 (1888), p. 220.

could distinctly hear, above the splashing noise of the Northmen's boats as they returned to the ship, the cries of agony and death from his countrymen, as they were slaughtered and thrown into the deep sea. There were some Christians with the expedition, but probably few; it is hoped none took part in this slaughter.

(p. 223)

Whimsy, by contrast, is the mode of a short piece of self-consciously anachronistic 'anti'-Columbian history published in 1885.[14] Mr and Mrs Thorfinn Karlsefne are well-to-do tourists from Greenland ('With eager minds and a long purse they were only waiting to hear of some place of sufficient novelty before setting out' [p. 295]), who lead a long and eventful tour to the balmy shores of Narragansett Bay ('so popular as a resort ever since' [p. 296]), where, during a mild winter, 'Mrs Karlsefne gave lawn parties and picnics in the woods' (p. 297). Turning in their graves when they hear the news of Columbus's discovery, Mr Karlsefne exclaims:

> I wish to gracious, Godrid, I could get up out of this, and tell what I know! Why, that scalawag has been up to Iceland and read the whole historical account of our voyages! (p. 295)

In nineteenth-century poetry, the Norse 'discovery' of America was celebrated as an encounter with the territorial rather than the racial Other. The removal of the native presence is perhaps the most striking difference between American verse and prose Vínland narrative to 1926. Although the period of composition of most of the poems discussed below coincides with the violent native–European confrontations triggered by the displacement of Native Americans to regions west of the Mississippi in the 1830s and the acquisition of Texas and California in the 1840s, it is not until the early twentieth-century novels of Ottilie Liljencrantz and Charles Rann Kennedy's play, *The Winterfeast*, that the Native American enters the literary discourse of Viking America.

As a student of Amerindian languages, admirer of Amerindian culture, and author of *Song of Hiawatha*, Longfellow knew better of course, as did Whittier, whose 'Mogg Megone' (1835) is a poem about friction between early New England settlers and Native Americans. For their American Viking verse, however, Longfellow, Whittier, Lowell, and Lanier borrow the rhetoric of the discovery narratives of Lewis and Clark, Zebulon Pike, and John C. Frémont, which tropes the West as virgin and makes 'discovery' the aesthetic response to a landscape whose unveiling and appropriation are authorized by the gaze of the beholder.[15]

---

14 Emma Sherwood Chester, 'Karlsefne versus Columbus', *Scandinavia* 2/12 (December, 1885), 295–9.

15 See Bruce Greenfield, *Narrating Discovery: the Romantic Explorer in American Literature 1790–1855* (New York, 1992), pp. 96–111; *idem*, 'The Problem of the Discoverer's Authority in Lewis and Clark's *History*', in Jonathan Arac and Harriet Ritvo, eds, *Macropolitics of Nineteenth-Century Literature. Nationalism, Exoticism, Imperialism* (Durham and London, 1995), pp. 12–36.

The Fireside Vikings

For James Russell Lowell, Viking visits to America are an integral part of the myth of national foundation; but whereas Whittier's image of Bradford, Massachusetts, concentrates on the enduring link between primeval and present-day local landscape, Longfellow's inspiration for the reworking of the West Atlantic Viking voyages is shaped primarily by his image of ancient Scandinavia.

Both Whittier and Longfellow claimed archaeological finds of alleged Norse provenance in Massachusetts as inspiration for their Viking poems, although their common ground ends there. Scandinavian voyages to New England are a trigger for reflection in Whittier's lyric, 'The Norsemen' (1841), in which a crew of lusty, blue-eyed, yellow-haired Norsemen sail up the Merrimack to the site of modern Bradford, Massachusetts, not in storm-tossed confusion but in purposeful seasonal migration to warmer climes. Joyfully disencumbered of their shaggy winter hides, these honourably weary warriors seek no more from the land than a breath of its balmy air:

> What sound comes up the Merrimac?
> . . .
> Joy glistens in each wild blue eye,
> Turned to green earth and summer sky.
> Each broad, seamed breast has cast aside
> Its cumbering vest of shaggy hide;
> Bared to the sun and soft warm air,
> Streams back the Norseman's yellow hair.   (*Works* I, 38)

'The Norsemen' follows the pattern of those New England poems on rivers where the speaker derives comfort from the contemplation of fluvial constancy throughout the vicissitudes of history,[16] here marked by the brief ripple of the Vínland voyages on the Merrimack's timeless journey. The poem's dramatic focus is the contrast between, on the one hand, the diurnal round of the cosy world of contemporary Bradford – farms, schools, houses, trains, churches, and the river rippling with the movement of sailboats and rowboats – and, on the other, the surge of Viking ships and the exultant voices of their crews along the ancient Merrimack.

According to its headnote, 'The Norseman' was prompted by 'a fragment of a statue, rudely chiselled from dark gray stone . . . found in the town of Bradford, on the Merrimac',[17] about whose provenance Whittier is coolly cautious:

---

16 See Lawrence Buell, *New England Literary Culture. From Revolution Through Renaissance* (Cambridge Mass., 1986), pp. 289–90.
17 *The Works of John Greenleaf Whittier*, 7 vols (Boston and New York, 1892), I, 37.

'Its origin must be left entirely to conjecture' (*ibid.*).[18] Whether the gray stone is a fragment of the statue of a berserkr, or of a mythological figure, matters less, says the poem's speaker, than the evidence it bears of God's gift of imagination to humankind:

> My spirit bows in gratitude
> Before the Giver of all good,
> Who fashioned so the human mind,
> That, from the waste of Time behind,
> A simple stone, or mound of earth,
> Can summon the departed forth.

Longfellow moves out of the purely regional frame of reference in 'The Skeleton in Armor', published in the same year as 'The Norsemen'. The origins of Longfellow's poem go back to the summer of 1835, which, in pursuit of his lifelong passion for Scandinavia as a repository for romantic inspiration, he had spent in Stockholm and Copenhagen.[19] In a journal entry three years later, he raises the possibility of a series of New England ballads with a Viking prelude:

> I have been looking at the old Northern Sagas, and thinking of a series of ballads or a romantic poem on the deeds of the first bold viking who crossed to this western world, with storm-spirits and devil-machinery under water. New England ballads I have long thought of. This seems to be an introduction. I will dream more of this. (3 May 1838; *Life* 1, 297)

By the following year, Longfellow's interest seems to have drifted away from the 'Northern Sagas' and towards alleged local Viking remains. In another journal entry he refers to his 'plan of a heroic poem on the Discovery of America by the Northmen, in which the Round Tower at Newport and the Skeleton in Armor have a part to play. The more I think of it, the more I like it' (24 May 1839). A disappointed-sounding parenthetical comment from Samuel Longfellow follows the last sentence: '[No epic came of this; only a lyric]' (*Life*, 1, 335). There was no series of Viking ballads either. After the lyric in question, 'The Skeleton in Armor', in which unnamed shores far to the west of Scandinavia become the refuge for a Viking warrior and a Norwegian princess in flight from the wrath of her father, Longfellow turned to the subject matter of Scandinavian legend, which produced the best known of his poems on Norse themes, 'The Saga of King Olaf'.

The Newport Tower is that structure in Newport, Rhode Island, claimed by Rafn as a medieval Scandinavian church but now almost universally acknowledged as a seventeenth-century construction. Longfellow was cheerfully sceptical about its alleged Scandinavian provenance but regarded it as 'sufficiently

---

18 According to Samuel Eliot Morison, 'The "Bradford statue," of course, turned out to be English colonial' (*The European Discovery of America. The Northern Voyages A.D. 500–1600* [New York, 1971], p. 75).

19 See above, Chapter 2, pp. 54–5.

well established for the purpose of a ballad' (*Works* I, 50). The skeleton, a body bearing metal plate, was discovered in Fall River in 1831 and put on display in a local museum which was destroyed by fire around 1843.[20] Although the remains were discounted as Norse by archaeological opinion of the day, there were those who were eager to identify it as a Viking warrior.[21]

Longfellow may have derived his initial inspiration for 'The Skeleton in Armor' from the Vínland sagas, but it is Tegnér's *Frithiofs saga*, where, after many adventures including a perilous sea journey, the low-born hero marries a princess, which provides its narrative framework.[22] Gaunt, glittering-eyed, and long-dead, a Viking warrior, thrusts himself upon the poet,

'Speak! speak! thou fearful guest!
Who, with thy hollow breast
Still in rude armour drest,
    Comest to daunt me!
Wrapt not in Eastern balms,
But with thy fleshless palms
Stretched, as if asking alms,
    Why dost thou haunt me?'

Then, from those cavernous eyes
Pale flashes seemed to rise.   (ll. 1–10)[23]

and tells the history of his life. After a wild, Viking youth, he woos and wins his timid but passionate princess in the forests of Norway; when her father, Prince Hildebrand, scornfully dismisses his suit, he carries her off to sea; Hildebrand perishes in pursuit of the couple, who sight land after a storm-tossed, three-week journey westwards. Here, says the speaker, he built a tower for his lady, who, after many years of blissful union, lies buried there.

Although 'The Skeleton in Armor' refers neither to the lovers' landfall nor to the tower by name, as originally printed in *Knickerbocker's Magazine* the poem was accompanied by marginal notes which identify their landing site as Newport.[24] These annotations were removed by Longfellow for reprinting in *Ballads and Other Poems* and are lacking in all subsequent editions:

Three weeks we westward bore,
And when the storm was o'er,   Driven westward
Cloud-like we saw the shore   by a fierce storm;

---

20 Samuel Ward, 'Days With Longfellow', *The North American Review* 134 (1882), 460; *Longfellow's Works*, ed. Samuel Longfellow, 14 vols (Boston and New York, 1886–91), I (*The Poetical Works of Henry Wadsworth Longfellow*), p. 50.

21 For a full description of the skeleton, see, for example, Justin Winsor, *Narrative and Critical History*, I, 105. Richard Clark identified the body as that of Þorvaldr Eiríksson ('America Discovered and Christianized', p. 224).

22 See Hilen, *Longfellow and Scandinavia*, pp. 63–4.

23 *Longfellow's Works*, I, 55.

24 The *Knickerbocker* version of the poem is printed in *Longfellow's Works*, I, 312–15.

Stretching to lea-ward;
There for my lady's bower
Built I the lofty tower,
Which, to this very hour,
Stands looking sea-ward.

but at length makes
land near Newport,
and builds the
Round Tower.

(*Works* I, 315)

Elsewhere Longfellow calls 'The Skeleton in Armor' 'a national ballad, as *The Wreck of the Hesperus* is' (*Works* I, 53), but culturally and, for the most part, geographically, the poem remains outside any discernible American framework. 'I think I have succeeded in giving the whole a Northern air', he wrote in a letter to his father on 13 December 1840.[25] Sam Ward's report of a conversation with Longfellow, who claimed, after a visit to the Fall River Skeleton in 1838, to have 'challenged my sister [Julia Ward Howe], in their home gallop over the Newport beaches, to make a poem out of the rusty hauberk and grim bones they had been inspecting',[26] hints at essentially agonistic inspiration for the work. Longfellow's skeleton in fact owes more to the image of dead Viking kings in their burial mounds in his *Frithiofs Saga* essay ('Their bones are within; skeletons of warriors mounted on the skeletons of their steeds, and Vikings sitting gaunt and grim on the plankless ribs of their pirate ships')[27] than to a local curiosity.[28]

Whereas Whittier's Vikings leave no permanent mark on the landscape, Longellow's warrior stakes some claim to settlement with his tower, and there is, perhaps, an oblique suggestion that he and his princess are the progenitors of a nation, since, in the course of their life together, '[s]he was a mother'. But the principal arena of 'The Skeleton in Armor' is the wild 'Northern Land' which forms the background for the life and adventures of the speaker. Most of the poem is devoted to his recollections of piratical exploits in the Baltic and moves westward only in the concluding five of its twenty stanzas. The dark, virgin forest to which the speaker retreats and takes his life after the death of his beloved,

Hateful to me were men.
The sunlight hateful!
In the vast forest here,

---

25 Andrew Hilen, ed., *The Letters of Henry Wadsworth Longfellow*, 2 vols (Cambridge, Mass., 1966) II (*1837–1843*), p. 269.

26 Sam Ward, 'Days with Longfellow', *The North American Review* 134 (1882), 460.

27 *The North American Review* 45 (1837), 152.

28 George LeRoy White sees other similarities between 'The Skeleton in Armor' and Tegnér's *Frithiofs saga* and suggests that the line 'Washed up by the tide, the bones of the outlaw'd Viking may lie' may have provided some inspiration for the poem's composition ('Longfellow's Interest in Scandinavia during the years 1835–1847', *Scandinavian Studies* 17 [1942], p. 76). Hilen calls the poem 'an amalgam of literary influences', which extend to Drayton and Shelley ('Longfellow and Scandinavia Revisited', in *Papers Presented at the Longfellow Commemorative Conference, April 1–3, 1982* [Longfellow National Historic Site, 1982], p. 8).

> Clad in my warlike gear,
> Fell I upon my spear.

is the lonely counterpart of the Norwegian Arcadia where they plighted their troth ('And in the forest's shade/ Our vows were plighted'). The forest description echoes Longfellow's imagined haunts, in the *Frithofs saga* essay, of the solitary 'old Scald'

> In the vast solitudes around him, the heart of Nature beat against his own. From the midnight gloom of groves the deep-voiced pines answered the deeper-voiced and neighboring sea. (p. 151)

and his modern counterpart in the forests of Sweden:

> Almost primeval simplicity reigns over this Northern land, – almost primeval solitude and stillness . . . Around you are forests or fir . . . the air is warm and balmy.
> (p. 152)

'The Skeleton in Armor' is less an 'heroic poem of the Discovery of America' than a Viking romance with a New World epilogue. In transferring the spirit of *Frithiof's Saga* to a cryptically encoded Rhode Island, Longfellow reverses the common practice among nineteenth-century adapters and retellers of the Vínland voyages. Instead of 'Americanizing' Tegnér's version of an Old Norse narrative by making New England locations and modern-day place-names the focus of the poem, he takes inspiration from a regional landmark and the New England wilderness for a romantic reconstruction of the Viking past among the pine forests of Norway.

The Newport Tower and 'The Skeleton in Armor' continued to inspire American writers over the next sixty-five years. Playfully quoting from 'Professor Rafin' [sic] in a note to her poem, 'The Newport Tower', published in the collection *Scenes In My Native Land* (1844), Lydia Howard Sigourney claims to be convinced 'that all who are familiar with Old Northern Architecture will concur that this building was erected at a period decidedly not later than the twelfth century'.[29] She exercises Yankee curiosity ('the creed/ Of Yankee people is, that through the toil/ Of questioning, there cometh light, and gain/ Of knowledge to the mind') concerning its possible origins:

> Say, reared the plundering hand
> Of the fierce buccaneer thy massy walls,
> A treasure-fortress for his blood-stained gold?
> Or wrought the beings of an earlier race
> To form thy circle, while in wonder gazed
> The painted Indian? (p. 240)

29 Mrs L. H. Sigourney, 'The Newport Tower', *Scenes in My Native Land* (London, 1844), pp. 242, 243.

In 'The American Legend', a poem delivered to the Phi Beta Kappa Society at Harvard in 1850, Bayard Taylor pays tribute to Longfellow's evocation of memories of America's past through indirect allusions to a number of his works and makes the following reference to 'The Skeleton in Armor':

> Honor to him who from his Baltic home
> Followed the Viking over the unploughed foam,
> And heard the sob, when, clad in warlike gear,
> Beside the tower he fell upon his spear.[30]

Ottilie Adeline Liljencrantz prefaced her novel of life in legendary Scandinavian America, *Randvar the Songsmith* (1906), with the full text of the poem and made the Tower the residence of its hero, the son of Longfellow's Viking and princess.

'The Norsemen' and 'The Skeleton in Armor' were analysed as historical poems in the journal *Poet-lore*. 'What have the poets to tell of the great stages in American Life and History?' is the question posed at the beginning of the first of a series of three articles published in 1895,[31] each headed 'School of Literature'. 'The Norsemen' is praised for its 'picturesque allusions' to sites of Viking activity, for its specific and 'effective geographical allusions . . . that take us really to the homes and hearts of the Vikings', and for its insights into Viking culture ('The mention of . . . chants and rhymes . . . give us glimpses of a still more intimate kind, of the Poetry and Religion, the Conquests and the Monuments, of the Northern race' [p. 107]).[32] 'The Skeleton in Armor' is commended in similar terms for the 'picturesque allusions that place before us characteristic habits of Northern life' (p. 47) in the speaker's recollections of hunting, skating, and piracy. Both Longfellow and Whittier are, however, gently and indirectly chided for not having drawn upon the substance of the Vínland sagas themselves:

> Longfellow prefers to invent a romantic story in connection with the unearthed skeleton of Rhode Island, and the supposed Norse Tower. Whittier sees visions in his own fashion over a Norse relic almost as doubtful as the tower.[33]

The writer, 'P.A.C.', endorses the merit of the sagas' claim to a place in the poetic history of America – 'these Norse legends provide a genuine element which should never be lacking from the poetic story of American life and

---

30 *The American Legend. A poem before the Phi beta kappa society of Harvard University, July 18, 1850* (Cambridge, 1850). Micropublished in *American Poetry, 1609–1900: Segment II* (New Haven, 1975), p. 22.
31 P.A.C., 'School of Literature. Poems Illustrative of American History: Longfellow's "Skeleton in Armor" ', *Poet-lore* 7 (1885), 41.
32 P.A.C., 'School of Literature. Poems Illustrative of American History: Whittier's "The Norsemen" ', *Poet-lore* 7 (1895), 106, 107.
33 'School of Literature. Poems Illustrative of American History: Longfellow's "Skeleton in Armor" ', p. 46.

history' – but has to concede that the closest connection of 'The Skeleton in Armor' with American life is 'through the poet's own personality and genius'.[34] The 'historicity' of these poems is, the writer concludes, a cultural one, which furnishes accurate information about Viking life and customs that constitute a higher 'poetic' truth.

Poetic truth and the testimony of the sagas were one thing; the authenticity of New England Viking archaeology was another. In the second series of his satiric *The Biglow Papers* (1867), James Russell Lowell, Longfellow's friend and successor as Smith Professor of the French and Spanish Languages and Professor of Belles Lettres at Harvard, overtly ridiculed Rafn, the inscriptions on the Dighton Rock, and the circumlocutory disclaimers of detraction from the glory of Columbus by those who accepted Leifr Eiríksson as the first European discoverer of America:

> I would by no means be understood as wishing to vilipend the merits of the great Genoese, whose name will never be forgotten so long as the inspiring strains of 'Hail Columbia' shall continue to be heard. Though he must be stripped also of whatever praise may belong to the experiment of the egg, which I find proverbially attributed by Castilian authors to a certain Juanito or Jack, (perhaps an offshoot of our giant-killing mythus,) his name will still remain one of the most illustrious of modern times. But the impartial historian owes a duty likewise to obscure merit . . .
>
> Touching Runic inscriptions, I find that they may be classed under three general heads: 1. Those which are understood by the Danish Royal Society of Northern Antiquaries, and Professor Rafn, their secretary; 2. Those which are comprehensible only by Mr. Rafn; and 3. Those which neither the Society, Mr. Rafn, nor anybody else can be said in any definite sense to understand, and which accordingly offer peculiar temptations to enucleating sagacity.[35]

The object of this witty piece by Lowell's model of New England pedantry, the Reverend Homer Wilbur, is his decoding of a runic stone which reveals the happy news that the doomed Bjarni Grímólfsson of *Eiríks saga rauða* returned to America in later life and discovered the joys of tobacco:

> I was now, and justly, as I think, satisfied of the conscientious exactness of my interpretation. It is as follows:-
>
>
>
> HERE
> BJARNA GRIMOLFFSON
> FIRST DRANK CLOUD-BROTHER
> THROUGH CHILD-OF-LAND-AND-WATER:
>
>
>
> that is, drew smoke through a reed stem. In other words, we have here a record of the first smoking of the herb *Nicotiana Tabacum* by a European on this continent

34 *Ibid.*, pp. 45, 48.
35 *The Poetical Works of James Russell Lowell*, Cambridge edition, revised and with a new Introduction by Marjorie R. Kaufman (Boston, 1978), pp. 253–4. All quotations from Lowell's works are from this edition.

... It is double pleasant, therefore, to meet with this proof that the brave old man arrived safely in Vinland, and that his declining years were cheered by the respectful attentions of the dusky denizens of our then uninvaded forests.

(pp. 254–5)

Nevertheless, Lowell saw the Vínland voyages as fundamental to the myth of national foundation. *The Voyage to Vinland and Other Poems* was his preferred title for a verse collection – 'I liked the poem, thought no title so good as "The Voyage to Vinland, and Other Poems" ', he wrote to Charles Eliot Norton in 1868[36] – otherwise inferior both in his opinion and that of his biographer,[37] which had been written over a period of some twenty years (part of the poem dates back to 1850) and was eventually published as *Under the Willows* (1869). Bjarni Herjólfsson's west-of-Greenland voyage is also briefly mentioned in Lowell's 'Columbus' (in the 1843 collection *Miscellaneous Poems*). Here, on his westward voyage, Columbus muses upon ancient travellers' tales, among them the Vínland voyages, which have inspired his journey:

> I heard Ulysses tell of mountain-chains
> Whose adamantine links, his manacles,
> The western main shook growling, and still gnawed.
> I brooded on the wise Athenian's tale
> Of happy Atlantis, and heard Björne's keel
> Crunch the gray pebbles of the Vinland shore.   (p. 58)

Although Lowell was not a student of Scandinavian literature, *The Biglow Papers* and 'The Voyage to Vinland' demonstrate a familiarity with the material of the Vínland sagas, Old Icelandic verb forms,[38] Norse mythology, and what the poet calls, in the same letter to Norton (*Letters* II: 2), 'the law of the Icelandic alliterated stave'.

Lowell had originally conceived his Vínland poem as a playful piece for himself, entitled 'The Voyage of Leif', in a proposed multi-speakered collection of story and verse, to be framed by the fictional visit of half a dozen old friends to his home in Cambridge, Massachusetts:

> I am to read my poem of the "Voyage of Leif" to Vinland, in which I mean to bring my hero straight into Boston Bay, as befits a Bay-state poet.[39]

In the intervening years the poem progressed from regional entertainment to national epic. Its ultimate stimulus to completion was not contemplation of the Vínland voyages themselves, but, as Lowell relates in another letter to Norton,

36 Charles Eliot Norton, ed., *Letters of James Russell Lowell*, 2 vols (New York, 1977), II, 2.

37 'Lowell's evaluation of the volume needs no revising' (Martin Duberman, *James Russell Lowell*, [Boston, 1966], p. 243).

38 In disputing the claim by the 'Rev. Jonas Tutchel' that the said runic inscription is Þorvaldr Eiríksson's grave stone, Wilbur comments in *The Biglow Papers*: 'He must indeed be ingenious who can make out the words *hèr hvílir* from any characters in the inscription in question' (p. 255).

39 Lowell to C. F. Briggs, 23 January 1850, *Letters* I, 171.

his reading, a few months after the outbreak of the Civil War, of George Webbe Dasent's translation of *Njáls saga*.[40]

'The Voyage to Vinland' is a narrative of mental and geographical discovery by Bjarni Herjólfsson ('Biörn'), which rises to an allegorical crescendo of national achievement when the ideals of the New World – Wisdom, Justice, and Mercy – conquer the follies of the Old. In three parts – (I) 'Biörn's Beckoners'; (II) 'Thorwald's Lay'; (III) 'Gudrida's Prophecy' – the poem charts Biörn's romantic yearning and his response to a skald's exhortation at a Yuletide feast to pursue Opportunity. Thus inspired to set sail in search of his heart's desire,

> 'A ship', he muttered, 'is a wingëd bridge
> That leadeth every way to man's desire,
> And ocean the wide gate to manful luck.'   (p. 312)

Biörn finds it better to travel than to arrive. He experiences only a sense of disappointment when, after a month at sea, he beholds the apparently unprepossessing object of his quest:

> Low in the west were wooded shores like cloud.
> They shouted as men shout with sudden hope;
> But Biörn was silent, such strange loss there is
> Between the dream's fulfilment and the dream,
> Such sad abatement in the goal attained.   (p. 313)

The disenchanted Biörn is abruptly excised from the Vínland story at this point, not in favour of Leifr Eiríksson, but of a prophetess, Gudrida, who proclaims the future glory of the New Land. The Northmen, she says, are fated to be excluded from this paradise ('Yours to behold it, Not to possess it' [p. 313]), which will ultimately be the prize in a contest of mythological proportions between the Old World and the New. The 'old gods', Odin and Thor, will be vanquished by Christ, and an ideal realm, godly, peaceful, pastoral, hospitable, hard-working, self-reliant, egalitarian, just, and merciful, will rise from the ashes of this Götterdämmerung in a classic statement of Puritan values:

> Here men shall grow up
> Strong from self-helping;
> Eyes for the present
> Bring they as eagles,
> Blind to the Past.
>
> They shall make over
> Creed, law, and custom;
> Driving-men, doughty
> Builders of empire,
> Builders of men.
>
> . . .

40 See above, Chapter 2, p. 62.

> Over the ruin
> See I the promise;
> Crisp waves the cornfield,
> Peace-walled, the homestead
> Waits open-doored.
> . . .
> Here shall a realm rise
> Mighty in manhood;
> Justice and Mercy
> Here set a stronghold
> Safe without spear.   (III: 313–14)

In the final four stanzas of the poem the land is figured as a Sleeping Beauty, whose awakening will be attended by the adoration of the meek and the guardianship of the brave:

> Beauty of promise,
> Promise of beauty,
> Safe in the silence
> Sleep thou, till cometh
> Light to thy lids!
>
> Thee shall awaken
> Flame from the furnace,
> Bath of all brave ones,
> Cleanser of conscience,
> Welder of will.
>
> Lowly shall love thee,
> Thee, open-handed!
> Stalwart shall shield thee,
> Thee, worth their best blood,
> Waif of the West!
>
> Then shall come singers,
> Singing no swan-song,
> Birth-carols, rather,
> Meet for the man child
> Mighty of bone.   (III: 314)

In the same year that Lowell began the composition of his Vínland poem, Bayard Taylor evoked the sounds of Viking wassail in 'The American Legend' as a distant counterpoint to the Pilgrims' singing of their 'pious staves' around the nation's cradle:

> Around thy cradle, rocked by wintry waves,
> The Pilgrim Fathers sang their pious staves,
> While like an echo, wandering dim and vast
> Down the snow-laden forests of the Past,
> The Norsemen's hail through bearded lips rang out,
> Frothy with mead, at every wassail-bout.

130

By the middle of the century, poetic celebration of Norse landings in America was moving beyond the commemoration of local landmarks of doubtful provenance and into a wider and more significant frame of reference. By the time of the Centennial, the Vínland voyages were ready for incorporation into the American epic.

Centennial Vínland

James Russell Lowell and Sidney Lanier had in common the composition of odes, narratives on medieval themes, and politically polemical 'dialect poems'.[41] They also appear to be the only two nineteenth-century American poets to have drawn directly on written sources for their accounts of Viking voyages to the West Atlantic. Like Longfellow, Lanier was a student of medieval literature and a professional scholar, who taught at Oglethorpe College, Georgia, between 1859 and 1861 and was appointed lecturer in English Literature at Johns Hopkins University in 1879. Commissioned by *Lippincott's Magazine*, 'Psalm of the West' was originally intended to be set to music.[42] A native of Georgia but an avowedly 'non-regional' writer,[43] Lanier adapts the Vínland voyages, probably via one of the adaptations of *Antiquitates Americanæ*,[44] into a poetic framework which is entirely American: nothing less than the broad sweep of European American history from the pre-Columbian era to 1876.

Whereas Lowell's underlying metaphor for the Vínland voyages is a literary one – when 'yellow-bearded kings' haunt Biörn's dreams, 'Strange sagas read he in their sea-blue eyes' (I: 311); his ship becomes the instrument of the first textual record of American history ('the brave prow that cut on Vinland sands/ The first rune in the Saga of the West' II: 312) – Lanier's is primarily symphonic. Just as the Pilgrim Fathers sing their 'pious staves' to a background of Viking toasts in 'The American Legend', so the Vínland voyages strike the opening chords of Lanier's national symphony.

The Norse chapter in this history of the United States is the first of two 'discovery' sections, where the uncovering of the new land is relayed in images of darkness and light which culminate in Columbus's sighting of light ashore. The Vínland voyages take the form of twin sequences, in which the voyages of Bjarni Herjólfsson and Ari Mársson[45] are separated from those of the family of Eiríkr and Karlsefni by a 28-line iambic apostrophe to a night-time landscape of the West. Bjarni's tentative incursion into New World waters comes in response

41 Roy Harvey Pearce, *The Continuity of American Poetry* (Princeton, 1961), p. 239.
42 *The Centennial Edition of the Works of Sidney Lanier*, ed. Charles R. Anderson, 10 vols (Baltimore, 1945), I (*Poems and Poem Outlines*), p. xlviii. All quotations are from this edition.
43 Edd Winfield Parks, *Sidney Lanier: the Man, the Poet, the Critic* (Athens, Ga., 1968), p. 41.
44 Lanier makes no specific reference to his source in correspondence between March and May 1876 which concerns the composition of the poem (*Works of Sidney Lanier*, IX, 340–66).
45 See above, Chapter 1, p. 31.

to the poem's speaker's plea to God that the vacuum of the western 'Sea of Darkness' should be visited by humankind. His actions are those of a sleep-walker, a pallid strayer to an ice-bound 'waste hell of slate' which is identified in a second stanzaic sequence as Helluland:

> Into the Sea of the Dark doth creep
>   Björne's pallid sail,
> As the face of a walker in his sleep,
>   Set rigid and most pale,
> About the night doth peer and peep
>   In a dream of an ancient tale.
>
> . . .
>
> *God save such land! Go by go by,*
>   *Here may no mortal rest,*
> *Where this waste hell of slate doth lie*
>   *And grind the glacier's breast.*   (pp. 65–6)

These dark waters are only momentarily illuminated by the lamps of Björne's crew, who, stirred by his waking cry, search for whatever ghost has disturbed his slumber:

> *Let us see the ghost* – his household fly
>   With lamps to search the night –
> So Norsemen's sails run out and try
>   The Sea of the Dark with light.

Timid Bjarni is overtaken in the second half of this ten-stanza sequence by the more robust figure of Are Marson, who careers southwards to Hvítra-mannaland, which is located, where Rafn placed it,[46] in the southern United States. The warmth and lushness of Georgia, Florida, and Carolina are in striking opposition to the dark and chilly landscape of the preceding stanzas, and Are's voyage becomes the prelude to a four-stanza hymn of praise to the verdant South, in which the paradisial attributes of Vínland in *Grænlendinga saga* – temperate climate and abundance of natural resources – are transferred to Hvítramannaland:

> Stout Are Marson, southward whirled
>   From out the tempest's hand,
> Doth skip the sloping of the world
>   To Huitramannaland,
> Where Georgia's oaks with moss-beards curled
>   Wave by the shining strand,
>
> And sway in sighs from Florida's Spring
>   Or Carolina's Palm –
> What time the mocking-bird doth bring

---

46 See *AA*, p. XXXVII.

The woods his artist's-balm,
Singing the Song of Everything
   Consummate-sweet and calm –

Land of large merciful-hearted skies,
   Big bounties, rich increase,
Green rests for Trade's blood-shotten eyes,
   For o'er-beat brains surcease,
For Love the dear woods' sympathies,
   For Grief the wise woods' peace,

For Need rich givings of hid powers
   In hills and vales quick-won,
For Greed large exemplary flowers
   That n'er have toiled nor spun,
For Heat fair-tempered winds and showers,
   For Cold the neighbor sun.

Land where the Spirits of June-heat
   From out their forest-maze
Stray forth at eve with loitering feet,
   And fervent hymns upraise
In bland accord and passion sweet
   Along the Southern ways.

The political bias towards the South which Lanier studiously avoided in his writing becomes topographical instead. The first two verses in the second stanzaic sequence, which relates Leif's visit to Taunton, Massachusetts, are prefaced by a three-stanza apostrophe to New England, where Vínland is a forbidding land of strong winds, lowering mountains, and angry rivers:

Land where the strenuous-handed Wind
   With sarcasm of a friend
Doth smite the man would lag behind to frontward of his end;
Yea, where the taunting fall and grind
   Of Nature's Ill doth send

Such mortal challenge of a clown
   Rude-thrust upon the soul,
That men but smile where mountains frown
   Or scowling waters roll,
And Nature's front of battle down
   Do hurl from pole to pole.

Succeeding Vínland voyages are incorporated into another iambic interlude which ends with the murder of Helgi and Finnbogi ('Hellboge and Finnge'):

Now long the Sea of Darkness glimmers low
With sails from Northland flickering to and fro –
Thorwald, Karlsefne, and those twin heirs of woe,
Hellboge and Finnge, in treasonable bed

> Slain by the ill-born child of Eric Red,
> Freydisa false . . .

Darkness descends again, and the land returns to a state of nothingness, to await the arrival of the Niña, the Pinta, and the Santa Maria.

The Vínland voyages reappear towards the end of the poem in a synoptic recapitulation of the history of the United States. The progress of its European history is delineated in a concert of song and verse, to which the arrival of Bjarni and his crew provides a faint and distant overture:

> Ghostly rhymes of Norsemen pale
> Staring by old Björne's sail,
> Strains more noble of that night
> Worn Columbus saw his Light,
> Psalms of still more heavenly tone,
> How the Mayfellow tossed alone,
> Olden tale and later song
> Of the Patriot's love and wrong,
> Grandsire's ballad, nurse's hymn –

Fifty years later, another creative or, as one reviewer called it, 'subjective' history of America,[47] William Carlos Williams's collection of prose essays *In the American Grain* (1925),[48] began with the stories of Eiríkr rauði and Freydís. Instead of making the Vínland story a self-contained prelude to the post-Columbian conquest of America, Williams integrates it into a conception of American history which, Bryce Conrad argues, underlies the work as a whole: the successful defence by the female New World against the 'implantation of the sperm'.[49] In the first part of 'Red Eric', Eric gives a first-person account of his thrusting through the ice to found the Greenland settlement; the second part of the essay is the third-person story of Freydis. Eric successfully inseminates Greenland; Freydis's actions bring Viking voyages to America to an end and so provide a 500-year reprieve for the New World from the next wave of her Old World ravishers.[50]

---

47 Kenneth Burke, 'Subjective History', *New York Herald Tribune Books*, March 14, 1926. On the early reception of this book, see Bryce Conrad, *Refiguring America. A Study of William Carlos Williams' In the American Grain* (Urbana and Chicago, 1990), pp. 1–11.

48 *In the American Grain. Essays by William Carlos Williams*, introd. Horace Gregory (Harmondsworth, 1989).

49 See Conrad, *Refiguring America*, pp. 104–55.

50 'The truculent Freydis becomes the defender of the New World's matriarchal essence. Her bloody deeds are what drives the tide of history from the shores of America, restoring the New World to that state of "immaculate fulfillment" that continues inviolate until Columbus' symbolic rape' (Conrad, *Refiguring America*, p. 139).

Early twentieth-century Vínland

It was not until the publication of *The Thrall of Leif the Lucky* (1902) by Ottilie Liljencrantz, the most successful American writer of Scandinavian historical fiction, that the Vínland story took fully fledged fictional form. Her novels and those of her successors to the mid-1920s, when stories of modern immigrant life became the predominant subject of the Scandinavian experience in American narrative, are informed by an ideology very different from the popular imperialist ideals of the superiority of Northern efficiency, masculinity, and race which underpin the Vínland fiction of late Victorian and early twentieth-century British writers. In the pattern of missionary discourse which was to continue in early twentieth-century American novels of medieval Scandinavia,[51] religious imperialism is the governing ethos of Liljencrantz's Vínland fiction. The Vínland voyages are related as an episode in the conversion of the North in *The Thrall of Leif the Lucky*, and, in *The Vinland Champions* (1904), as religious exemplum. *Randvar the Songsmith: A Romance of Norumbega* (1906) invites interpretation as a moral fable. Liljencrantz's works, says the biographical note in *A Viking's Love* (1911), a posthumously published collection of stories of ancient Scandinavia, 'are all morally wholesome'.

The *Thrall of Leif the Lucky* was as popular in America as *The Norsemen in America* was in England.[52] The *New York Times* reviewer found it 'interesting and absolutely clean' and likely to hold the attention of its readers through a single sitting'.[53] Infused with an evangelical zeal more strident than that of *Eiríks saga rauða*, *The Thrall of Leif the Lucky* is also strongly influenced by the Aryan supremacist views of Charles Kingsley, who is cited, among a raft of historians, scholars, and eccentrics, as a source of inspiration in the book's 'Note of Acknowledgment'.[54] The Vikings in this novel are exemplars of the master race, their brutality tempered by purity and truth, 'as', says the Foreword, 'befits the boyhood of the mighty Anglo-Saxon race'. Stern, broad-shouldered, hawk-nosed, and steely-eyed, Leif Ericsson, although celibate, is otherwise a muscular Christian in the Charles Kingsley mode. He is 'the Lucky' because he is a Christian and, despite his pagan reprobate father, has found favour with Olaf Tryggvason. Leif is prepared to suffer martyrdom for his faith and expects his men to be ready to do the same:

---

51 See George LeRoy White, *Scandinavian Themes in American Fiction* (Philadelphia, 1937), pp. 23–5, 31–5. Genevra Snedden's children's story *Leif and Thorkel: Two Norse Boys of Long Ago* (1922), which is largely concerned with Leif's childhood and youth in Norway, is the exception here.
52 By late 1904 it had gone through eight printings. See White, *Scandinavian Themes*, p. 26.
53 *New York Times*, May 31, 1902, p. 361.
54 Liljencrantz acknowledges a debt to the studies of 'Rafn, Torfeus, Vigfusson, Mallet, Keyser, Anderson, Du Chaillu, Endnader, Rink, Tegner', and also the 'works of John Fiske, Eben Norton Horsford, Thomas Wentworth Higginson, Alexander von Humboldt, J. S. C. Abbott, Bayard Taylor, Charles Kingsley, William Cullen Bryant, Aaron Goodrich, and others'. All references are to O. A. Liljencrantz, *The Thrall of Leif the Lucky* (London, Melbourne, Toronto, 1904).

And not only am I a Christian, but every man who calls himself mine is also one, and will let blood-eagles be cut in his back rather than change his faith.   (p. 145)

Viking violence, indulgently attributed in the Foreword to 'the unchastened turbulence of youth' but extending to acts of savage discipline, such as the flogging of young Alwin, the nobly-born Anglo-Saxon who is the titular thrall of the novel, can be read as Liljencrantz's expression of the primeval Teutonic energy or *thumos* which Charles Kingsley identified as the life force of manliness.[55]

Unlike the infantilized indigenes of English imperial Vínland narrative, Liljencrantz's New World natives ('Skraellings') evolve from sadistic executioners in *The Thrall of Leif the Lucky*, to instruments of God's vengeance in *The Vinland Champions*, and, in *Randvar the Songsmith*, unspoiled sons of the earth. In repellent contrast to the manly Norsemen in *The Thrall of Leif the Lucky*, the Skraellings are scrawny, swarthy, animalistic pygmies with 'fierce beast-mouth and . . . small tricky eyes in . . . great sockets', who communicate in bestial grunts:

> They were not imposing . . . Two of their lean arms would not have made one of the Wrestler's magnificent white limbs, and the tallest among them could not have reached above Alwin's shoulders. Skins were their only coverings; and the coarseness of their bristling black locks could have been equalled only in the mane of a wild horse . . . When they began talking together, it was in a succession of grunts and growls and guttural sounds that bore more resemblance to animal noises than to human speech. (p. 323)

Their sole narrative function is to visit a hellish fate upon the novel's villain, a treacherous compatriot of Leif's named Kark, who suffers an offstage but lingering despatch. 'Evidently it is not the excitement of fighting which they enjoy, but the pleasure of torturing' (p. 330), exclaims Alwin's friend, Rolf, who is inclined to suspect that the killers must be trolls.

The natives' demonic presence asserts itself only in the presence of evil. Vínland otherwise remains a virgin paradise of vines, wheat, and honey-sweet dew. A mingling of metaphors from 'The Song of Solomon' and 'The Battle Hymn of the Republic' tropes its conquest by the Norsemen as a divinely authorized act:

> To plunge unstinted hands into the hoarded wealth of ages, to be the first to hunt in a game-stocked forest and the first to cast hook in a fish-teeming river, – to have the first skimming of nature's cream-pans as it were, – was a delight so keen that, saving war and love, they could imagine nothing to equal it.
>
> Like children upon honey, they fell upon the gift that had tumbled out of nature's horn of plenty, and swept through the vineyard in a devastating army.

---

55 On this subject see, for example, David Rosen, 'The volcano and the cathedral: muscular Christianity and the origins of primal manliness', in Donald E. Hall, ed., *Muscular Christianity. Embodying the Victorian Age* (Cambridge, 1994), pp. 30–1.

Snuffing the sweet scent of the sun-heated grapes, they ate and sang and jested as they gathered, in the most innocent carousel of their lives.   (pp. 296–7)

Not until the final stages of *The Thrall of Leif the Lucky* is it revealed that the Vinland enterprise has served a cause far greater than the discovery of America, namely, the extension of the empire of Christ. On his triumphant return to Greenland, Leif receives homage from the Norse Greenlanders, gives honour and glory for his Vinland voyage to God, and inspires *en masse* conversion by the hitherto recalcitrantly pagan populace, thereby enacting the evangelizing mission of the Spanish in the New World in reverse. As he bows before the Cross, a chorus of voices declare their allegiance to Christ. In the closing lines Leif himself is elevated to Christ-like stature when Alwin pledges his lifelong fealty by kissing the hem of his cloak:

'What I have done I have been able to do by the help of my God whom you reject. To Him I give the thanks and the glory.'
In that humility which is higher than pride, he raised the silver crucifix from his breast and bent his head before it. Out of the hush that followed, a man's voice rang strongly, – the voice of one of Greenland's foremost chiefs.
'Hail to the god of Leif Ericsson! The God that helped him must be all-powerful. Henceforth I will believe that he and no one else is the only God. Hail to the Cross!'
. . . Alwin bent and touched the scarlet cloak-hem with his lips . . . 'So faithful will I be to you hereafter.'   (pp. 353–4)

The primary concern of Liljencrantz's next novel, *The Vinland Champions*, is the forfeiture of Vinland through the sin of Cain in an act committed not, as in *Grænlendinga saga*, by Freydís upon her fellow countrymen, but by a Norse settler upon a Skrælling. In the interests of strengthening the Vinland settlement, acquiring knowledge of the land's topography, and enjoying profitable trading relations, Thorfinn Karlsefne initially insists, like Ballantyne's Karlsefin, that they make 'friends' (p. 51)[56] of the natives. Figured in the first part of the novel as a form of game, these are 'creatures' (p. 23) to be stalked as objects of observation rather than as prey. Karlsefne's nephew, Alrek Ingolfsson, and his friend, Gard, make a trip one night to the grave of Thorwald Ericsson for some Skrælling spotting:

– the Skraellings! Some had been trapped and had not yet escaped, and it was going to fall to him to get sight of them. To succeed where all the rest had failed! To be the one to give Kaarlsefne the information he wanted!   (pp. 36–7)

Gard accuses him of scaring them away and getting 'all the sport' (p. 42) for himself. Predicting that, in time to come, 'a white face . . . will become to the

---

56 References are to Ottilie A. Liljencrantz, *The Vinland Champions* (London, Melbourne, Toronto, 1911).

wild men a token of bloodshed' (p. 165), Karlsefne declares the Skrællings a protected species and makes killing them a capital offence.

Prior to the homicide, the Skraellings are harmlessly bovine: one feeds upon curds 'with half-shut eyes and an air of solemn content' (p. 142). When they arrive at Karlsefne's camp to trade their furs, they are briefly humanized as 'wild men' (p. 141) and 'forest men' (p. 146) but are also reduced by synecdoche, as in Nevil Shute's *An Old Captivity*, to body parts. In the furs-for-dairy products exchange, a 'copper-coloured palm' (p. 142) receives a cheese ball, and a Norse bondmaid ladles curds into a 'gaping mouth' (*ibid.*). After the murder, of which Alrek is falsely accused, the Skrællings metamorphose into a sinister and threatening force. At the same time as a large host attacks the settlement from the sea, another army of ghost-like 'Things' (pp. 238, 239), malevolent 'creatures with gaudy-coloured bodies naked as earthworms, and bristling black heads feathered like monstrous birds' (p. 243) flit menacingly through the forest. Only the appearance of a raging bull scares them to flight.

Ultimately they become a divine scourge, invading 'in herds and shoals and swarms' (p. 268). This plague, says Karlsefne, is retribution for the settlers' failure to keep what he calls their own 'beast-cravings' (p. 249) in check. At the very moment when Alrek faces a grapevine noose, the killer is finally revealed as his kinsman, Hallad. A higher power has nevertheless condemned the Norsemen to suffer the collective punishment of being drummed out of Eden. Karlsefne explains:

> they will always come in herds and shoals and swarms, as when the Lord sends a plague of creatures on a country. For I think it is as a plague they have come upon us. Here the All-Father had spread a Heaven-like land, and stored it with food and property for all . . . It might have been a never-emptied treasure-house for all our race, a peace-land for Northmen of all time. The trouble that has come into it is of our own bringing, brought in blood as vermin are brought in ships. The hand of the Lord is against us; it is my advice that we bow before His wrath. Natures such as ours have no right to softer things than Greenland cold and Iceland rock. It is my ruling that when the spring comes we shall go back over the ocean.
>
> (pp. 268–9)

The Thrall of Leif the Lucky and *The Vinland Champions* were regarded as rewarding reading for English adolescents. An end page, headed 'Gift Books for Boys', of the 1911 edition (by Ward, Lock & Co.) of *The Vinland Champions* lists *The Thrall of Leif the Lucky* and *The Vinland Champions* among 'A New Series of Boys' Books . . . The greatest care has been exercised in the selection of the tales included, and no more beautiful prize or gift books have ever been offered to the public'. One such prizewinner was the original owner of the pristine copy of *The Thrall of Leif the Lucky* now held in the State Library of Victoria, Australia. According to its bookplate, the novel was awarded to Archibald Fitzgibbon of Albert Park School, Melbourne, as a swimming prize in 1924. Perhaps a copy of Ballantyne's *The Norsemen in the West* might have shown more signs of readerly wear than this often grisly story of stern morality, which is unrelieved by that novel's scenes of cosy domesticity, genial frustrating of native knavish tricks, and seductive descriptions of the North American wilderness.

Randvar the Songsmith: A Romance of Norumbega takes the story of Norse America from Vínland to mythical Norumbega and continues the tale of Long-fellow's lovers in 'The Skeleton in Armor', here named Rolf and Freya, into the next generation through their son, Randvar. The moral of the novel is that homespun Northern integrity is superior to the decadence of southern Euro-pean manners. The corruption of the Francophile Old World is pitted against the integrity of the plain-speaking man and the noble savage of the New. Norumbega, under the rule of a certain Starkad Jarl at the time of the Norman Conquest, is no 'straggling line of cabins, no huddle of tented booths' (p. 83)[57] but a prosperous town of two thousand inhabitants, graced by vine-clad hills, great estates, tree-lined avenues, and broad thoroughfares. Its courtly society presents a dazzling pageant of aristocratic high-life. The spectators to a hunt arrive in stately procession on the heels of the hounds:

> The din passed at last, and on its heels came a colorful train – stately old priests and chieftains gravely discussing the hunts of their youth, high-born maidens with shining uncovered locks, and matrons whose lace veils floated cloudily from their moon like faces, stocky young thralls bent under hampers and wine-skins, and towering leather-clad guardsmen bearing bright spears on their shoulders.
>
> (pp. 8–9)

Ladies of the court assemble for a feast in a shining spectacle of gold, silk, and flowing tresses:

> Through the broad portal was advancing a train of court-women, walking far apart because of the trailing length of their silken robes, stately matrons with towering head-dresses, and white-armed maidens whose bright tresses fell free from golden bands.   (p. 95)

Destined to win the love of Starkad's daughter, Brynhild, Randvar lives an antithetically simple life as a forester with his foster-mother and the ageing remnants of Rolf's crew on the fringes of Norumbega, in the draughty ruins of Longfellow's 'Skeleton in Armor' Tower. But glittering appearance is an unreli-able mark of true character. The fine manners of Olaf, the French-reared rival wooer of Brynhild, disguise his moral shallowness; Starkad's son, Helvin is a werewolf and patricide; and Randvar's royal pedigree cannot be obliterated by his rustic lifestyle. 'If my King's blood cannot show itself through a layer of deerskin', he tells Brynhild, 'I hold it for a spring that is run dry' (p. 33).

Here, for the first time, Liljencrantz acknowledges Native Americans as 'that new-world race which the early Norse explorers called Skraellings' (p. 5) and upgrades them from bestial to botanical simile. One, for example, has 'hair as

---

57 References are to Ottilie A. Liljencrantz, *Randvar the Songsmith. A Romance of Norumbega* (New York and London, 1906).

black as freshly turned leaf-mould, and a shining naked body of the hue of an oak-leaf in November' (*ibid.*). A brave, referred to only as 'Red man', and Randvar, who has learned his language, are companions. In insights which are never credited to the natives in contemporary English Vínland literature, their conversation reveals that 'Red man' knows all too well that the white man sees him as an animal, who regards his homeland as no more than a feeding ground, and with whom interaction is solely a means of profit:

> He comes among us as one who comes among animals – driving them out to possess himself of their feeding-ground – dealing with them only when he wants profit out of their hides. (p. 12)

Randvar in turn declares his admiration for the native Norumbegans, whose love of freedom, fearlessness, and artistic talents embody, he says, the (implicitly lost) ideals of the heroic Viking past.

Music provides the means of cultural rapprochement when, in order to show his fellows that the 'forest men' share their own values of 'strong simplicity' (p. 107), Randvar, Helvin's 'song-maker', entertains the court retainers at a banquet with a song about a self-sacrificing Skrælling chief. The 'Skrælling love-song' (p. 114) with which Randvar serenades Brynhild persuades her that the natives must be human after all: 'When I hear you sing, creatures who have seemed to me no more than beasts become human like myself' (p. 115). The Skrællings are, moreover, prepared to dedicate their fighting skills to Randvar against the increasingly deranged and tyrannical Helvin:

> Say to the white chief that the men of the stone-axe race have set up their houses around him. Say to him that they turn their weapons whither he points. Say to him that they will bring him the white sachem's red scalp whenever he gives the sign. (p. 301)

Randvar's foster-brother, Eric, is forced to concede that 'ugliness' is an unreliable guide to true worth:

> when your experience of life has been as broad as mine has, sooner will you choose their ugly worth than the fair falseness of the Town-people. (p. 301)

Substance eventually triumphs over show, and the plain-speaking hero becomes the ruler of glamorous Norumbega. Randvar and Brynhild abandon the false splendour of Helvin's court for the forest Tower, only to be recalled in the last pages of the novel to take their places as Starkad's successors after Helvin's death. With Randvar at the helm, allied by a formal trading treaty with an indigenous people who are the spiritual heirs of the 'gothic' credo, the New World looks to a glorious future.

Hervey Allen's undistinguished poem, 'Saga of Leif the Lucky', published in *The Bookman* in 1923, writes the subsequent history of Norumbega from a contrastingly pessimistic perspective. Vínland fails not through the short-comings of its colonists but because the Black Death severs its economic lifeline to Greenland. Darkness and decay enshroud once-bustling Norumbega. The poem's dominant 'light versus darkness' metaphor constructs a crudely racist image of Vinland's natives. Demonized monsters, dark of spirit, and useless of purpose, they serve only to effect the racial degeneration of the settlement's dwindling survivors:

> The Redmen and the *Skraelings*
> Kept the coasts,
> With darkness in their brains,
> Stealing up and down a little way
> On useless, evil errands
> Like painted demon ghosts;
> . . .
> And the youths followed old desires
> Finding flat nosed brides beside the *Skraeling* fires;
> Stone axes took the place of steel;
> Bears' claws the teeth of seal;
> Black hair the fair.[58]

Leif is restored to the pinnacle of greatness in the closing section of the poem – and the Leifr vs. Columbus contest is neatly resolved – when his spirit emerges from a 400-year sleep to inspire and guide Columbus to the shores of San Salvador:

> And Leif was there the night
> That they saw the mysterious light;
> . . .
> Leif was the first on the shore,
> When they fired the glad salve
> On San Salvador.   (p. 403)

The only twentieth-century American play to draw on the Vínland story, Charles Rann Kennedy's *The Winterfeast*, which opened at the Savoy Theatre on Broadway in November 1908, casts interracial union in a more romantic light. Set in an Icelandic farmhouse twenty years after the conversion of Iceland, the action hinges on a love triangle between Valbrand, son of the resolutely heathen Thorkel; Thorkel's foster-son, Bjorn; and Valbrand's wife, Herdisa. The *New York Times* reviewer applauded this five-act melodrama as 'a tragedy of great spiritual and pictorial beauty' but considered its four-hour duration, which covers the time from seven to ten o'clock on the stormy night of 14 October 1020, too taxing for most playgoers.[59] Time has eroded its impact and scrambled its semiotics. Late twentieth-century audiences are likely to be disconcerted by the author's stage directions for a set swathed in 7–8 foot

---

58 Hervey Allen, 'Saga of Leif the Lucky', *The Bookman* (New York) 58 (1923), 401.
59 'Kennedy's Tragedy. "The Winterfeast" ', *New York Times*, December 1, 1908, p. 9.

tapestries patterned in swastikas (p. 14)[60] and unlikely to be awed by the play's ponderous 'Norse' English, as typified in its opening lines:

THORKEL. What is thy task, thrall?
ODD. I mend Valbrand's sword, Master Thorkel.
THORKEL. So? How brake he his sword?
ODD. Nay, the sword is good enow. I do but bind it with hemp round the haft – to hold by. (p. 19)

A cryptic and provocative reference early in the play, by a Christian priest named Ufeig, to a tale told by Thorkel on his return, alone, from a trip to Vineland with Bjorn some twenty years earlier, suggests that the consequences of that voyage will constitute the action of the piece, an impression heavily reinforced by stage direction and italics:

UFEIG. I would talk of that old tale of thine which thou didst spin twenty years ago, Thorkel – *that day when thou wert come from Vineland over the seas.* 'Twas the only time in all thy life what thou wert known to play the skald.

[A curious change comes over THORKEL.]

THORKEL. Ssh! What canst thou have to say – of *that?*
UFEIG. *All that there is to know of it, I know.* (pp. 26–7)

Although attenuated, pagan–Christian conflict has a significant part in the drama. In a situation which has its parallels with the rivalry between Kjartan and Bolli for the hand of Guðrún in *Laxdœla saga*,[61] Bjorn and Thorkel are both said to have sought Herdisa in marriage. Twenty years later, Thorkel tells Valbrand that his motivation for the trip to Vineland, which left Bjorn stranded there, was not only to remove Bjorn from contention in the marriage suit but also to distance himself from the irritant of Christianity. On his return from Vineland, Thorkel delivered an insulting and fallacious salutation to Herdisa from Bjorn, and she consequently married Valbrand. Long presumed dead, Bjorn gives warning of his imminent return on the day of the Winterfeast through a message and token which have been given to Ufeig by an apparent stranger on a ship recently arrived in Iceland. Tensions mount, the play climaxes with the killing of Bjorn by Valbrand, and ends with the death of most of the cast.

Kennedy adds a new dimension to the Vínland story – and ventures into territory occupied in real life by John Rolfe, John Smith, and Pocahontas in the seventeenth century;[62] by Chateaubriand in *Atala* (1800); and by writers of

---

60 References are to Charles Rann Kennedy, *The Winterfeast* (New York and London, 1908).
61 Ed. Einar Ól. Sveinsson, *Íslenzk fornrit* 5 (Reykjavík, 1934); trans. Magnus Magnusson and Hermann Pálsson (Harmondsworth, 1969), chs 41–43.
62 For Smith's account of his capture by Powhatan and rescue by Pocahontas, see *Captain John Smith: A select edition of his writings*, ed. Karen Ordahl Kupperman (Chapel Hill and London, 1988), pp. 58–67.

popular late eighteenth-century American fiction and early nineteenth-century drama (James N. Barker's play *The Indian Princess* was written in 1808, and George Washington Custis's *Pocahontas* some twenty years later)[63] – in making an unnamed princess of 'the Red Folk' Bjorn's liberator and lover. Her role, however, remains restricted to Bjorn's narrative, and she is doubly voiceless because, as Bjorn tells his listeners, verbal communication between them was impossible: 'Forsooth, the poor soul scarce gathered a word of mine all the year I lived with her. We spake two tongues, she and I' (p. 64). The princess, he says, delivered Thorkel and himself from certain death at the hands of her kin. After leading Bjorn and his company safely to their ships, she fled into the forest. Bjorn jumped ship to rescue her from retribution, but by the time he had accomplished his mission, the fleet had sailed, and a hostile crowd of Red Folk had gathered on the shore. In the couple's ensuing flight, she saved his life six more times. They cohabited for twelve months, after which she died, having borne him a son, Olaf.

Vineland itself serves only as spawning ground for the tragedy. When, '[c]lean-shaven, and clad in byrnie and shining Viking helm with eagle feathers' (p. 112), Olaf makes his appearance at the end of Act 3, he has shed all outward trace of his Amerindian ancestry except for the plumage on his helmet. The land of his birth is swiftly dismissed as an object of interest in itself and his allegiance swiftly transferred to Iceland when he falls in love with Valbrand's daughter, Swanhild:

SWANHILD. 'Tis a fair land hath grown thee. Tell me thereof.
OLAF. 'Tis far off, over the sea. Much have I loved my land, and counted it the only land for me. Now I have found another. (p. 120)

Olaf's mother, who has served solely as aristocratic progenitor in a liaison clearly doomed beyond the shores of Vineland, exists only as a distant and inarticulate memory.

Clara Sharpe Hough's melodramatic novel *Leif the Lucky* (1926) directly links passion and conversion. The untimely arrival in Greenland of Leif's Hebridean mistress, Brenda, and their child, Cormic, puts an end to Leif's aspirations for the hand of the relentlessly virtuous Gudrid, who, appalled at the evidence of his incontinence, plights her troth to Karlsefni instead. Thwarted desire turns the previously sunny-tempered Leif the Lucky into a murderous monster, who abandons his burgeoning interest in Christianity for the old pagan ways in order to win Gudrid by fair means or foul. Only after his blasphemous prayers to Christ backfire and result in the death of his brother, Thorwald, and Brenda deliberately, although not lethally, drinks from the poisoned chalice prepared by Leif for Karlsefni at the wedding feast, does he

---

63 On this theme in late eighteenth-century American fiction, see Louise R. Barnett, *The Ignoble Savage: American Literary Racism, 1790–1890* (Westwood, Conn., 1975), p. 113.

repent and embrace both Brenda and Christianity. They marry and sail off to Vineland with Cormic as the novel ends:

> This was Brenda who could dare the sea like a Viking's daughter, who was fit mate for Leif the Lucky, bold and fearless as himself . . . But she was a saucy jade!
>
> The *Long Serpent* was late that morning hoisting sail, but before the sun reached the noon-mark in the heavens, she was sliding down the fjord to turn her nose toward Vineland.
>
> She had to wait for Leif Eriksson, her master, who was hours late to get to the quay, but who came, when he did come, striding down the sunny hill with his son set on his shoulder.   (p. 346)[64]

Leif, Brenda, and their descendants will, we assume, live happily ever after in the New World.

*

American poetry and prose from the middle of the nineteenth century to the first quarter of the twentieth celebrate individual acts of enterprise and heroism which take the Norsemen to the New World and present them to the reader as precursors of national greatness. For poets of the mid-nineteenth century, the trailblazing and sometimes one-way voyage to a New World empty of prior claimants is the dominant motif of Norse landfalls west of Greenland. Although Leifr and Karlsefni are either anonymous or minor players in the Viking voyages of Whittier, Longfellow, and Lowell, these poets share a common vision of the new land as arena for present and future bold and noble deeds. Some thirty-five years later, Sidney Lanier grafted the Vínland voyages onto the national genealogical tree in commemoration of the American Centennial. Whereas the 1870s gave rise to the first stirrings of imperial anxiety in England, where fiction writers confronted the material of the Vínland sagas as a story of failed colonization, the decade of the Centennial brought with it increasing confidence in the power, prosperity, and destiny of the United States. In the late nineteenth- and early twentieth-century novels of Ottilie Liljencrantz, Vínland is less prospective profitable colony, except insofar as it extends the empire of Christ, than promised land for heroes whose physical strength is matched by their moral integrity.

---

64 Clara Sharpe Hough, *Leif the Lucky. A romantic saga of the sons of Erick the Red* (New York and London, 1926).

Epilogue: Postcolonial Vínland

Post-World War II literature in English has brought radical shifts of perspective to the Vínland voyages. Missionary zeal and popular imperialism have been replaced by reworkings of the story from feminist and indigenous perspectives. Joan Clark, for example, tells the story from the point of view of Freydís. The folly of unenlightened colonialism is demonstrated by Francis Berry. Amerindian prior right of occupancy is acknowledged by Paul Metcalfe and George Mackay Brown. The consequences of the Old World's impact upon the environment and ecology of the New are anticipated by Mackay Brown, William T. Vollman, and Thomas Pynchon. Vínland itself has been re-evaluated in a number of ways: as doomed paradise; as semi-legendary haven for the weary; as beautiful but deadly destination; as idyllic context for hardworking pioneers; as lush land of Lotus-Eaters. In Kim Robinson's short story, 'Vinland the Dream' (1991),[1] the tale of Vínland is itself revealed to be an entirely modern construct: the artefacts at L'Anse-aux-Meadows were planted less than two hundred years ago, and the accounts of the Vínland voyages in *Grœnlendinga saga* and *Eiríks saga rauða* are forged insertions dating from the early nineteenth century.

The discovery of evidence of Norse occupation at L'Anse-aux-Meadows prompted a retelling of the Vínland voyages by Charles Olson in *Maximus Poems* (1975), a survey of the whole of American history from the perspective of the seaport of Gloucester, Massachusetts. Without mention of the saga principals – Bjarni, Leif, Karlsefni, Guðríðr – Olson makes the heroes of his historical-mythic epic of North America the fishermen of Gloucester and other early settlers of the northeast seaboard, who come not as fortune hunters or land-grabbers but as tillers of the sea. The Vínland voyages are introduced through the eyes of a local fisherman, George Decker, the spokesman for the residents of L'Anse-aux-Meadows, who in 1960 directed Helge Ingstad to the bumps and ridges, just south of the village at the tip of the Great Northern Peninsula, which contained the evidence of Norse presence. Decker is foregrounded in the opening lines of the poem:

---

1 In *Remaking History* (New York, 1991), pp. 108–19.

George Decker: A fisherman told him,
                George Decker, over at
Lancey Meadow   l'Anse aux Meadow   l'Anse aux Meadow

And George Decker, (when he got there) sd
Anything goes on
At Lancey Meadow
I know – there is
evidence down at
Black Duck Beach.
There was. Norse
persons
by carbon date
1006 had
come ashore
here Had built
houses, had set up
a peat bog iron
forge. Were
living
Lancey Meadow
1006
AD   (p. 76)[2]

Carbon dating, not the Vínland sagas, provides the evidence of the presence of the Norsemen, who are 'Los Americans/ Number One (after/ Skraelings)'.

In the second half of Paul Metcalfe's poem 'Shick Shock' (1976),[3] passages quoted from Magnus Magnusson and Hermann Pálsson's translation of *Græn-lendinga saga* and *Eiríks saga rauða* (*The Vínland Sagas*)[4] and from one of the legends on the Vínland Map execute a progressive textual takeover of the indigenous history of America. 'Shick Shock' begins with the crossing of the Bering Strait by natives of Siberia and goes on to relate the settlement of North America, Greenland, and Mexico by groups of different tribes. In the last third of the poem, the native history of the Americas is overwhelmed by the arrival of Europeans. This event takes the form of large, intrusive chunks of *The Vínland Sagas*, the aggressive and overwhelming nature of which is signified in upper case. Tribal migrations come to a halt, and the textual march of *Grænlendinga saga* is interrupted only by Amerindian observation of 'the Whites' converging from all directions on the land:

---

2 Charles Olson, *The Maximus Poems. Volume Three*, eds Charles Boer and George F. Butterick (New York, 1975).

3 In *Apalache* (Berkeley, 1976).

4 Magnus Magnusson and Hermann Pálsson, trans. and introd., *The Vinland Sagas: The Norse Discovery of America. Grænlendinga Saga and Eirik's Saga* (Harmondsworth, 1965).

BJARNI ORDERED HIS MEN TO SHORTEN SAIL AND
NOT TO GO HARDER THAN SHIP AND RIGGING COULD STAND . . .

> . . . persons floating in from the east: the Whites
> were coming.

SOME TIME LATER, BJARNI HERJOLFSSON SAILED
FROM GREENLAND TO NORWAY AND VISITED EARL
EIRIK, WHO RECEIVED HIM WELL. BJARNI TOLD THE
EARL ABOUT HIS VOYAGE AND THE LANDS HE HAD
SIGHTED. (p. 117)

Towards the end of the poem, the European narrative looms more threaten-
ingly, in larger font and in italics, and the poem moves to its conclusion with
the 'discovery' of a new land:

*AS THE VERY BEATING AND SURGE
OF THE SEA OUERFLOWED THEM*

> . . . where persons were floating in from the north and from the south: the Whites
> . . .

BY GOD'S WILL, AFTER A LONG VOYAGE FROM THE
ISLAND OF GREENLAND TO THE SOUTH TOWARD
THE MOST DISTANT REMAINING PARTS OF THE
WESTERN OCEAN SEA, SAILING SOUTHWARD AMIDST
THE ICE, THE COMPANIONS BJARNI AND LEIF EIRIKS-
SON DISCOVERED A NEW LAND . . . (pp. 121–2)

Constance Irwin also punctuates her telling of the story, *Gudrid's Saga. The
Norse Settlement in America. A Documentary Novel* (1974), with excerpts from
Grænlendinga saga and *Eiríks saga rauða* which are also closely based on the
Magnusson and Pálsson translation. This novel views Wineland and its future
prospects through the eyes of Gudrid, the only one of its characters whose faith
in the land remains unshaken. Although her dreams in Greenland of a perfect
place 'where no man's hand had ever been raised in anger against another' (p.
147) are interrupted by news of Thorvald's massacre of the Wineland natives,
Gudrid urges Karlsefni to search for a land where children can grow up in the
sun. Peaceful co-existence with the Skrælings and mutually beneficial trade, not
exploitation, are her aim: 'Why shouldn't we trade as friends. There's land
enough for all' (p. 174), she declares.

Karlsefni's goal in *Gudrid's Saga* is not the founding of a colony but of an
eventually independent nation:

> Yes, every new land requires help from a mother country. Wineland's – like Green-
> land's – will come from Iceland. Not as a colony. Greenland is free. Iceland is free.
> Wineland too will be independent. (p. 175)

A bright future of rewarding hard work seems to be within the grasp of these
pioneers. While Gudrid gazes at the virgin forest in the distance and at the

stumps felled by Norse axes around their homestead, Karlsefni chews sweet grapes as he takes a break from his sweaty labour. Despite Gudrid's expressed readiness to die for her new land, however, Karlsefni refuses to stay after they are attacked by Skrælings. Freydis's Wineland expedition is relegated to the background by being related largely, and without comment, as a direct quotation from *Grænlendinga saga* (ch. 8). Disengagement from the new land is attributed neither to faintheartedness nor Freydis's crimes, but to the intervention of momentous events in mainland Scandinavia – Knut's assumption of the English throne, a change of ruler in Norway, and the consolidation of Christianity there – which deflect interest from speculative expeditions to the fringes of the Scandinavian world. The West simply vanishes from the Norse sphere of interest:

> Wineland? Who should bother about it now? . . . Few Icelanders now shook hairy fists at old gods who displeased them, and few set out a-viking. The old wild ways were dying with the old fierce gods. The North was becoming part of Europe.
>
> (pp. 237, 239)

Even the Church, as Gudrid discovers on her pilgrimage to Rome, has no interest in extending its empire across the Atlantic. In old age, she decides that the promised land which she has sought for so long is a spiritual one and, in the final sentences of the novel, steps across the threshold of the cloister:

> As Gudrid saw it, a new frontier had opened a land of the mind and spirit – She stepped out of the saga into her seventh, and the door creaked shut behind her.
>
> (pp. 241, 242)

Francis Berry's *I Tell of Greenland* (1977)[5] projects the Vínland story through less idealistic eyes. The novel's Preface relates a fictional, first-person, twentieth-century traveller's tale of codicological serendipity: the discovery in an Icelandic farmhouse of the 'autobiography' of Ingolf Mordsson, an imagined contemporary of Thorfinn Karlsefni. Like Maurice Hewlett in the Preface to *Gudrid the Fair*, Berry makes some observations on the 'objective' nature of the *Íslendingasögur* (p. xvi) and supplies the desired 'subjectivity' to his narrative through the opinionated voice of Ingolf, who intrudes into the families of Leif and Thorfinn by having affairs with both Freydis and Gudrid and has a sardonic eye for character and motivation. *I Tell of Greenland* supplies an answer to the question implicit in both *Grænlendinga saga* and *Eiríks saga rauða*: why does Leif never make a return voyage to Vínland? The answer is that he is burdened with too many family responsibilities in Greenland to do so in the forseeable future, although he actively encourages Karlsefni's plans for settlement.

The encounter of European and native is informed by the author's conception of the prejudices of an eleventh-century Greenlander, who finds the natives

---

5 Francis Berry, *I Tell of Greenland. An Edited Translation of the Sauðarkrokur Manuscripts* (London, 1977).

of Vinland incomprehensible, stupid, repulsive, and 'even more treacherous, spiteful, dirty and thieving than those in Greenland' (p. 147). Only Christian conversion, thinks Ingolf, will ultimately dispel their resistance to Scandinavian hegemony:

> All we wanted was to clear the timber, till the land and graze like good Christian people. But these skraelings could not be treated in a Christian manner. . . . Though great in their numbers, they should be all killed, or render themselves our slaves, so that we, who understand these arts . . . should be able to use their land as it should be used. . . . Leif Eiriksson . . . had set foot in Vinland, finding there innumerable heathen souls who might one day both own the faith and confess us to be masters for bringing them that wisdom.   (pp. 147, 161, 165)

Ingolf's experiences in Vínland demonstrate the disastrous effects of the misinterpretation of foreign custom in the meeting of Old World and New. When, for example, one of Karlsefni's party rapes and mutilates the wife of a 'skraeling', Karlsefni sentences the offender to hang, a form of retribution which, as Ingolf points out, is unknown in Greenland and Iceland. Instead of serving to placate them, the execution is interpreted by the 'skraelings', who have seen a crucifix left behind by one of Thorwald Eiriksson's company, as an act of worship. At every turn, mutual cultural misunderstanding frustrates Karlsefni's efforts to ingratiate his company with the indigenous Vinlanders. Moreover, Ingolf implies, a detrimental effect of conquest is the erosion of the conqueror's own values. Not only is death by hanging an alien punishment in Greenland and Iceland, so is the flogging which Karlsefni decrees for any member of his company who trades in weapons with the natives:

> flogging was a practice, no less than hanging, in the crueller and slave-like king-ruled lands of Norway and England. . . . [T]he English . . . when they first began to settle their land, encountered vast numbers of people who resisted them . . . they . . . and to impose harsh penalties on them – until they submitted; which penalties the English still shamefully impose even on their own kind. So we too, far from our own kind, and among a wicked and low people, and beset with perils, had to do outrageous things.   (p. 151)

In Val Manning's sensational Viking romance *Valkyrie Queen* (1975),[6] the goal becomes escape from, not the quest for or settlement in, a deceptively para-disial but ultimately hellish Vínland. This novel also draws on Magnusson and Pálsson's translation but, in a series of narrative inversions, provides a new slant on particular events in *Grænlendinga saga* and *Eiríks saga rauða*. Ragnar, an out-of-favour retainer of Halfdan-the-Black, who is unofficially exiled with the order to 'carve yourself a kingdom in some uncharted sea' (p. 75); Astrid, a beautiful captive Saxon woman; and Astrid's son, Kol, are blown off course from Iceland to a strange land which Astrid initially takes for Paradise. When Ragnar decides to winter there, Astrid is apprehensive about being stranded with a pack of sex-

---

6 Published in paperback as *Viking Queen* (London, 1978). References are to this edition.

starved Vikings. Having fended off the advances of and wounded one of them, she flees into the forest. In a reversal of the actions of Freydís in *Eiríks saga rauða*, this time it is the *skraelings* who are led by a female warrior and slaughter some of Ragnar's men. Astrid kills a *skraeling* and becomes the target of vengeance. Kol disappears. Ragnar has an overwhelming premonition 'that only death would release them from Vinland' (p. 113). In a variation on the milk (*Grœnlendinga saga*) and cloth (*Eiríks saga rauða*) exchange for furs episodes, milk and coloured fabric are unsuccessfully offered by Ragnar as ransom for Kol, who is discovered in the company of the *skraelings*. Ragnar's ship, the *Valkyrie Queen*, is struck by a burning arrow in a *skraeling* attack. Astrid is fatally injured by the fallen mast. Ragnar refuses to leave her as the vessel goes up in flames and they enter Valhalla together in the last lines of the novel. Chosen as the heir of the ageing *skraeling* chief, Kol remains in Vinland with a couple of Ragnar's faithful followers. The implication is that he will found a Norse–Amerindian dynasty.

Vínland is a less tangible prospect in Jane Smiley's *The Greenlanders* (1988), a sombre chronicle of the rigours of life in the Greenland colony from 1352 to the years leading up to its demise a century later. Although an early episode of the work concerns a mission to timber- and fur-rich Markland led by a certain Thorleif, the double impetus for which is the memory of 'the famous adventures of Leif Eriksson and his kin, and of the paradise to be found in the west' (p. 22),[7] Vinland never actually appears in the novel. It is said to be a place of riches, and even the Garden of Eden itself, but entry to it is barred by dangerous obstacles like the islands and strong tidal streams in the Vinland–Markland area. Another of Thorleif's companions expresses doubt about allegations that Vinland is Eden: 'No priest has ever been to Vinland itself, only to Markland, and so it is not easy to know about the Garden of Eden' (p. 27). Thorleif's expedition runs into bad weather and bad luck. There are fatalities among the crew and severe damage to the ship in the storm. Ill-feeling erupts, and they find neither game nor fish ashore: 'everything seemed to have vanished, as if by some curse' (p. 28). Even the trophies of the voyage, timber and furs, lose their lustre: 'these treasures now seemed somehow of little worth and yet cumbersome' (p. 28).

The foreign and unknown in *The Greenlanders* are either perilous, like the route to Vinland, or actively malevolent, like the natives of Greenland. The indigenous people of Greenland and Markland are not perceived as prospective trading partners, labourers, or converts. This is the story of a settlement in decline, not one with ambitions to colonial expansion. Vinland is a distant, fabled refuge, whose fragile promise of a better land underscores the doomed fortunes of medieval Greenland. Towards the end of the novel, a party of Greenlanders, fifteen men and fifteen women, sail into the sunset in search of this place, where 'men may rest from their labors from time to time' (p. 575), after

---

7 Jane Smiley, *The Greenlanders* (London, 1988).

rampagers from Bristol have all but destroyed the settlement at Garðar. The expedition is never heard of again, but, since there is no evidence of a ship-wreck, the novel leaves open the possibility that they may have reached their Shangri-La.

The most recent tellings of the Vínland story are less interested in the fact of Bjarni and Leif's 'discovery' than in its impact on the New World. The Columbus quincentenary produced only a desultory revival of the Leifr Eiríksson movement which dogged the quatercentenary, anti-Columbian senti-ment this time focusing upon the depredations perpetrated upon the New World by the Old. Whereas Nevil Shute idealized the industrialization and urbanization of America in *Vinland the Good*, Thomas Pynchon's contemporary Vineland in *Vineland* (1990) is an urban and suburban wasteland. In *The Ice-Shirt* (1990), the first in William T. Vollmann's seven-novel series *Seven Dreams: A Book of North American Landscapes*, present-day Vinland is the heir of the envi-ronmental and moral deterioration which Freydís sets in train in *Grœnlendinga saga*. In George Mackay Brown's *Vinland* (1992) on the other hand, Vinland is a paradise from which Leif deliberately expels himself and his company for an act of desecration which he foresees as repeated on a larger scale in the future.[8]

The narrative focus of *The Ice-Shirt* is Freydis's trip to Vinland at the behest of the satanic spirit of the Greenland glacier Blue-Shirt (*Bláserkr*), who seeks to extend his dark domain through the transformation of Vinland's landscape from hospitably temperate to mercilessly icebound. 'You must', he says to her, 'plant the frost-seed in the blood of your own kind' (p. 300).[9] Freydis and her men plunder the natural riches of Vinland, murder their compatriots, and return to Greenland, leaving Vinland's natives to suffer the misery of its newly harsh climate. Her implicit legacy to twentieth-century Vinland is the spurious glitter of cities, where 'hoarfrost has become whorefrost' (p. 326) and the gold-lettered forests of night are the semiology of advertising. In a *Note* at the end of the novel Vollmann asks, 'Did the Norsemen – really come to the New World bearing ice in their hearts? – Well, of course they did not. But if we look upon the Vinland episode as a precursor of the infamies there, of course they did'.

Leif's voyage in Mackay Brown's *Vinland* is motivated solely by discovery, and his landfall is blessed with good fortune. An almost magical calm descends just before he and his company on board the *West-Seeker* reach an apparently pre-lapsarian shore. Leif cautiously declares the country *terra nullius* and gives it cartographical substance by propping himself against a rock and drawing his own version of the Vinland Map on a piece of parchment. The land's abundant riches – fresh water, woodlands, and abundant game – are extolled in fishy

8 For a discussion of the influence of Old Norse literature on the works of George Mackay Brown, see Julian D'Arcy, *Scottish Skalds and Sagamen. Old Norse Influence on Modern Scottish Literature* (East Linton, 1996), pp. 242–83.
9 William T. Vollmann, *The Ice-Shirt* (New York, 1990). On the use of Icelandic source material in *The Ice-Shirt*, see Peter Christiansen, 'William T. Vollmann's "The Ice-Shirt": updating Icelandic traditions', *Critique: Studies in Contemporary Fiction* 38 (1996), 52–68.

metaphor when Leif relates the story of his voyage back in Greenland: 'Greenland is like a poor gnawed fish-bone and Vinland is like a huge sturgeon brimming with oil and stuffed with roe' (p. 28).[10]

For a brief period the Norsemen bask harmoniously in a Golden Age of innocence with the ethnic Other. The first contact with the natives of this Edenic world is a disinterested greeting between child and child. When Ranald Sigmundson, the central character of the novel, who, as a young boy in Orkney, stows away on the *West Seeker*, and a native boy make eye contact, they have no difficulty in interpreting body language: 'The boy raised his hand, palm spread outwards: a greeting' (p. 12). Ranald reciprocates, but their silent understanding is soon corrupted by material exchange and botched attempts at cross-cultural communication. The former is detrimental to the Amerindians, not because of its unequal nature but because of its very nature. The latter, like the hanging in *I Tell of Greenland*, entails a misunderstanding of ritual, this time on the part of the Norsemen. Exchange here is not a question of barter or trade but of mutual peace-offering. The painted 'shore-dwellers' bring baskets of salmon, venison, and small bunches of fruit, which turn out to be grapes. Leif reciprocates with ale horns, ale, and goat cheese. The 'forest people' consume the ale with gusto and break into an exuberant war dance, which Leif, but not everyone else, sees as being performed in their honour, and which ends in the killing of one of the dancers by Leif's cook, Wolf. In the ensuing mêlée, one of Leif's men is scalped. As reluctance to stay there grows among his company, Leif decides that the place where they have landed is, in fact, 'unlucky' and that 'Things have been wrongly done here' (p. 21). He resolves to explore further south, with a view to permanent and peaceful settlement, after he has made a return trip to Greenland to repair his ship, and to pick up supplies, sailors, women, harps, honey-hives, and horses.

Leif acknowledges their failure of communication with the Vinland natives but is optimistic about the future: 'We did an evil thing when we broke their dance of welcome. When we return we will know how to give them gifts, and how to receive the gifts they offer us. It may be, there will be perpetual peace between us Norsemen and the Vinlanders' (pp. 21–2). Leif also endorses the Vinlanders' superior appreciation of ecology. When, on the homeward voyage to Greenland, Wolf laments the lack of opportunity to kill a passing whale which could have provided dinners throughout the next winter, Leif rebukes him with a speech about the native Vinlanders' understanding of nature:

The skraelings, that we thought so savage and ignorant, were wiser than us in this respect. They only killed as many deer and salmon as they needed for that day's hunger. We are wasteful gluttons and more often than not leave carcasses to rot after a hunt – a shameful thing. Did you not see what reverence the Vinlanders had for the animals and the trees and for all living things? It seemed to me that the

10 B. George Mackay Brown, *Vinland* (London, 1992).

Vínlanders had entered into a kind of sacred bond with all the creatures, and there was a fruitful exchange between them, both in matters of life and death. (p. 24)

Back in Greenland, Leif has a disturbing dream which he interprets as a vision of the ecological vandalism that will result from the greed of future New World settlers. Skraelings, animals, and trees dance together until a fair-haired man, wearing a gold mask, joins the dance. Immediately the dancers begin to disappear, until only he is left and is joined by an armada, which claims the land for itself. The dream supplies another answer to the question concerning Leif's failure to return to Vínland: appalled at the prospects for its future, he abandons the entire enterprise. Just as the loss of Vínland in *Grœnlendinga saga* can be read as a demonstration that *radix malorum est cupiditas*, in *Vinland* the land is explicitly renounced by Leif himself as penance for the rapaciousness of future generations.

One such potential vandal is Olaf Tryggvason, who, drawing upon some of the more sensational aspects of *Eiríks saga rauða*, says that he has heard that Vinland is populated by repulsive unipeds, but that it is also a rich source of raw materials. 'It seems to us a pity that the oil and fruit and mines from such a land should be wasted on the greedy Greenland and Iceland merchants' (p. 47), he tells Ranald. Like Smiley's Greenlanders, however, Olaf is deterred from Vinland ventures by the hazards of the voyage, although his considerations are purely economic: 'whirlpools, shipwrecks, icebergs and sea monsters' (p. 47) make financial investment risky.

In adulthood, Ranald prospers in Orkney, but he and his companions yearn for the balmy climate of Vinland. Ranald's dream of returning is never realized, and, although his often told story of the westward voyage with Leif is fondly remembered by the older generation, the younger loses interest in it. Unlike Smiley's *The Greenlanders*, where recollections of the tales of Eric the Red and Leif the Lucky provide inspiration for the people of Greenland in the final pages of the novel, constant retelling of the Vinland voyage robs it of its magic.

Leif's worst fears in *Vinland* are realized in Pynchon's apocalyptic *Vineland*, where Vínland has been transposed to the West Coast, to Cabrillo's rather than Leif's shores, and become a paradise for property developers who compete for space with New Age flower children. Shangri-La is there, but it has been reconstituted as a sauna, 'the Shangri-La Sauna – Vineland County's finest' (p. 321),[11] which ministers not to despairing Greenlanders but to weary loggers. Vineland, capital of Vineland County, is an incipient piece of urban blight off Highway 101 in northern California's redwood country, whose nerve centres are the Vineland Mall, the Vineland Lanes, and the Vineland International Airport. Vestiges of its natural beauty are concealed behind the Cucumber Lounge, 'a notorious Vineland County roadhouse' (p. 8), which extends 'back from the disreputable neon roadhouse itself into a few acres of virgin redwood grove. Dwarfed and overshadowed by the towering dim red trees were two

---

11 References are to Thomas Pynchon, *Vineland* (London, 1991).

dozen motel cabins with woodstoves, porches, barbecues, waterbeds, and cable TV' (p. 9). The future nightmare of a 'Eureka-Crescent City-Vineland megalopolis' threatens to engulf a forested coastline, once nudged only by the fishing settlements of the Yurok and Tolowa.

The conclusion of Joan Clark's *Eiriksdottir. A Tale of Dreams and Luck* (1994) examines the negative impact of Edenic Vínland upon those who find it. Leifsbudir itself, the site of much of the action, is, as one Icelander puts it, 'a far cry from Paradise' (p. 262).[12] Attracted by Leif's reports of Vinland, Freydis, who lives in squalor in Greenland with her oafish husband Thorvard, sees the new land as a place where she might 'improve her luck' (pp. 7, 14) and organizes an expedition there in partnership with the Icelanders, Helgi and Finnbogi. Tensions erupt between Greenlanders and Icelanders at Leifsbudir. Helgi determines to go in search of Leif's Vinland, an uninhabited 'place of untold wealth', filled with 'wine grapes and honey, fruits and nuts, cargo wood of every kind' (p. 261). Having duped Freydis into supplying the sail, he sets a southerly course in a boat which has been built for her. Helgi does not return, most of the Icelanders who remain at Leifsbudir are massacred, and, with Freydís in command, the Greenlanders take Finnbogi's ship and return home. Talk of the incident finally subsides in Greenland, where Vinland has acquired a murky reputation:

> Folk seldom told tales of Vinland, for many were convinced that the place held more evil than Luck. Gradually the details of the final voyage faded until Vinland become little more than a mythical country hovering on the outermost reaches of the Greenlanders' minds. (p. 342)

In the meantime, Helgi and his crew have sailed into a heightened version of the Vínland landscape of *Grænlendinga saga*, which some of them think must be their desired destination, although the sight of cultivated grain makes many of them anxious about an attack by 'skraelings'. Helgi's notion of Vínland proper is a place where such fears are irrelevant:

> 'For me the real Vinland is some distance yet,' Helgi said. Now that he had come this far, Helgi was greedy to find a land that surpassed this one and was empty of skraelings. (p. 347)

Continuing south, they come upon a tropical virgin land of white beaches, warm lagoons, bright flowers, fruits, unsown wheat, and forests which extend to the shoreline. This, they all agree, must be Vínland. Ravished by the landscape, their senses feast on a cornucopia of sight, sound, and taste:

> They were much affected by the peacefulness of the place: the soughing trees, the falling waves, the droning bees, the scent of rose bushes and wild pea blossoms – Huge clusters of grapes hung from arbours. This sight was so wondrous that the men stood slack jawed with awe. (pp. 349, 350)

12 Joan Clark. *Eiriksdottir. A Tale of Dreams and Luck* (Toronto, 1994).

Then they discover that Vínland is also a gourmet's paradise: 'It was the nature of Vinland that no sooner did someone express a desire for a certain kind of food than the wish was granted' (p. 352). Gradually their energies, other than sexual, are sapped. An endless supply of wine and the midday heat are so soporific that all thoughts of wood-cutting, ship-building, winter provisions, the passage of time, Leifsbudir, and Iceland recede. Equally mellow, the women abandon the chore of baking, since an abundance of delicacies is there for the plucking. Wine-induced delirium leads to the death of one man by drowning, and then another disappears in suspected similar circumstances. Despite resolutions to get to work, they lose not only the desire but also the capacity for it. Well-groomed beachcombers when they first arrive,

> The men smelled better themselves from having spent so much time bathing – The women had taken to wearing fragrant beach pea and roses in their hair and shell ankle bracelets which rustled pleasantly when they walked. Together these things made them more attractive than they had been before.   (p. 353)

they become slothful and slovenly as they yield to the torpor of the warmth, wine, and riches of Vinland. The rot sets in:

> They lost all interest in seeing themselves as others might. They lay in the sun, their lips stained the colour of overripe plums. They stopped washing their hair and combing their beards. They no longer bathed or kept themselves clean. The Vinlanders lost their fresh tangy smell. Instead they took on the musty odour of decaying fruit.   (p. 361)

Having achieved the object of their quest, Helgi and his crew enjoy only occasional glimmers of the wisdom of the proverb about the consequences of fulfilled desire before they eventually surrender to the grip of the grape. Formerly renowned as a man of action and adventure, Helgi suggests that they abandon all attempts to return to Leifsbudir and thoughts of responsibility towards kin in Iceland. Whereas, despite the pioneering efforts of Gudrid and Karlsefni, Vinland is lost in Irwin's *Gudrid's Saga* and is probably ever out of reach in Smiley's *The Greenlanders*, those to whom Vínland offers itself without challenge in *Eiriksdsottir* are destroyed by the willing forfeiture of their own identity.

In its demonstration of the consequences of excess, an exemplum arguably played out several centuries before in *Grænlendinga saga*, *Eiriksdottir* brings the Vínland story full circle. The concerns of *Eiríks saga rauða* too, continue to exert their allure: the geographical quest for Vínland, which began in that saga, continues; and the 1000-year anniversary of Leif's 'discovery' in 2000 promises to re-ignite interest in the pre-Columbian Scandinavian presence in America. In the meantime, as an enduringly potent symbol of promise, plenty, opportunity, and temptation, literary Vínland – 'the Wineland of our dreams' –[13] remains

---

13 Henry Hardel Richardson, *Maurice Guest* (Melbourne, 1965), p. 37.

accessible as a destination of the mind and as a vehicle for the interrogation of the moral and ideological ramifications of the European fascination with the lands west of Greenland from the Middle Ages to the present day.

BIBLIOGRAPHY

Note: Anonymous primary sources are listed alphabetically by title. Icelandic patronymics are listed alphabetically by first names. Authors' names are given as they appear on title pages.

Abbot, John S. C. *The History of Maine* (Augusta, Maine, 1882).

Adam of Bremen. 'Gesta Hammaburgensis ecclesiae Pontificum: Descriptio Insularum Aquilonis', in *Quellen des 9. und 11. Jahrhunderts zur Geschichte der Hamburgischen Kirche und des Reiches*, ed. Werner Trillmich (Berlin, 1961).

———. *History of the Archbishops of Hamburg-Bremen*, trans. Francis J. Tschan (New York, 1959).

Adams, Herbert Baxter. *Thomas Jefferson and the University of Virginia*, U.S. Bureau of Education, Circular of Information No. 1 (Washington, DC, 1888).

Allen, Hervey. 'Saga of Leif the Lucky', *The Bookman* (New York) 58 (1923), 395–403.

Allen, Ralph Bergen. *Old Icelandic Sources in the English Novel* (Philadelphia, 1933).

Almqvist, Bo. *Norrön Niddiktning. Traditionshistoriska studier i versmagi*, I (Stockholm and Uppsala, 1965).

Anderson, Rasmus. *America Not Discovered by Columbus. An Historical Sketch of the Discovery of America by the Norsemen in the Tenth Century*, 3rd enlarged edn (Chicago, 1883).

———. *Life Story of Rasmus B. Anderson, written by himself, with assistance of Albert O. Barron*, 2nd revised edn (Madison, Wis., 1917).

Anon. Review of John Reinhold Forster, *History of the Voyages and Discoveries made in the North. Translated from the German of John Reinhold Forster*, *The Critical Review* 62 (1786), 331–7.

Anon. Review of John Reinhold Forster, *History of the Voyages and Discoveries made in the North. Translated from the German of John Reinhold Forster, J.U.D.*, *The Monthly Review or Literary Journal* 76 (1787), 611–24.

Anon. 'The discovery of Vinland, or America, by the Icelanders', *The American Museum* 6 (1789), 159–62; 7 (1790), 340–4.

Anon. Review of Washington Irving, *A History of the Life and Voyages of Christopher Columbus*, 4 vols (London, 1828), *The Monthly Review* 7 (1828), 419–34.

Anon. Review of Washington Irving, *A History of the Life and Voyages of Christopher Columbus*, 4 vols (London, 1828), *The Athenæum* 9 (22 February 1828), 131–3; 10 (26 February 1828), 150–1.

Anon. Review of Henry Wheaton, *History of the Northmen* (London, 1831), *The American Quarterly Review* 10 (1831), 311–34.

Anon. Review of Henry Wheaton, *History of the Northmen* (London, 1831), *The Athenæum* 194 (16 July 1831), 453–5.

Anon. Review of Henry Wheaton, *History of the Northmen* (London, 1831), *The Westminster Review* 15 (1831), 442–57.

Anon. Review of Henry Wheaton, *History of the Northmen* (Philadelphia, 1831), *The American Monthly Review* (March 1832), pp. 245–6.

Anon. Review of *Antiquitates Americanæ*, *Dublin Evening Post*, 19 April 1838 (unpaginated).

Anon. Review of *Antiquitates Americanæ* ('Scandinavians in the Tenth Century'), *Journal of the Royal Geographical Society of London* 8 (1838), 115–29.

Anon. Review of *Antiquitates Americanæ*, *The Knickerbocker* 11 (1838), 288–9.

Anon ('L.B.'). Review of *Antiquitates Americanæ*, *The Western Messenger* 5 (1838), 217–30.

Anon. 'Wild Sports of the Far West; or, a few weeks' adventures among the Hudson's Bay Company's fur traders, in the autumn of 1836', *Tait's Edinburgh Magazine* 5 (1838), 648–55.

Anon. Review of N. L. Beamish, *Discovery of America by the Northmen*, *The Monthly Review* 155 (1841), 337–41.

Anon. Review of N. L. Beamish, *Discovery of America by the Northmen*, *Tait's Edinburgh Magazine* 8 (1841), 471.

Anon. Review of N. L. Beamish, *Discovery of America by the Northmen*, *The Athenæum* 714 (3 July 1841), 499–501.

Anon. 'The Successive Discoveries of America', *Dublin Review* 11 (1841), 277–310.

Anon. Review of B. F. De Costa, *The Pre-Columbian Discovery of America, by the Northmen, with translations from the Icelandic sagas* (Albany, NY, 1868), *The North American Review* 109 (1869), 265–72.

Anon. Review of R. M. Ballantyne, *The Norsemen in the West*, *The Athenæum* 2351 (16 November 1872), 633.

Anon. Review of Gabriel Gravier, *Découverte de l'Amérique par les Normands au Xe siècle* (Paris, 1874), *The North American Review* 119 (1874), 166–82.

Anon. 'The Historical Value of the Vinland Sagas', *The Atlantic Monthly* 60 (1887), 856.

Anon. 'The Discovery of America by the Northmen', *The Nation* 8 (21 January 1869), 53.

Anon. Review of Arthur Reeves, *The Finding of Wineland the Good* ('Wineland the Good'), *The Saturday Review* 70 (1890), 568.

Anon. Review of Arthur Reeves, *The Finding of Wineland the Good* ('The Norse Discovery of America'), *The Scottish Review* 18 (1891), 341–66.

Anon ('C.R.M.'). Review of Arthur Reeves, *The Finding of Wineland the Good*, *Proceedings of the Royal Geographical Society*, n.s. 13 (1891), 127–8.

Anon. Review of Arthur Reeves, *The Finding of Wineland the Good* ('The Icelandic Discovery of America'), *The Nation* 52 (1891), 54–6.

Anon. Review of Ottilie Liljencrantz, *The Thrall of Leif the Lucky* (Chicago, 1902), *The New York Times*, May 31, 1902, p. 361.

Anon. 'Kennedy's Tragedy. "The Winterfeast" ', *The New York Times*, December 1, 1908, p. 9.

Antiqvitates Americanæ sive Scriptores Septentrionales Rerum Ante-Columbianarum in America. Samling af de i Nordens Oldskrifter indeholdte Efterretninger om de gamle Nordboers Opdagelsesreiser til America fra det 10de til det 14de Aarhundrede. Edidit Societas Regia Antiqvariorum Septentrionalium (Hafniæ [Copenhagen], 1837); rpr. Osnabrück, 1968.

Appelbaum, Stanley. *The Chicago World's Fair of 1893. A Photographic Record* (New York, n.d.).

Ari Þorgilsson. *Íslendingabók*, ed. Jakob Benediktsson, in *Íslendingabók. Landnámabók*, Íslenzk fornrit I (i) (Reykjavík, 1968).

The Arna-Magnæan Manuscript 557 4to containing inter alia the History of the first Discovery of America, Corpus Codicum Islandicorum Medii Ævi, vol. 13, ed. Dag Strømback (Copenhagen, 1940).

Arnold, Guy. *Held Fast for England. G. A. Henty, Imperialist Boys' Writer* (London, 1980).

Ashe, Geoffrey (ed.) *The Quest for America* (London, 1971).

Babcock, William H. *Early Norse Visits to North America*, Smithsonian Miscellaneous Collections, Vol. 59, no. 19 (Washington, DC, 1913).

Baldwin, John D. *Ancient America, in notes on American archæology* (New York, 1872).

Ballantyne, R. M. *The Norsemen in the West, or America before Columbus. A Tale* (Toronto, 1872).

———. *Ungava. A Tale of Esquimau Land*, new edn (London, Edinburgh, New York, 1894).

Bancroft, George. *History of the United States from the Discovery of the American Continent*, 5 vols (London, 1854).

———. *History of the United States of America, from the discovery of the continent. The Author's Last Revision*, 6 vols (New York, 1888).

Bancroft, Hubert Howe. *The Works of Hubert Howe Bancroft*, 39 vols (San Francisco, 1874–90).

Barnes, Geraldine. 'Vinland the Good: Paradise Lost?', *Parergon*, n.s. 12 (1995), 75–96.

———. 'Reinventing Paradise: Vínland 1000–1992', in *Old Norse Studies in the New World*, eds Geraldine Barnes, Margaret Clunies Ross, and Judy Quinn (Sydney, 1994), pp. 19–30.

———. 'The Lost (Christian) Colony of Vinland', in *Treasures of the Elder Tongue*, ed. Katrina Burge (Melbourne, 1995), pp. 127–36.

———. 'The Fireside Vikings and the Boy's Own Vinland', in *Reinventing the Middle Ages and the Renaissance: Constructions of the Medieval and Early*

Modern Periods, ed. William F. Gentrup (Turnhout, Belgium, 1998), pp. 147–65.

Barnett, Louise R. *The Ignoble Savage: American Literary Racism, 1790–1890* (Westwood, Conn., 1975).

Barnum, L. H. 'The Discovery of America by the Northmen', *The Cornell Review* 1 (1874), 246–55, 342–53.

Bárðar Saga. Ed. and trans. by Jón Skaptason and Phillip Pulsiano (New York, 1984).

Barrow, John. *A Chronological History of Voyages into the Arctic Regions* (London, 1818).

Bartlett, Robert. *The Making of Europe. Conquest, Colonization and Cultural Change 950–1350* (London and New York, 1993).

—— and Angus MacKay (eds) *Medieval Frontier Societies* (Oxford, 1989).

Bartolomé de Las Casas, trans. Nigel Griffin. *A Short Account of the Destruction of the Indies* (London, 1992).

Bartram, John. *Observations on the Inhabitants, Climate, Soil, Rivers, Productions, Animals, and other matters worthy of Notice made by Mr. John Bartram, In his Travels from Pensilvania to Onondago, Oswego and the Lake Ontario, In Canada* (London, 1751).

Batho, Edith. 'Sir Walter Scott and the Sagas: Some Notes', *Modern Language Notes* 24 (1929), 409–15.

Baudet, Henri. *Paradise on Earth: Some Thoughts on European Images of Non-European Man* (New Haven, 1965).

Baumgartner, Walter. 'Freydís in Vinland oder Die Vertreibung aus dem Paradies', *Skandinavistik* 23 (1993), 16–35.

Baxter, James Phinney. 'The Present Status of Pre-Columbian Discovery of America by the Norsemen', *Annual Report of the American Historical Association For the Year 1893* (Washington, DC, 1894), pp. 101–10.

Beamish, North Ludlow. *The Discovery of America by the Northmen in the Tenth Century, with notices of the early settlements of the Irish in the Western Hemisphere* (London, 1841).

Beauvois, M. E. 'Migration des Gaels en Amérique au Moyen-Age', *Congrès International des Américanists, Huitième Session* (Paris, 1890), pp. 200–1.

Beck, Richard. 'George P. Marsh and Old Icelandic Studies', *Scandinavian Studies* 17 (1943), 195–203.

Becker, Carl L. *Cornell University: Founders and the Founding* (Ithaca, 1943).

Belknap, Jeremy. *American Biography*, I (Boston, 1794).

Bennett, J. A. W. *The History of Old English and Old Norse Studies in England from the Time of Francis Junius till the end of the Eighteenth Century*, unpubl. D.Phil. thesis, University of Oxford, Bodl. MS. D.Phil. d. 287 (1938).

——. 'The Beginnings of Norse Studies in England', *Saga-Book of the Viking Society* 12 (1937–1945), 35–42

Benson, Adolph B. 'The Beginning of American Interest in Scandinavian Literature', *Scandinavian Studies and Notes* 8 (1924–25), 133–41.

———. 'Scandinavians in the Works of Washington Irving', *Scandinavian Studies and Notes* 9 (1926), 207–23.

———. 'Henry Wheaton's Writings on Scandinavia', *Journal of English and Germanic Philology* 29 (1930), 546–61.

Bergesen, Robert. *Vinland Bibliography: Writings relating to the Norse in Greenland and America* (Tromsø, 1997).

Berkhofer, Robert F., Jr. *The White Man's Indian. Images of the American Indian from Columbus to the Present* (New York, 1978).

Berry, Francis. *I Tell of Greenland. An Edited Translation of the Sauðarkrokur Manuscripts* (London, 1977).

Bessason, Haraldur. 'New Light on Vinland from the Sagas', *Mosaic* 1 (1967), 52–65.

Bideaux, Michel (ed.) *Jacques Cartier: Relations* (Montreal, 1966).

Biggar, H. P. (ed.) *The Precursors of Jacques Cartier 1497–1534. A Collection of Documents relating to the early history of the Dominion of Canada*, Publications of the Canadian Archives No. 5 (Ottawa, 1911).

Bishop, Morris. *Early Cornell 1865–1900* (Ithaca, 1962).

Bitterli, Urs, trans. Ritchie Roberston. *Cultures in Conflict. Encounters Between European and Non-European Cultures, 1492–1800* (Cambridge, 1989; rpr. 1993).

Bjarni Einarsson. 'On the Status of Free Men in Society and Saga', *Mediaeval Scandinavia* 7 (1974), 52–5.

Björn Þorsteinsson. 'Some Observations on the Discoveries and the Cultural History of the Norsemen', *Saga-Book of the Viking Society* 16 (1962–65), 173–91.

Blackwell, I. A. (ed.) *Northern Antiquities . . . New edition, revised throughout and considerably enlarged* (London, 1847).

Blind, Karl. 'The Forerunners of Columbus', *New Review* 7 (1892), 346–57.

Boas, George. *Essays on Primitivism and Related Ideas in the Middle Ages* (Baltimore, 1948).

Boehmer, Elleke. *Colonial & Postcolonial Literature* (Oxford and New York, 1995).

Boer, R. C. (ed.) *Ǫrvar-Odds saga* (Leiden, 1888).

Boon, James A. *Other Tribes, Other Scribes: Symbolic Anthropology in the Comparative Study of Cultures, Histories, Religions, and Texts* (Cambridge, 1962).

Borning, Laurent Etienne. *Notices on the Life and Writings of Carl Christian Rafn* (Copenhagen, 1864).

Boyd, Kelly. 'Exemplars and Ingrates: Imperialism and the Boys' Story Paper, 1880–1930', *Historical Research* 67 (1994), 143–55.

Brantlinger, Patrick. *Rule of Darkness. British Literature and Imperialism, 1830–1914* (Ithaca and London, 1988).

Braudel, Fernand, and Michel Mollat du Jourdin (eds) *Le Monde de Jacques Cartier* (Montreal and Paris, 1984).

Brent, Peter. *The Viking Saga* (London, 1975).

Bristow, Joseph. *Empire Boys: Adventures in a Man's World* (London, 1991).

Brown, George Mackay. *Vinland* (London, 1992).

Brown, Marie A. 'The Norse Discovery of America', *Notes and Queries*, 7th ser. 2 (1886), 145–6.

———. *The Icelandic Discoveries of America; or Honour to whom Honour is Due* (London, 1887).

Brownell, Henry. *The Pioneer Heroes of the New World* (Cincinnati, 1857).

Bryant, William Cullen, and Sydney Howard Gay. *A Popular History of the United States, from the first discovery of the western hemisphere by the Northmen, to the end of the first century of the Union of the States*, I (London, 1876).

Buchan, John. *John Macnab* (London and Aylesbury, 1935).

Buell, Lawrence. *New England Literary Culture. From Revolution Through Renaissance* (Cambridge, Mass., 1986).

Bull, Sara. 'Leif Erikson', *Magazine of American History* 19 (1888), 217–23.

Burne-Jones, Edward. *The paintings, graphic and decorative work of Sir Edward Burne-Jones 1833–98* (The Arts Council of Great Britain, 1975).

Burne-Jones, Georgiana, introd. John Christian. *Memorials of Edward Burne-Jones* (London, 1993).

Burritt, Elihu. 'The Narrative of Thorstein Ericsson. Translated from the Icelandic', *The American Eclectic* 1 (1841), 109–11.

Cabot, J. Elliot. 'Discovery of America by the Norsemen', *Massachusetts Quarterly Review* 6 (1849), 189–214.

Cahill, T. A. *et al.* 'The Vinland Map, Revisited: New Compositional Evidence on Its Inks and Parchment', *Analytical Chemistry* 59 (1987), 829–33.

Calloway, Colin G. 'What Will We Do Without Columbus? American History and American Indians after the Quincentennial', *Reviews in American History* 21 (1993), 369–73.

Campbell, Mary B. *The Witness and the Other World: Exotic European Travel Writing, 400–1600* (Ithaca and London, 1988).

Carlyle, Thomas. 'Early Kings of Norway', *Critical and Miscellaneous Essays*, Vol. 5 (London, 1899).

Carpenter, W. H. 'Recent Work in Old Norse', *American Journal of Philology* 3 (1882), 77–80.

———, Wm. H. 'A Fragment of Old Icelandic', *Modern Language Notes* 3 (1888), 59–62.

———, William Henry. 'Willard Fiske in Iceland', *Papers of the Bibliographical Society of America* 12 (1918), 107–15.

Carr, Helen. *Inventing the American Primitive. Politics, Gender and the Representation of Native American Literary Traditions, 1789–1936* (New York, 1996).

Cartier, Jacques. *Voyages au Canada. Avec les relations des voyages en Amérique de Gonneville, Verrazano et Roberval*, eds Ch.-A. Julien, R. Herval, and Th. Beauchesne (Paris, 1981) [originally published as *Les Français en Amérique dans la première moitié du XVIe siècle*, Paris, 1946].

Champlain, Samuel, ed. H. P. Biggar. *The Works of Samuel Champlain*, 6 vols (Toronto, 1922–36).

Chapman, Paul. *The Norse Discovery of America* (Atlanta, Ga., 1981).

Charvat, William. *The Origins of American Critical Thought 1810–1835* (Philadelphia, 1936).

Chaunu, Pierre, trans. Katherine Bertram. *European Expansion in the Later Middle Ages* (Amsterdam, 1979).

Chester, Emma Sherwood. 'Karlsefne versus Columbus', *Scandinavia* 2/12 (December 1885), 295–9.

Christiansen, Peter. 'William T. Vollmann's "The Ice-Shirt": updating Icelandic traditions', *Critique: Studies in Contemporary Fiction* 38 (1996), 52–68.

Clark, Joan. *Eiriksdottir. A Tale of Dreams and Luck* (Toronto, 1994).

Clark, Richard H. 'America Discovered and Christianized in the Tenth and Eleventh Centuries', *The American Catholic Quarterly Review* 13 (1888), 211–37.

———. 'The First Christian Northmen in America', *The American Catholic Quarterly Review* 14 (1889), 598–615.

———. 'The Norse Hierarchy of America', *The American Catholic Quarterly Review* 15 (1890), 249–66.

Clunies Ross, Margaret. *Skáldskaparmál. Snorri Sturluson's ars poetica and medieval theories of language* (Odense, 1987).

———. 'The Development of Old Norse Textual Worlds: Genealogical Structure as a Principle of Literary Organisation in Early Iceland', *Journal of English and Germanic Philology* 92 (1993), 371–85.

———. 'Percy and Mallet – The genesis of *Northern Antiquities*', in *Sagnaþing, helgað Jónasi Kristjánssyni sjötugum 10. april 1994*, eds Gísli Sigurðsson, Guðrún Kvaran, and Sigurgeir Steingrímsson (Reykjavík, 1994), pp. 107–17.

———. 'Textual Territory. The Regional and Genealogical Dynamic of Medieval Icelandic Literary Production', *New Medieval Literatures* 1 (1997), 9–30.

———. *The Norse Muse in Britain, 1750–1820* (Trieste, 1998).

———. *Prolonged Echoes. Old Norse myths in medieval Northern society*, 2 vols (Odense, 1998).

———. 'Land-Taking and Text-Making in Medieval Iceland', in *Text and Territory: Geographical Imagination in the European Middle Ages*, eds Sylvia Tomasch and Sealy Gilles (Philadelphia, 1998), pp. 159–84.

Coen, Rena N. 'Longfellow, Hiawatha and some Nineteenth-Century AmericanPainters', in *Papers Presented at the Longfellow Commemorative Conference, April 1–3, 1982* (Longfellow National Historic Site, 1982), pp. 69–91.

Cohen, J. M. (ed. and trans.) *Christopher Columbus: The Four Voyages* (London, 1969).

Colker, Marvin L. 'America Rediscovered in the Thirteenth Century?', *Speculum* 54 (1979), 712–26.

Conrad, Bryce. *Refiguring America. A Study of William Carlos Williams' In the American Grain* (Urbana and Chicago, 1990).

Conroy, Patricia. '*Laxdœla saga* and *Eiríks saga rauða*', *Arkiv för nordisk filologi* 95 (1980), 116–25.

Cook, Ramsay (introd.) *The Voyages of Jacques Cartier* (Toronto, Buffalo, London, 1993).

Cosser, Jeffrey. Review of Ólafur Halldórsson, *Grœnland í miðaldaritum*, *Saga-Book of the Viking Society* 20 (1980), 222–7.

Cowan, Edward J. 'Icelandic Studies in Eighteenth- and Nineteenth-Century Scotland', *Studia Islandica* 31 (1972), 109–51.

Crantz, David. *The History of Greenland: containing a description of the country, – and its inhabitants: and particularly, A Relation of the Mission, carried on for above these Thirty Years by the Unitas Fratrum at New Herrnhuth and Lichten-fels, in that Country. Translated from the High-Dutch*, 2 vols (London, 1767).

Crosby, Alfred W. *Ecological Imperialism: The Biological Expansion of Europe, 900–1900* (Cambridge, 1986).

Curtis, William Eleroy. 'Recent Disclosures Concerning Pre-Columbian Voyages to America in the Archives of the Vatican', *National Geographic Magazine* 5 (1893–94), 197–234.

D'Arcy, Julian Meldon. 'George Mackay Brown and *Orkneyinga saga*', in *Northern Antiquity. The Post-Medieval Reception of Edda and Saga*, ed. Andrew Wawn (Enfield Lock, 1994), pp. 305–27.

———. *Scottish Skalds and Sagamen. Old Norse Influence on Modern Scottish Literature* (East Linton, 1996).

Dasent, George Webbe. *A Grammar of the Icelanders or Old Norse Tongue translated from the Swedish of Erasmus Rask* (London, 1843).

Davin, Anna. 'Imperialism and motherhood', in *Patriotism: The Making and Unmaking of British National Identity*, I: *History and Politics*, ed. Raphael Samuel (London and New York, 1989), pp. 203–35.

Davis, Asahel. *A Lecture on the Discovery of America by the Northmen, Five Hundred Years before Columbus. Delivered in New York, New Haven, Philadelphia, Baltimore, Washington, and other cities: also in some of the first literary institutions of the Union*, 5th edn (New York and Boston, 1840).

De Bellis, Jack. *Sidney Lanier* (New York, 1972).

De Costa, B. F. *The Pre-Columbian Discovery of America, by the Northmen, with translations from the Icelandic sagas*, 2nd edn (Albany, NY, 1890).

De Roo, P. *History of America Before Columbus*, II, *European Immigrants* (Philadelphia and London, 1900).

Dewey, John. *Experience and Nature*, 2nd edn (London, 1929).

Dictionary of American Biography. Eds Allen Johnson and Dumas Malone (New York, 1946–58).

The Dictionary of National Biography. Eds Leslie Stephen and Sidney Lee (London, 1917–).

Dixon, Robert. *Writing the Colonial Adventure. Race, gender and nation in Anglo-Australian popular fiction, 1875–1914* (Cambridge and Melbourne, 1995).

Dougherty, Carol. *The Poetics of Colonization. From City to Text in Archaic Greece* (New York and Oxford, 1993).

Dreyer-Eimbcke, Oswald. *Island, Grönland und das nörliche Eismeer im Bild der Kartographie seit dem 10. Jahrhundert* (Hamburg, 1987).

Duberman, Martin. *James Russell Lowell* (Boston, 1966).

DuBois, B. H. 'Did the Norse Discover America?', *Magazine of American History* 27 (1892), 362–77.

Dunae, Patrick. 'Boys' Literature and the Idea of Race: 1870–1900', *Wascana Review* (Spring 1977), pp. 84–107.

——. 'Boys' Literature and the Idea of Empire, 1870–1914', *Victorian Studies* 24 (1980), 105–21.

——. 'New Grub Street for boys', in *Imperialism and juvenile literature*, ed. Jeffrey Richards (Manchester and New York, 1989), pp. 12–33.

Ebel, Else. 'Fiktion und Realität in den Vínlandsagas', in *Festschrift für Heinrich Beck*, ed. Heiko Uecker (Berlin and New York, 1994), pp. 89–100.

Edwards, P. D. *Frances Cashel Hoey*, Victorian Fiction Research Guides 8 (Department of English, University of Queensland, 1982).

Egge, Albert E. 'Scandinavian Studies in the United States', *Modern Language Notes* 3 (1888), 66–8.

Einars þáttr Sokkasonar (Grœnlendinga þáttr). Ed. Matthías Þórðarson, in *Eyrbyggja saga. Grœnlendinga sǫgur*, Íslenzk fornrit 4 (Reykjavík, 1935).

Eiríks saga rauða. Ed. Matthías Þórðarson, in *Eyrbyggja saga. Grœnlendinga sǫgur*, Íslenzk fornrit 4 (Reykjavík, 1935).

Eiríks saga rauða. Texti Skálholtsbókar AM 557 4to. Ed. Ólafur Halldórsson, Íslenzk fornrit 4 (suppl.) (Reykjavík, 1985).

Eiríks saga viðfǫrla. Ed. Helle Jensen, Editiones Arnamagnæanæ, Series B, Vol. 29 (Copenhagen, 1983).

Elliot, Charles W. *The New England History, from the discovery of the continent by the Northmen, A.D. 986*, 2 vols (New York, 1857).

Elliott, J. H. *The Old World and the New 1492–1650* (Cambridge, 1970; Canto edn, 1992).

Emerson, Ralph Waldo. *The Collected Works of Ralph Waldo Emerson*, I, *Nature, Addresses, and Lectures*, introd. Robert E. Spiller; text established by Alfred R. Ferguson (Cambridge, Mass., 1971).

——. *The Journals and Miscellaneous Notebooks of Ralph Waldo Emerson*, ed. William Gilman *et al.*, 16 vols (Cambridge, Mass., 1960–82).

Enterline, James Robert. *Viking America: the Norse Crossings and their legacy* (New York, 1972).

Everett, Alexander Hill. Review of Washington Irving, *A History of the Life and Voyages of Christopher*, 3 vols (New York and London, 1828), *The North American Review* 28 (1829), 103–34.

——. Review ('The Discovery of America by the Northmen') of *Antiquitates Americanæ*, *United States Magazine and Democratic Review* 2 (1838), 85–96, 143–58.

Everett, Edward. Review ('The Discovery of America by the Northmen') of *Antiquitates Americanæ*, *The North American Review* 46 (1838), 161–203.

Eyrbyggja saga. Ed. Einar Ól. Sveinsson, in *Eyrbyggja saga. Grœnlendinga sǫgur*, Íslenzk fornrit 4 (Reykjavík, 1935).

Falnes, Oscar J. 'New England Interest in Scandinavian Culture and the Norsemen', *The New England Quarterly* 10 (1937), 211–42.

Farley, Frank Edgar. *Scandinavian Influences in the English Romantic Movement*, Studies and Notes in Philology and Literature 9 (Boston, 1903).

Fernández-Armesto, Felipe. *Before Columbus. Exploration and Colonisation from the Mediterranean to the Atlantic 1229–1492* (London, 1987).

Fisher, Peter, and Hilda Ellis Davidson (trans. and eds) *Saxo Grammaticus: History of the Danes I–II* (Cambridge, 1979–80).

Fiske, John. *The Discovery of America, with some account of Ancient America and the Spanish Conquest*, 2 vols (Boston and New York, 1892).

Fiske, Willard. *Chess in Iceland and in Icelandic literature* (Florence, 1905).

———. *Life and Correspondence. A Biographical Study by his literary executor Horatio S. White* (New York, 1925).

Flateyjarbók. En Samling af Norske Konge-sagaer, eds Guðbrandur Vigfusson and C. R. Unger, 3 vols (Christiania, 1860–68).

Fleming, Robin. 'Picturesque History and the Medieval in Nineteenth-Century America', *American Historical Review* 100 (1995), 1080–4.

Flóamanna saga. Eds Þorhallur Vilmundarson and Bjarni Vilhjálmsson, in *Harðar saga*, Íslenzk fornrit 13 (Reykjavík, 1991).

Flom, George T. *A History of Scandinavian Studies in American Universities, together with a bibliography*, Iowa Studies in Language and Literature 11 (Iowa City, 1907).

Folsom, George. Review ('Discovery of America by the Northmen') of *Antiquitates Americanæ*, *The New York Review* 2 (1838), 352–71.

Foote, P. G. 'A Question of Conscience', *Opuscula Septentrionalia. Festskrift til Ole Widding*, ed. Bent Chr. Jacobsen *et al.* (Copenhagen, 1977), pp. 11–18.

———, Peter. 'Observations on "syncretism" in early Icelandic Christianity', *Aurvandilstá. Norse Studies* (Odense, 1984), pp. 84–100.

———. 'On the Vínland Legends on *The Vinland Map*', *Saga-Book of the Viking Society* 17 (1966–69), 73–89.

Føroya Kvæði. Corpus Carminum Færoensium, I, eds N. Djurhuus, N and Chr. Matras (Copenhagen, 1951–63).

Forster, John Reinhold. *History of the Voyages and Discoveries made in the North, translated from the German of John Reinhold Forster* (London, 1786).

Fostbrœðra saga. Ed. Guðni Jónsson, in *Vestfirðinga sǫgur*, Íslenzk fornrit 6 (Reykjavík, 1943).

Franklin, Benjamin. *The Papers of Benjamin Franklin*, ed. Leonard W. Labaree *et al.*, 34 vols (New Haven and London, 1959–98).

Franklin, Wayne. *Discoverers, Explorers, Settlers. The Diligent Writers of Early America* (Chicago and London, 1979).

Friedman, John Block. *The Monstrous Races in Medieval Art and Thought* (Cambridge, Mass., 1981).

Frobisher, Martin. *The Three Voyages of Martin Frobisher, in search of passage to*

Cathaia and India by the North-West, A.D. 1576–8, ed. Richard Collinson (London, 1867).

———. *The Three Voyages of Martin Frobisher. In search of a passage to Cathay and India by the North-West, A.D. 1576–8. From the original 1578 text of George Best*, ed. Vilhjalmur Stefansson, 2 vols (London, 1838).

Frost, Alan. 'New South Wales as *Terra Nullius*: the British Denial of Aboriginal Land Rights', *Historical Studies* 19 (1981), 513–23.

Frost, John. *The Pictorial History of the United States of America*, 4 vols (London, 1843).

Gathorne-Hardy, G. M. *The Norse Discoverers of America. The Wineland Sagas translated & discussed* (Oxford, 1921).

Gerbi, Antonello, trans. Jeremy Moyle. *Nature in the New World. From Christopher Columbus to Gonzalo Fernández de Oviedo* (Pittsburgh, 1985).

Gering, Hugo. Review of Arthur Reeves, *The Finding of Wineland the Good* (London, 1890), *Zeitschrift für deutsche Philologie* 7 (1892), 353–6.

Goodrich, Aaron. *A History of the Character and Achievements of the So-Called Christopher Columbus* (New York, 1874).

Gravier, Gabriel. *Découverte de l'Amérique par les Normands au xe siècle* (Rouen, 1874).

Gray, Edward F. *Leif Eriksson Discoverer of America A.D. 1003* (London, 1930).

Greenblatt, Stephen. *Marvelous Possessions. The Wonder of the New World* (Oxford, 1991).

Greenfield, Bruce. *Narrating Discovery. The Romantic Explorer in American Literature, 1790–1855* (New York, 1992).

———. 'The Problem of the Discoverer's Authority in Lewis and Clark's *History*', in *Macropolitics of Nineteenth-Century Literature: Nationalism, Exoticism, Imperialism*, eds Jonathan Arac and Harriet Ritvo (Durham and London, 1995).

Gribbin, John, and H. H. Lamb. 'Climatic change in historical times', in *Climatic Change*, ed. John Gribbin (Cambridge, 1978), pp. 68–82.

Grøndal, Benedict (ed.) *Breve fra og til Carl Christian Rafn, med en Biographi* (Copenhagen, 1869).

Grænlendinga saga. Ed. Matthías Þórðarson, in *Eyrbyggja saga. Grænlendinga sǫgur*, Íslenzk Fornrit 4 (Reykjavík, 1935).

Grænlendinga þáttr. See *Einars þáttr Sokkasonar*.

Grønlands historiske Mindesmærker, 3 vols (Copenhagen 1838–45).

Gudbrand Vigfusson and F. York Powell. *An Icelandic Prose Reader* (Oxford, 1879).

——— (eds and trans.) *Origines Islandicae. A Collection of the more important sagas and other native writings relating to the settlement and early history of Iceland*, 2 vols (Millwood, NY; Kraus Reprints, 1976).

Gunnars saga Keldugnúpsfífls. Ed. Jóhannes Halldórsson, in *Kjalnesinga Saga*, Íslenzk fornrit 14 (Reykjavík 1959).

Guralnick, Eleanor (ed.) *Vikings in the West. Papers presented at a symposium sponsored by The Archaeological Institute of America, Chicago Society, and the*

Museum of Science and Industry of Chicago; held at the Museum of Science and Industry, *Aoruk 3, 1982* (Chicago, 1982).

Hálfdanar saga Brǫnufóstra. Ed. Guǒni Jónsson, in *Fornaldar sögur Norǒurlanda* 4 (Reykjavík, 1954).

Halldór Hermannsson. *Bibliography of the Icelandic Sagas and Minor Tales*, *Islandica* 1 (Ithaca, 1908; rpr. 1966).

——. *The Northmen in America*, *Islandica* 2 (Ithaca, 1909).

——. *The Problem of Wineland*, *Islandica* 25 (Ithaca and New York, 1936).

——. *The Vinland Sagas, edited with an introduction, variants and notes*, *Islandica* 30 (Ithaca and New York, 1944).

Hannabuss, Stuart. 'Ballantyne's message of empire', in *Imperialism and juvenile literature*, ed. Jeffrey Richards (Manchester and New York, 1989), pp. 53–71.

Hanse, Harry. *Longfellow's New England* (New York, 1972).

Haraldur Bessason. 'New Light on Vinland from the Sagas', *Mosaic* 1 (1967–68), 52–65.

Harbert, Earl N., and Robert A. Rees. *Fifteen American Authors Before 1900: Bibliographical Essays on Research and Criticism*, rev. edn (Madison, Wis., 1984).

Harley, J. B., and David Woodward (eds) *Cartography in Prehistoric, Ancient, and Medieval Europe and the Mediterranean* (Chicago, 1987).

Hart, Albert Bushnell, and Edward Channing. 'Extracts from the Sagas Describing the Voyages to Vinland', *American History Leaflets* 3 (New York, 1892).

Harvey, P. D. A. *Medieval Maps* (Toronto, 1991).

Hastrup, Kirsten. 'Cosmology and Society in Medieval Iceland', *Ethnologica Scandinavica* (1981), 63–78.

——. 'Establishing an Ethnicity. The emergence of the "Icelanders" in the early Middle Ages', in *Semantic Anthropology*, ed. David Parkin (London, 1982), pp. 145–60.

——. *Culture and History in Medieval Iceland: An anthropological analysis of structure and change* (Oxford, 1985).

——. *Island of Anthropology: Studies in past and present Iceland* (Odense, 1990).

Haugen, Einar. 'History of the Department of Scandinavian Studies at the University of Wisconsin 1869–1931', Typescript (University of Wisconsin, Madison, Archives).

——. 'Wisconsin Pioneers in Scandinavian Studies: Anderson and Olson, 1875–1931', *Wisconsin Magazine of History* (Autumn 1950), pp. 29–36.

Hauksbók. Eds Eríkur Jónsson and Finnur Jónsson (Copenhagen, 1892–96).

Haynes, Henry. 'The Historical Character of the Norse Sagas', *Proceedings of the Massachusetts Historical Society* 5 (1890), 332–40.

——. 'A few Words more about Leif Ericson and the Norse Sagas', *Proceedings of the Massachusetts Historical Society* 7 (1892), 349–54.

Hazlett, John D. 'Literary Nationalism and Ambivalence in Washington Irving's

The Life and Voyages of Christopher Columbus', *American Literature* 55 (1983), 560–75.

Hedges, William L. *Washington Irving: An American Study, 1802–1832* (Baltimore, 1965).

Henderson, Ebenezer. *Iceland; or the journal of a residence in that island during the years 1814 and 1815*, 2nd edn (Edinburgh, 1819).

Hennig, Richard. *Terrae Incognitae: Eine Zusammenstellung und kritische Bewertung der wichtigsten vorcolumbischen Entdeckungsreisen an Hand der darüber vorliegenden Originalberichte*, 4 vols, 2nd edn (Leiden, 1944–56).

Herbermann, Charles G. *The History of ancient Vinland by Thormod Torfason. Translated from the Latin* (New York, 1891).

Hermann Pálsson. 'Íslenzkar fornsögur og Isidor frá Seville', *Tímarit Þjóðræknisfélags Íslendinga* 49 (1968), 35–8.

—— and Paul Edwards (trans.) *The Book of Settlements. Landnámabók* (Winnipeg, 1972).

Herval, René (trans.) 'Voyage de Giovanni da Verrazano à la «Francesca» (1524)', in *Jacques Cartier: Voyages au Canada. Avec les relations des voyages en Amérique de Gonneville, Verrazano et Roberval* (Paris, 1981).

Hewlett, Maurice. *The Light Heart* (London, 1920).

——. *Gudrid the Fair* (London, 1924).

Higginson, Thomas Wentworth. *A Book of American Explorers* (Boston and New York, 1877).

Hilen, Andrew. *Longfellow and Scandinavia. A Study of the Poet's Relationship with the Northern Languages and Literature*, Yale Studies in English 107 (New Haven and London, 1947).

——. 'Longfellow and Scandinavia Revisited', in *Papers Presented at the Longfellow Commemorative Conference, April 1–3, 1982* (Longfellow National Historic Site, 1982), pp. 1–12.

Hodge, Frederick W. (ed.) *Handbook of American Indians North of Mexico*, 2 vols (Washington, DC, 1906; republ. New York, 1960).

Hodgetts, J. F. *Edric the Norseman. A Tale of Adventure and Discovery, The Boy's Own Paper* 10/455–72 (October 1887–January 1888).

Hodgson, Amanda. *The Romances of William Morris* (Cambridge, 1987).

Holland, Henry M. D. 'Preliminary Dissertation on the History and Literature of Iceland', in Sir George Steuart Mackenzie, *Travels in the Island of Iceland during the summer of the year MDCCCX* (Edinburgh, 1812).

Holtsmark, Anne. *Studier i Snorres Mytologi* (Oslo, 1964).

Honour, Hugh. *The New Golden Land* (London, 1975).

Honti, John Th. 'New Ways to Vinland Problems', *Acta Ethnologica* (1938), 17–30.

——. 'Vinland and Ultima Thule', *Modern Language Notes* 54 (1939), 159–72.

Horsford, Eben Norton. *Discovery of America by Northmen. Address at the Unveiling of the Statue of Leif Eriksen, delivered in Faneuil Hall, Oct. 29, 1887*

(Boston and New York, 1888). Also printed in the *Boston Evening Transcript*, Saturday, October 29, 1887 (unpaginated).

———. *The Discovery of the Ancient City of Norumbega. A Communication to the President and Council of the American Geographical Society at their special session in Watertown, November 21, 1889* (Cambridge, Mass., n.d.)

———. *The Problem of the Northmen. A Letter to Judge Daly, The President of the American Geographical Society* (Cambridge, Mass., 1889).

———. *The Defences of Norumbega; and a review of the reconaissances of Col. T. W. Higginson, et al.: A Letter to Judge Daly* (Boston and New York, 1891).

———, and Cornelia Horsford. *Leif's House in Vineland. Graves of the Northmen* (Boston, 1893).

Horsman, Reginald. *Race and Manifest Destiny. The Origins of American Racial Anglo-Saxonism* (Cambridge, Mass., 1981).

Hough, Clara Sharpe. *Leif the Lucky. A romantic saga of the sons of Erik the Red* (New York and London, 1926).

de Humboldt, Alexander. *Examen critique le l'histoire de la geographie du nouveau continent et des progrès de l'astronomie nautique aux quinzième et seizième siècles*, 5 vols (Paris, 1836–39).

von Humboldt, Alexander. *Cosmos: A Sketch of a Physical Description of the Universe, translated from the German by E. C. Otté* (London, 1849).

Hungrvaka. Ed. Jón Helgason (Copenhagen, 1938).

Hustvedt, Lloyd, *Rasmus Bjørn Anderson. Pioneer Scholar* (Northfield, Minn., 1966).

Huyghe, Patrick. *Columbus Was Last* (New York, 1992).

Ingstad, Anne Stine. *The Discovery of a Norse Settlement in America: Excavations at L'Anse aux Meadows, Newfoundland, 1961–1968*, I (Oslo, Bergen, Tromsø, 1977).

———, and Helge Ingstad. *The Norse Discovery of America I–II* (Oslo, 1985).

Irving, Washington. *A History of New York, from the beginning of the world to the end of the Dutch dynasty, The Works of Washington Irving*, 1 (London, 1883).

———. *The Life and Voyages of Christopher Columbus; together with the Voyages of His Companions*, author's revised edn, 2 vols, *The Works of Washington Irving*, 6 (London, 1883).

———. *The Life and Voyages of Christopher Columbus*, ed. John Harmon McElroy, *The Complete Works of Washington Irving*, 9 (Boston, 1981).

———. Review of Wheaton's *History of the Northmen*, *The North American Review* 35 (1832), 342–71.

Irwin, Constance. *Gudrid's Saga. The Norse Settlement in America. A Documentary Novel* (New York, 1974).

Jakob Benediktsson. 'Hafgerðingadrápa', in *Speculum Norroenum. Norse Studies in Memory of Gabriel Turville-Petre*, eds Ursula Dronke, Guðrún P. Helgadóttir, Gerd Wolfgang Weber, Hans Bekker-Nielsen (Odense, 1981), pp. 27–32.

James, Louis. 'Tom Brown's Imperialist Sons', *Victorian Studies* 17 (1973–74), 89–99.

Jansson, Sven B. F. *Sagorna om Vinland*, I, *Handskrifterna til Erik den rödes saga* (Lund, 1944).

Jefferson, Thomas. *Notes on the State of Virginia*, ed. Thomas Perkins Abernethy (New York, 1964).

Jelič, Luka. 'L'Évangélisation de l'Amérique avant Christophe Colomb', in *Compte rendu du troisième congrès scientifique international des Catholiques tenu à Bruxelles 1894* (Brussels, 1895), pp. 3–7.

——. 'L'Évangélisation de l'Amérique avant Christophe Colomb', *Le Missioni Francescane* 8 (1897), 556–60.

——. 'L'Évangélisation de l'Amérique avant Christophe Colomb', in *Compte rendu du congrès scientifique international des Catholiques tenu à Paris 1891* (Paris, 1891), pp. 170–84.

—— (with manuscript notes by John Shipley). *Najstariji kartografski spomenik o rimskoj pokrajini Dalmaciji* (Sarajevo, 1898).

Jesch, Judith. *Women in the Viking Age* (Cambridge, 1991).

Jett, Stephen C. 'Pre-Columbian Transoceanic Contacts', in *Ancient Native Americans*, ed. Jesse D. Jennings (San Francisco, 1978), pp. 593–656.

Jochens, Jenny. *Old Norse Images of Women* (Philadelphia, 1996).

Jón Jóhanneson. 'Aldur Graenlendinga sögu', *Nordaela* (Reykjavík, 1956), 150–7; trans. Tryggvi J. Oleson as 'The Date of the Composition of the Saga of the Greenlanders', *Saga-Book of the Viking Society* 16 (1962), 54–66.

——, trans. Haraldur Bessason. *A History of the Old Icelandic Commonwealth* (Winnipeg, 1974).

Jón Hnefill Aðalsteinsson. *Under the Cloak. The Acceptance of Christianity in Iceland with particular Reference to the Religious Attitudes Prevailing at the time* (Uppsala, 1978).

Jones, Gwyn. *The North Atlantic Saga*, 2nd edn (Oxford and New York, 1986).

Julien, Ch.-A. (introd.) *Les Français en Amérique pendant la première moitié du XVI siècle: textes des voyages de Gonneville, Verrazano, J. Cartier et Roberval* (Paris, 1946).

Kålund, Kr. (ed.) *Alfræði Íslenzk. Islandsk Encyklopædisk Litteratur*; 3 vols (Copenhagen, 1908–18).

——. Review of A. M. Reeves, *The Finding of Wineland the Good* (London, 1890), *Arkiv för nordisk filologi* 7 (1891), 383–6.

Katz, Wendy. *Rider Haggard and the Fiction of Empire* (Cambridge, 1987).

Kaups, Matti Enn. 'Shifting Vinland – Tradition and Myth', *Terrae Incognitae* 2 (1971), 29–60.

Keen, Benjamin (trans.) *The Life of the Admiral Christopher Columbus by his son Ferdinand* (New Brunswick, NJ, 1959).

Kellett, Ernest Edward. *The Passing of Scyld and Other Poems* (London, 1902).

——. *Ex Libris: Confessions of a Constant Reader* (London, 1940).

Kennedy, Charles Rann. *The Winterfeast* (New York and London, 1908).

Kingsley, Charles. *The Works of Charles Kingsley* (London, 1885).

Kingston, W. G. H. *Peter the Whaler* (London, 1930).

Kipling, Rudyard. *Many Inventions* (London and New York, 1893).

Koeman, C. *The History of Abraham Ortelius and his Theatrum Orbis Terrarum* (Lausanne, 1964).

Kolbrún Haraldsdóttir. 'Flateyjarbók', in *Medieval Scandinavia: An Encyclopedia*, ed. Phillip Pulsiano (New York, 1993), pp. 197–8.

Konungsannáll. Ed. Guðni Jónsson, in *Annálar og Nafnaskrá* (Reykjavík, 1953).

Konungs Skuggsiá. Ed. Ludvig Holm-Olsen, rev. edn (Oslo, 1983).

Kretschmer, K. Review of Arthur Reeves, *The Finding of Wineland the Good* (London, 1890), *Deutsche Litteraturzeitung*, 20 February, 1897, pp. 258–60.

Laing, Samuel. *The Heimskringla; or Chronicle of The Kings of Norway. Translated from the Icelandic of Snorro Sturleson, With a Preliminary Dissertation*, 3 vols (London, 1844).

Lamb, H. H. *Climate Past, Present, and Future* (London, 1977).

Lammers, Donald. 'Nevil Shute and the Decline of the "Imperial Idea" in Literature', *Journal of British Studies* 16 (1977), 123–4.

Landnámabók. Ed. Jakob Benediktsson, Íslenzk fornrit, 1, i–ii (Reykjavík, 1968).

Lang, Andrew. *Essays in Little*, new and revised edn (London, 1892).

———. *The Light Heart* (London, 1920).

Lanier, Sidney. *The Centennial Edition of the Works of Sidney Lanier*, ed. Charles R. Anderson, 10 vols (Baltimore, 1945).

Larsson, Mats G. 'The Vinland Sagas and Nova Scotia. A Reappraisal of an Old Theory', *Scandinavian Studies* 64 (1992), 305–35.

The Laws of Early Iceland, Grágás I. Trans. Andrew Dennis, Peter Foote, and Richard Perkins (Winnipeg, 1980).

Laxdœla saga. Ed. Einar Ól. Sveinsson, Íslenzk fornrit 5 (Reykjavík, 1934).

Levin, David. *History as Romantic Art: Bancroft, Prescott, Motley, and Parkman* (New York and Burlingame, 1959).

Lieder, Paul Robert. 'Scott and Scandinavian Literature. The Influence of Bartholin and Others', *Smith College Studies* 2 (1920), 8–57.

Liljencrantz, Ottilie Adeline. *The Thrall of Leif the Lucky. A Story of Viking Days* (London, Melbourne, Toronto, 1904).

———. *Randvar the Songsmith. Ar omance of Norumbega* (New York and London, 1906).

———. *The Vinland Champions* (London, Melbourne, Toronto, 1911).

Lindow, John. 'Supernatural Others and Ethnic Others: A Millennium of World View', *Scandinavian Studies* 67 (1995), 8–31.

Litzenberg, Karl. *The Victorians and the Vikings: A Bibliographical Essay on Anglo-Norse Literary Relations*, University of Michigan Contributions in Modern Philology 3 (1947).

Lodewyckx, A. 'Freydís Eiríksdóttir rauða and the Germania of Tacitus', *Arkiv for nordisk filologi* 70 (1955), 182–7.

Longfellow, Henry Wadsworth. *Longfellow's Works. The Works of Henry Wadsworth Longfellow, with bibliographical and Critical Notes and His Life, with extracts from his journals and correspondence, edited by Samuel Longfellow*, 14 vols (Boston and New York, 1886–91).

———. *Life of Henry Wadsworth Longfellow, with Extracts from his Journals and Correspondence*, edited by Samuel Longfellow, 3 vols (*Longfellow's Works*, Vols 12–14) (Boston and New York, 1886–91).

———. 'A review of the fifth edition of Tegnér's poem, and a German and English translation', *The North American Review* 45 (1837), 149–83.

———. *The Letters of Henry Wadsworth Longfellow*. Ed. Andrew Hilen, 2 vols (Cambridge, Mass., 1966).

Lowell, James Russell. *Letters of James Russell Lowell, edited by Charles Eliot Norton*, 2 vols (New York, 1893; rpr. 1977).

———. *The Poetical Works of James Russell Lowell. Revised and with a New Introduction by Marjorie R. Kaufman* (Boston, 1978).

Lowenthal, David. 'G. P. Marsh and Scandinavian Studies', *Scandinavian Studies* 29 (1957), 41–52.

———. *George Perkins Marsh, Versatile Vermonter* (New York, 1959).

Lunenfeld, Marvin (ed.) *1492: Discovery, Invasion, Encounter. Sources and Interpretations* (Lexington, Mass., and Toronto, 1991).

Lyschander, Claus. *C. C. Lyschander's Digtning 1579–1623*, ed. Flemming Lundgreen-Nielsen (Copenhagen, 1989).

MacKenzie, John M. *Propaganda and Empire: the manipulation of British Public Opinion, 1880–1960* (Manchester, 1984).

MacLean, J. P. *A Critical Examination of the Evidences Adduced to Establish the Theory of the Norse Discovery of America* (Chicago, 1892).

Maddox, Lucy. *Removals. Nineteenth-Century American Literature and the Politics of Indian Affairs* (New York and Oxford, 1991).

Madsen, Deborah L. *The Postmodernist Allegories of Thomas Pynchon* (New York, 1991).

Mallet, Paul Henri. *Introduction a l'histoire de Dannemarc, ou l'on traite de la Réligion, des Loix, des Mœurs & des Usages des Anciens Danois* (Copenhagen, 1755).

———. *Introduction a l'histoire de Dannemarc, ou l'on traite de la Réligion, des Loix, des Mœurs & des Usages des anciens Danois, Seconde Edition revuë & corrigée*, 2 vols (Geneva, 1763).

Manning, Val. *Viking Queen* (London, 1978).

Marcus, G. J. *The Conquest of the North Atlantic* (Woodbridge, 1980).

Marsh, George P. *A Compendious Grammar of the Old-Northern or Icelandic Language, compiled and translated from the Grammars of Rask* (Burlington, Vt., 1838).

——— (trans.) 'The Origin, Progress and Decline of Icelandic Historical Literature, by Peter Erasmus Mueller, late Bishop of Zealand in Denmark. *Translated from the original in the Nordisk Tidsskrift for Oldkyndighed, 1. B. 1 H., with notes*', *The American Eclectic* 1 (1841), 446–68.

———. *The Goths in New-England. A Discourse delivered at the anniversary of the Philomathesian Society of Middlebury College, August 15, 1843* (Middlebury, Vt., 1843).

————. *The Origin and History of the English Language and of the early literature it embodies* (London, 1862).

————. *Catalogue of the Library of George Perkins Marsh* (Burlington, Vt., 1892).

Matthías Þórðarson. 'Um dauða Skalla-Gríms og hversu hann var heygður (Egils-Saga, LVIII. Kap.)', *Festskrift til Finnur Jónsson* (Copenhagen, 1928), pp. 109–12.

McDougall, Ian. 'The enigmatic einfœtingr of Eiríks saga rauða', in *Frejas Psalter: en psalter i 40 afdelinger til brug for Jonna Louis-Jensen på tresårsdagen den 21. oktober 1996*, eds Bergljót S. Kristjánsdóttir and Peter Springborg (Copenhagen, 1997), pp. 128–32.

McGhee, Robert. 'Contact Between Native North Americans and the Medieval Norse: A Review of the Evidence', *American Antiquity* 49 (1984), 4–26.

McGlinchee, Claire. *James Russell Lowell* (New York, 1967).

McGovern, Thomas H. 'The economics of extinction in Norse Greenland', in *Climate and History: Studies in past climates and their impact on Man*, eds T. M. L. Wigley, M. J. Ingram, and G. Farmer (Cambridge, 1981), pp. 404–33.

————. 'The Vinland Adventure: A North Atlantic Perspective', *North American Archaeologist* 2 (1980–81), 285–308.

McTurk, Rory. 'Approaches to the Structure of *Eyrbyggja saga*', in *Sagnaskemtmun. Studies in Honour of Hermann Pálsson*, eds Rudolf Simek, Jónas Kristjánsson, and Hans Bekker-Nielsen (Vienna, Cologne, Graz, 1986), pp. 223–37.

Merrill, William Stetson. 'The Vinland Problem Through Four Centuries', *The Catholic Historical Review* 21 (1936), 21–48.

Metcalfe, W. M. 'The Norse Discovery of America', *Scottish Review* 18 (1891), 341–66.

Metcalf, Paul. *Apalache* (Berkeley, 1976).

Meyers, Jeffrey. *Fiction & The Colonial Experience* (Ipswich, 1973).

Moldenhauer Joseph J. *The Maine Woods* (Princeton, 1972).

————. '*Pym*, the Dighton Rock, and the Matter of Vinland', in *Poe's* Pym: *Critical Explorations*, ed. Richard Kopley (Durham and London, 1992), pp. 75–94.

Montgomery, James. *The Poetical Works of James Montgomery collected by himself* (London, 1851).

————. *Greenland and Abdallah*, introd. Donald H. Reiman (New York and London, 1978).

Monumenta Historica Norvegiæ. Ed. Gustav Storm (Kristiania, 1880).

Moorehead, Alan. *The White Nile* (London, 1960).

Morison, Samuel Eliot. *The European Discovery of America: The Northern Voyages A.D.500–1600* (New York, 1971).

Morris, Charles. *The Aryan Race, its origin and its achievements* (Chicago, 1892).

————. 'Vineland and the Vikings', *Historical Tales. The Romance of Reality*, I (New York and Los Angeles, 1893), pp. 9–25.

Morris, William. *The Collected Letters of William Morris*, edited by *Norman Kelvin*, 4 vols (Princeton, 1987).

——, and Eiríkr Magnússon (trans.) *The Story of the Ere-Dwellers (Eyrbyggja Saga)* (London, 1892).

Moulton, Joseph, *History of the State of New York*, I (New York, 1824).

Münter, Frederik C. C. *Kirchengeschichte von Dænemark und Norwegen* I (Leipzig, 1823–33).

Murray, Hugh. *Historical Account of Discoveries and Travels in North America* (London, 1829).

Nansen, Fridtjof, trans. Arthur G. Chater. *In Northern Mists. Arctic Exploration in Early Times*, 2 vols (London, 1911).

Neukomm, Edmond. *Les dompteurs de la mer; les Normands en Amérique depuis le x jusqu'au xv siècle* (Paris, 1895).

——, trans. Mrs Cashel Hoey. *Tamers of the Sea. The Northmen in America from the Tenth to the Fifteenth Century* (London, 1887).

Nordby, Conrad Hjalmar. *The Influence of Old Norse Literature upon English Literature* (New York, 1901).

Ólafur Halldórsson (ed.) *Ólafs saga Tryggvasonar en mesta*, Editiones Arnamagnæanæ, Series A, 2 vols (Copenhagen, 1961).

Ólafur Halldórsson. *Grænland í miðaldaritum* (Reykjavík, 1978).

——. 'Lost Tales of Guðríðr Þorbjarnardóttir', in *Sagnaskemmtun. Studies in Honour of Hermann Pálsson on his 65th birthday, 26 May 1986*, eds Rudolf Simek, Jónas Kristjánsson, and Hans Bekker-Nielsen (Vienna, Cologne, Graz, 1986), pp. 239–46.

Ólsen, Björn Magnússon (ed.) *Den Tredje og Fjærde Grammatiske Afhandling i Snorres Edda Tilligemed de Grammatiske Afhandlingers Prolog og To Andre Tillæg* (Copenhagen, 1884).

Olson, Charles. *The Maximus Poems. Volume Three*, eds Charles Boer and George F. Butterick (New York, 1975).

Olson, Julius E. 'The Leif Erikson Monument', *The Nation* 45 (1887), 395–6.

Omberg, Margaret. *Scandinavian Themes in English Poetry, 1760–1800*, Acta Universitatis Upsaliensis, Studia Anglistica Upsaliensia, 29 (1976).

Ortelius, Abraham. *The Theatre of the Whole World* (London, 1606; rpr. Amsterdam, 1968), introd. by R. A. Skelton.

P.A.C. (Charlotte Porter and Helen A. Clarke?). 'School of Literature. Poems Illustrative of American History: Longfellow's "Skeleton in Armor" ', *Poet-lore* 7 (1895), 41–8.

——. 'School of Literature. Poems Illustrative of American History: Poems of Discoveries; Lowell's "Columbus" and Whitman's "Prayer of Columbus" ', *Poet-lore* 7 (1895), 161–6, 218–22.

——. 'School of Literature. Poems Illustrative of American History: Whittier's "The Norsemen" ', *Poet-lore* 7 (1895), 105–9.

Pagden, Anthony. *European Encounters with the New World. From Renaissance to Romanticism* (New Haven and London, 1993).

Parks, Edd Winfield. *Sidney Lanier: the Man, the Poet, the Critic* (Athens, Ga., 1968).

Pàroli, Teresa. 'Bishops and Explorers: On the structure of the Vínland Sagas', in *Sagnaþing helgað Jónasi Kristjánssyni sjötugum 10. apríl 1994*, ed. Gísli Sigurðsson, Guðrún Kvaran, Sigurgeir Steingrímsson (Reykjavík, 1994), pp. 641–52.

Pearce, Roy Harvey. *The Continuity of American Poetry* (Princeton, 1961).

Percy, Thomas. *Northern Antiquities: or, a Description of the Manners, Customs, Religion and Laws of the Ancient Danes, And other Northern Nations*, 2 vols (London, 1770).

Perkins, Richard. 'Norse Implications', in *The Strange Case of the Vinland Map*, ed. H. Wallis *et al.*, *Geographical Journal* 140 (1974), 199–205.

———. 'The Dreams of *Flóamanna Saga*, *Saga-Book of the Viking Society* 19 (1974–77), 191–238.

———. 'The Furðustrandir of *Eiríks saga rauða*', *Mediaeval Scandinavia* 9 (1976), 51–98.

———. *Flóamanna saga, Gaulverjabær and Haukr Erlendsson*, Studia Islandica 36 (Reykjavík, 1978).

Perkins, R. M. 'Eyrbyggja saga', *Reallexikon der Germanischen Altertumskunde*, ed. Heinrich Beck *et al.*, 8 (Berlin and New York, 1991), 49–57.

Phillips, J. R. S. *The Medieval Expansion of Europe* (Oxford, 1988).

Phillips, William D., Jr., and Carla Rahn Phillips. *The Worlds of Christopher Columbus* (Cambridge, 1992).

Poole, Russell. 'Constructions of Fate in Victorian Philology and Literature', in *Old Norse Studies in the New World*, eds Geraldine Barnes, Margaret Clunies Ross, and Judy Quinn (Sydney, 1994), pp. 110–19.

Prescott, William H. *History of the Conquest of Mexico*, ed. Wilfred Harold Munro (Philadelphia and London, 1904).

Priest, Josiah. *American Antiquities, and discoveries in the west: being an exhibition of the evidence that an ancient population of partially civilized nations, differing entirely from those of the present Indians, peopled America, many centuries before its discovery by Columbus*, etc. (Albany, NY, 1833).

Pynchon, Thomas. *Vineland* (London, 1991).

Quayle, Eric. *Ballantyne the Brave. A Victorian Writer and his Family* (London, 1967).

———. *The Collector's Book of Boys' Stories* (London, 1973).

Quinn, D. B. 'The Vínland Map: A Viking Map of the West?', *Saga-Book of the Viking Society* 17 (1966–69), 63–72.

Quinn, David B. *America from Concept to Discovery. Early Exploration of North America*, 5 vols (London and Basingstoke, 1979).

Quinn, Judy, and Margaret Clunies Ross. 'The Image of Norse Poetry and Myth in Seventeenth-Century England', in *Northern Antiquity. The Post-Medieval Reception of Edda and Saga*, ed. Andrew Wawn (Enfield Lock, 1994), pp. 189–210.

Rafn, Charles C. *America Discovered in the Tenth Century* (New York, 1838).

——, C. C. 'Bemærkninger om en gammel bygning i Newport', *Annaler for nordisk Oldkyndighed* (1840–41), 37–51.

——, Charles Christian (ed.) *Supplement to the* Antiquitates Americanæ (Copenhagen, 1841).

——. *Mémoire sur la découverte de l'Amérique au dixième siècle* (Copenhagen, 1843).

——, Charles. 'The Discovery of America by the Northmen', *Proceedings of the New Jersey Historical Society* 6 (1851–53), 166–70.

——, Charles C. 'The Discovery of America by the Northmen', *The New England Historical and Genealogical Register* 7 (1853), 13–14.

——, Prof. Ch. C. 'Northmen in America', *Journal of the American Geographical and Statistical Society* 1 (1857), 178–9.

——, C. C. *Cabinet d'antiquités américaines à Copenhague. Rapport ethnographique*, 2nd edn (Copenhagen, 1858).

Reeves, Arthur Middleton. *The Finding of Wineland the Good. The History of the Icelandic Discovery of America, edited and translated from the earliest records* (London, 1890).

Rehder, Alfred. 'Júglans', *Cyclopedia of American Horticulture*, ed. L. H. Bailey, III (New York, 1975), 846.

Reman, Edward. *The Norse Discoveries and Explorations in America* (Berkeley and Los Angeles, 1949).

Reynolds, Henry. *Dispossession. Black Australians and White Invaders* (London and Sydney, 1989).

Richardson, Henry Handel. *Maurice Guest* (1908; Melbourne, 1965).

Riding In, James. 'The Politics of the Columbus Celebration: A Perspective of Myth and Reality in United States Society', *American Indian Culture and Research Journal* 17 (1993), 1–9.

Riley, E. S., Jr. 'Pre-Columbian Discovery of America by the Northmen', *Southern Magazine* 13 (1873), 700–12.

Robertson, William. *The History of America*, 3 vols, fourteenth edn (London, 1821).

Robinson, Kim Stanley. 'Vinland the Dream', in *Remaking History* (New York, 1991), pp. 108–19.

Rosen, David. 'The volcano and the cathedral: muscular Christianity and the origins of primal manliness', *Muscular Christianity. Embodying the Victorian Age*, ed. Donald E. Hall (Cambridge, 1994), pp. 17–44.

Roux, Jean-Paul. *Les explorateurs au Moyen Age* (Paris, 1985).

Rudd, Martin B. *The Influence of Old Norse Literature on English Literature in the Eighteenth and Nineteenth Centuries*. Unpubl. MA thesis, University of North Dakota (1907).

Saga Óláfs Tryggvasonar af Oddr Snorrason munk. Ed. Finnur Jónsson (Copenhagen, 1932).

Said, Edward. *Culture and Imperialism* (London, 1993).

Sale, Kirkpatrick. *The Conquest of Paradise: Christopher Columbus and the Columbian Legacy* (London, 1991).

Samuel, Raphael (ed.) *Patriotism: The Making and Unmaking of British National Identity*, I: *History and Politics* (London and New York, 1989).

Sauer, Carl O. *Northern Mists* (Berkeley and Los Angeles, 1968).

Sayers, William. 'Vinland, the Irish, "Obvious Fictions and Apocrypha" ', *Skandinavistik* 23 (1993), 1–15.

Schach, Paul. *Icelandic Sagas* (Boston, 1984).

Schier, Kurt. 'Iceland and the Rise of Literature in 'Terra Nova', *Gripla* 1 (1975), 168–81.

Schoolcraft, Henry. 'The ante-Columbian history of America', *The American Biblical Repository* (April 1839), pp. 430–49.

—— R. *Personal Memoirs of a Residence of Thirty Years with the Indian Tribes on the American Frontiers: with brief notices of passing events, facts, and opinions, A.D. 1812 to A.D. 1842* (Philadelphia, 1851).

Schröder, Johan. 'Om Skandinavernes Fordna Upptåcktsresor Till Nordamerika', *Svea* 1 (1818), 197–226.

Scott, Sir Walter. *The Pirate, with Introductory Essay and Notes by Andrew Lang*, 2 vols (London, 1893).

Seaver, Kirsten. 'The "Vinland Map": New light on an old controversy; who made it, and why?', *The Map Collector* 70 (1995), 32–40.

——. *The Frozen Echo. Greenland and the Exploration of North America ca. A.D. 1000–1500* (Stanford, 1996).

Selmer, Carl. 'The Vernacular Translations of the *Navigatio Sancti Brendani*. A Bibliographical Study', *Mediaeval Studies* 18 (1956), 145–57.

—— (ed.) *Navigatio Sancti Brendani Abbatis from Early Latin Manuscripts* (Notre Dame, 1959).

Sephton, John. *Eirik the Red's Saga: A translation read before the Literary and Philosophical Society of Liverpool; January twelfth, 1880* (Liverpool, 1880).

Sertima, Ivan Van. *They Came Before Columbus* (New York, 1976).

Shipley, Marie A. (née Brown) and J. B. Shipley. *The English Rediscovery and Colonization of America* (London, 1890).

——, Mrs Marie A. (née Brown) 'The Missing Records of the Norse Discovery of America', *Congrès international des Américanistes, huitième session (Paris 1890)* (Paris, 1892), 190–200.

——, Marie A. (née Brown) *The Norse Colonization in America by the light of the Vatican finds* (Lucerne, 1899).

Showalter, Elaine. *Sexual Anarchy: Gender and Culture at the Fin de Siècle* (London, 1991).

—— (ed.) *Daughters of Decadence. Women Writers of the Fin-de-Siècle* (New Brunswick, NJ, 1993).

Shute, Nevil. *An Old Captivity* (London, 1940).

——. *Vinland the Good* (London and Toronto, 1946).

Sigourney, Mrs L. H. *Scenes in My Native Land* (London, 1844).

Simek, Rudolf. 'Elusive Elysia or Which Way To Glæsisvellir?', *Sagnaskemtmun. Studies in Honour of Hermann Pálsson*, eds Rudolf Simek, Jónas Kristjánsson, and Hans Bekker-Nielsen (Vienna, Cologne, Graz, 1986), pp. 248–75.

————. *Altnordische Kosmographie. Studien und Quellen zu Weltbild und Welt-beschreibung in Norwegen und Island vom 12. bis zum 14. Jahrhundert* (Berlin, 1990).

Simpson, John M. '*Eyrbyggja saga* and nineteenth-century scholarship', in *Proceedings of the First International Saga conference, University of Edinburgh 1971*, eds Peter Foote, Hermann Pálsson, and Desmond Slay (London, 1973), pp. 360–94.

Skelton, R. A., Thomas E. Marston, and George D. Painter. *The Vinland Map and the Tartar Relation* (New Haven and London, 1965).

Slafter, Rev. Edmund F. *The Discovery of America by the Northmen 985–1015* (Concord, NH, 1891).

Smiley, Jane. *The Greenlanders* (London, 1988).

Smith, Charles Sprague, 'The Vinland Voyages', *Journal of the American Geographic Society* 24 (1892), 510–35.

Smith, G. Barnett. *The Romance of Colonization. The United States from the earliest times to the landing of the Pilgrim Fathers* (London, 1897).

Smith, John. *Captain John Smith: A Select Edition of His Writings*, ed. Karen Ordahl Kupperman (Chapel Hill and London, 1988).

Smith, Joshua Toulmin. *The Discovery of America by the Northmen in the Tenth Century* (London, 1839).

Snedden, Genevra. *Leif and Thorkel: Two Norse Boys of Long Ago* (New York, 1925).

Spies, Marijke. *Arctic Routes to Fabled Lands. Olivier Brunel and the Passage to China and Cathay in the Sixteenth Century* (Amsterdam 1997).

Starke, Aubrey Harrison. *Sidney Lanier. A Biographical and Critical Study* (New York, 1964).

Stefán Einarsson. 'The Freydís-Incident in Eiríks Saga Rauða, ch. 11', *Acta Philologica Scandinavica* 13 (1938–39), 246–56.

Stevens-Arroyo, Anthony M. 'The Inter-Atlantic Paradigm: The Failure of Spanish Medieval Colonization of the Canary and Caribbean Islands', *Comparative Studies in Society and History* 35 (1993), 515–43.

Storm, Gustav. 'Studier over Vinlandsreiserne, Vinlands Geografi og Ethno-grafi', *Aarbøger for nordisk Oldkyndighed og Historie* 1887, pp. 293–372.

————. (ed.) *Islandske Annaler indtil 1578* (Christiania, 1888).

————. 'Ginnungagap i Mythologien og i Geografien', *Arkiv för nordisk filologi* 6 (1890), 340–50.

Stoutenburgh, John L., Jr. *Dictionary of the American Indian* (New York, 1960).

Strömback, Dag. *Sejd. Textstudier i nordisk religionshistoria* (Lund, 1935).

————, trans. Peter Foote. *The Conversion of Iceland. A Survey* (London, 1975).

Such, Peter. *Vanished Peoples. The Archaic Dorset & Beothuk People of Newfound-land* (Toronto, 1978).

Symington, Andrew James. 'Some Notable Men: I. Carl Christian Rafn', *The Fireside* (1889), pp. 53–7.

Taylor, Bayard. *The American Legend. A poem before the Phi beta kappa society of*

Harvard university, July 18, 1850 (Cambridge, 1850). Micropublished in *American Poetry, 1609–1900: Segment II* (New Haven, 1975).

Thalbitzer, William. 'Four Skræling Words from Markland (Newfoundland) in the Saga of Erik the Red (Eirikr Rauði)', *International Congress of Americanists. Proceedings of the XVIII Session* (London, 1912), pp. 87–95.

Torfaeus, Thormod. *Historia Vinlandiae antiquae* (Copenhagen, 1705).

Tucker, Susie I. 'Scandinavica for the Eighteenth-Century Common Reader', *Saga-Book of the Viking Society* 16 (1962), 233–47.

Turville-Petre, G. *Origins of Icelandic Literature* (Oxford, 1953).

Þórunn Sigurðardóttir (comp.) *Manuscript Material, Correspondence, and Graphic Material in the Fiske Icelandic Collection. A Descriptive Catalogue, Islandica* 48 (Ithaca and London, 1994).

Verduin, Kathleen. 'Medievalism and the Mind of Emerson', in *Medievalism in American Culture. Papers of the Eighteenth Annual Conference of the Center for Medieval and Early Renaissance Studies*, eds Bernard Rosenthal and Paul E. Szarmach (Binghamton, NY 1989), pp. 129–50.

Verrazzano, Giovanni, ed. Lawrence C Wroth. *The Voyages of Giovannni da Verrazzano 1524–1528* (New Haven and London, 1970).

——, trans. Susan Tarrow. 'Translation of the Cellère Codex', in Wroth, *The Voyages of Giovanni da Verrazzano 1524–1528*, pp. 133–43.

Vestfirðinga Sǫgur. Eds Björn K. Þórólfsson and Guðni Jónsson, Íslenzk fornrit 6 (Reykjavík, 1943).

Vilhjalmur Stefansson. *Iceland. The First American Republic* (New York, 1939).

——. *Ultima Thule. Further Mysteries of the Arctic* (London, 1942).

The Vinland Sagas. The Norse Discovery of America. Grænlendinga Saga and Eirik's Saga, trans. and introd. Magnus Magnusson and Hermann Pálsson (Harmondsworth, 1965).

Vollmann, William T. *The Ice-Shirt* (New York, 1990).

Wahlgren, Erik. 'Some Further Remarks on *Vinland*', *Scandinavian Studies* 40 (1968), 26–35.

——. 'Fact and Fancy in the Vinland sagas', in *Old Norse Literature and Mythology: a symposium*, ed. Edgar C. Polomé (Austin, Tx., and London, 1969), pp. 19–80.

——. *The Vikings and America* (London, 1986).

——. 'Vinland Map', *Medieval Scandinavia: An Encyclopedia*, ed. Phillip Pulsiano (New York, 1993), pp. 703–4.

Wahlund, Carl. *Die altfranzösische Prosaübersetzung von Brendans Meerfahrt* (Uppsala, 1900).

Wallace, Birgitta Linderoth. 'The Vikings in North America: Myth and Reality', in *Social Approaches to Viking Studies*, ed. Ross Samson (Glasgow, 1991), pp. 207–19.

Wallis, Helen. 'The Vinland Map: fake, forgery, or *jeu d'esprit?*', *The Map Collector* 53 (1991), 2–6.

——. 'The Vinland Map: Genuine or Fake', *Bulletin bibliophile* 1 (1991), 76–83.

180

Ward, Samuel. 'Days With Longfellow', *North American Review* 134 (1882), 456–66.

Warner, Philip. *The Best of British Pluck: The Boy's Own Paper* (London, 1976).

Washburn, Wilcomb E. 'The Meaning of "Discovery" in the Fifteenth and Sixteenth Centuries', *American Historical Review* 68 (1962), 1–21.

Watts, Pauline Moffitt. 'Prophecy and Discovery: On the Spiritual Origins of Christopher Columbus's "Enterprise of the Indies" ', *American Historical Review* 90 (1985), 73–102.

Wawn, Andrew. ' "The Courtly Old Carle": Sir Henry Holland and Nineteenth-Century Iceland', *Saga-Book of the Viking Society* 21 (1982–83), 54–79.

——. *The Icelandic Journal of Henry Holland 1818* (London, 1987).

——. *The Anglo Man. Þorleifur Repp, Philology and Nineteenth-Century Britain* (Reykjavík, 1991).

——. 'The Spirit of 1892: Sagas, Saga-Steads and Victorian Philology', *Saga-Book of the Viking Society* 23 (1992), 213–52.

——. Review of George Mackay Brown, *Vinland*, *Times Literary Supplement*, August 28, 1992, p. 18.

—— (ed.) *Northern Antiquity. The Post-Medieval Reception of Edda and Saga* (Enfield Lock, 1994).

——. 'The Cult of "Stalwart Frith-thjof" in Victorian Britain', *Northern Antiquity*, pp. 211–54.

Webb, J. F. (trans.) *Lives of the Saints* (Harmondsworth, 1965).

Webb, Thomas H. 'Communication on Professor Rafn', *Proceedings of the Massachusetts Historical Society* 8 (1865).

Weber, H., and R. Jamieson (eds) *Illustrations of Northern Antiquities* (Edinburgh, 1814).

Westrem, Scott D. (ed.) *Discovering New Worlds: Essays on Medieval Exploration and Imagination* (New York, 1991).

Wheaton, Henry. 'Scandinavian Literature', *The American Quarterly Review* 3 (1828), 181–90.

——. *History of the Northmen, or Danes and Normans; from the earliest times, to the Conquest of England by William of Normandy* (London, 1831).

——. 'Anglo-Saxon Language and Literature', *The North American Review* 33 (1831), 325–50.

——. Review of *Antiquitates Americanæ*, *The Foreign Quarterly Review* 21 (1838), 89–118.

White, George LeRoy, Jr. *Scandinavian Themes in American Fiction* (Philadelphia, 1937).

——. 'Longfellow's Interest in Scandinavia during the years 1835–1847', *Scandinavian Studies* 17 (1942), 70–82.

White, Horatio S. *Willard Fiske. Life and Correspondence. A Biographical Study* (New York, 1925).

Whittier, John Greenleaf. *The Works of John Greenleaf Whittier*, 7 vols (Boston and New York, 1892).

Williams, Stephen. *Fantastic Archaeology. The Wild Side of North American Prehistory* (Philadelphia, 1991).

Williams, William Carlos. *In the American Grain. Essays by William Carlos Williams*, introd. Horace Gregory (Harmondsworth, 1989).

Williamson, Hugh. *The History of Carolina*, 2 vols (Philadelphia, 1812).

Winsor, Justin. *Narrative and Critical History of America*, 8 vols (Boston and New York, 1889).

Wolf, Kirsten. 'Amazons in Vínland', *Journal of English and Germanic Philology* 95 (1996), 469–85.

———, and Julian Meldon D'Arcy. 'Sir Walter Scott og Eyrbyggia', *Skírnir* 162 (1988), 256–72.

INDEX

Abbot, John S. C.   85
Adam of Bremen   xin, xii
Allen, Hervey   140; 'Saga of Leif the Lucky'   140–1
Allen, Ralph Bergen   118
Anderson, Rasmus   55–6, 64, 66, 80
L'Anse-aux-Meadows   xvii, 145
Antiquitates Americanæ   xvii, xx, 36, 37, 44–51, 53–6, 58, 80, 81, 82, 84, 90, 117, 131
Ari Þorgilsson   3, 22
Auðr djúpúðga ('deep-minded')   4–5

Babcock, William   71
Baffin Island   xvi
Baldwin, John R.   85
Ballantyne, R. M.   91, 96, 107, 137; *The Norsemen in the West* 92–9, 101, 102, 118, 135, 138; *Ungava* 94, 113
Bancroft, George   47–8, 52, 53, 58, 63
Bancroft, Hubert Howe   81
Bárðar saga Snæfelláss   34, 35
Barrow, John   38
Bartholin, Thomas   90
Bartlett, James   46, 47n, 48n, 54
Bartlett, Robert   ix
Bartram, John   41
Baumgartner, Walter   2, 19, 23, 24
Baxter, James Phinney   69
Beamish, Nathaniel Ludlow   45, 50, 82, 90, 118
Beck, Richard   60n
Belknap, Jeremy   41, 42n, 73–4, 81, 86–7
Bennett, J. A. W.   38n
Beothuk   15–16, 71, 72–3, 74
Berry, Francis   145; *I Tell of Greenland* 148–9, 152
Best, George   18
Bitterli, Urs   xix, 15
Bjarni Grímólfsson   26, 31–2, 110, 127
Bjarni Herjólfsson   5, 6, 11–12, 58, 128, 129, 131, 145
Björn Þorsteinsson   30n
Bjǫrn Gilsson (Bishop)   1
Blackwell, I. A.   50–1

Blind, Karl   65, 80
Boehmer, Elleke   92n, 97n
Border Ruffians   62
Boyesen, Hjalmar   67n
The Boy's Own Paper   93
Brandr Sæmundarson (Bishop)   1
Brownell, Henry   82
Bryant, William Cullen (and Sydney Howard Gay) *A Popular History of the United States* 83, 118
Buchan, John   110; *John Macnab* 110–11
Bull, Ole   66, 67, 69
Bull, Sarah   69
Burne-Jones, Edward   68, 87
Burritt, Elihu   45, 52, 55

Cabot, J. Elliot   61
Campbell, Mary   xvi, xix
Carlyle, Thomas   51
Carpenter, W. H.   56n
Carr, Helen   81n, 87
Cartier, Jacques   xvi, xvii, 17, 18, 19, 21
Catlin, George   86
Channing, Edward   59
Chateaubriand, François René   143; *Atala* 143
Clark, Joan   145; *Eiriksdottir* 154–5
Clark, Richard   76–7, 80, 88, 119–20, 123n
Clark, William   88
Clunies Ross, Margaret   xvin, 2n, 8, 30n
Columbia University   56, 58, 67n
Columbus, Christopher   xvi, xvii, xviii, xix, 17, 18–19, 21, 36, 37, 42–4, 49, 50, 60, 64, 65, 68, 88, 127
Conrad, Bryce   134
Cook, Ramsay   xvi
Cornell University   55
Cowan, Edward J.   51n
Crantz, David   41, 73, 81, 89
Curtis, William Eleroy   67n, 77

Dasent, George Webbe   45, 53, 62
Davis, Asahel   61

De Costa, Benjamin   45, 49, 61, 63, 66, 83n, 87, 118, 119
De Roo, P.   85
Decker, George   145
Dewey, John   xviii
Dighton Rock   46, 48, 51, 69, 127
Dixon, Robert   91n
DuBois, B. H.   63n, 69n
Dunae, Patrick   95n

Eastman, Seth   86
Egils saga   20
Einarr Þorgeirsson   28
Einars þáttr Sokkasonar (Grœnlendinga þáttr)   3
Eiríkr blóðøx (King)   20–21
Eiríkr Gnúpsson (Bishop)   71–7, 79
Eiríkr rauði (Eric the Red)   x, 4, 5, 6, 10–12, 13, 14, 32, 35, 114, 131, 134
Eiríks saga rauða   x, xi, xiv, xv, xvi, xvii, xix, xx, 2, 3, 4, 7–8, 10–11, 13, 14, 15–21, 22, 25–33, 34, 36, 37, 44–5, 50, 54, 57, 58–9, 70, 84, 87, 90, 92, 101, 104, 107, 110, 111, 114, 115, 127, 145, 146, 147, 148, 149, 150, 153, 155
Eiríks saga viðfǫrla   xv
Elliott, J. H.   xvi
Emerson, Ralph Waldo   62
Everett, Alexander Hill   49, 80
Everett, Edward   xvii, 43, 49, 80
Everett, William   68
Eyrbyggja saga   29, 33, 38, 44, 90, 118

Fernández-Armesto, Felipe   xix
Finnur hin fríði   34–5
Finnur Magnússon   46, 69n
Fiske, Daniel Willard   48, 55, 56, 57, 66, 67, 69
Fiske, John   58, 67, 69
Flateyjarbók   3, 5
Fleming, Robin   62n, 64n, 88n
Flóamanna saga   3–4, 7, 9
Flom, George   57, 58n
Fóstbrœðra saga   3, 33n
Foerster, Johan Reinhold   38, 73, 74, 76, 81; *Geschichte der Entdeckungen und Schifffahrten im Norden (History of Discoveries and Voyages made in the North)*   38, 73
Folsom, George   49, 80
Franklin, Benjamin   41, 42
Frémont, John C.   120
Freydís Eiríksdóttir   xv, 6, 12, 13, 23–5,

27, 29–30, 32, 71, 72, 97, 114, 134, 137, 145
Frobisher, Martin   18

Gering, Hugo   57
Ginnungagap   xiii
Goodrich, Aaron   64, 81
Gosse, Edmund   118
Goths   39–40, 60
Gravier, Gabriel   70, 76, 104; *Découverte de l'Amérique par les Normands au Xe siècle*   70, 86
Greenblatt, Stephen   xix, 17, 21
Grettis saga   33
Gripla   xii, 34
Grœnlendinga saga   x, xi, xiii, xiv, xv, xvi, xvii, xix, xx, 1, 2, 4, 5, 7, 9–11, 13–14, 15–21, 22–6, 29–30, 32–3, 34, 36, 37, 44–5, 48, 50, 57, 58–9, 71, 78–9, 87, 92, 93, 97, 101, 104, 106, 119, 132, 137, 145, 146, 147, 148, 149, 150, 153, 154, 155
Grœnlendinga þáttr, see *Einars þáttr Sokkasonar*
Grœnlands annáll   xii, 34
Guðbrandur Vigfússon   55n, 56, 57, 58
Guðríðr Þorbjarnadóttir   xv, 1, 4, 7–9, 10, 19, 20, 21, 23–26, 28–29, 32–33, 77, 114
Gunnars saga Keldugnúpsfífls   34
Gunnlaugr Leifsson   3, 75
Gunnlaugs saga   57

Haki and Hekja (in *Eiríks saga rauða*)   26, 32, 98n, 100, 111
Hale, Edward Everett   67
Halldór Hermannsson   xiiin, 48n, 57n
Hálfdanar saga Brǫnufóstra   33–4
Hálfdanar saga Eysteinssonar   34
Haraldur Bessason   1
Hart, Albert Bushnell   59
Haugen, Einar   56
Haukr Erlendsson   xi, 2
Hauksbók   xi, 2, 8, 12, 26, 27, 28n, 31–2, 98n
Haynes, Henry   69
Hazlett, John D.   43n
Heimskringla   38
Helgi and Finnbogi (in *Grœnlendinga saga*)   23–5, 71, 72, 133
Helluland   xi, xii, xvi, 12, 13, 30, 33–4, 35
Henderson, Ebenezer   52
Henty, G. A.   93n

Hermann Pálsson 31
Hewlett, Maurice 106, 148; *Gudrid the Fair* 106–9, 148
Hilen, Andrew 117, 124n
Historia Norvegiæ 14n
Hodgetts, J. F. 92, 93, 99, 107; *Edric the Norseman* 92, 93, 100–3
Hoey, Frances Cashel 103
Holland, Sir Henry 38, 82
Horsford, Cornelia 70
Horsford, Eben Norton 62, 64, 65–7, 70, 78–9, 104
Horsman, Reginald 60n
Hough, Clara Sharpe 143; *Leif the Lucky* 143–4
Humboldt, Alexander von 47
Hungrvaka 72
Hvítramannaland 31–2, 118, 132

Ingstad, Anne xvii
Ingstad, Helge xvi–xvii, 145
Inuit 16, 18, 30n, 31n, 94, 113–14
Irving, Washington 42–3, 48, 52, 74; *The Life and Voyages of Christopher Columbus* 42–4; *Knickerbocker's History of New York* 43, 48
Irwin, Constance 147; *Gudrid's Saga* 147–8, 155
Isidore of Seville 27
Íslendingabók 3, 14, 15, 57

Jamestown 71
Jefferson, Thomas 39; *Notes on the State of Virginia* 39
Jelič, Luka 75, 78
Jesch, Judith 30n
Jett, Stephen C. xviii
Jochens, Jenny 30n, 102n
Jones, Gwyn xviin

Kalm, Peter 41
Kålund, Kristian xiii
Karlamagnús saga 26
Kaups, Matti Enn 38n
Kellett, Ernest Edward 109; 'Bjarni' 109–10
Kennedy, Charles Rann, *The Winterfeast* 120, 141–3
Kingsley, Charles 61, 62, 87, 135
Kingston, W.G.H. 94n
Kipling, Rudyard 106, 109; 'The Finest Story in the World' 106, 111
Knox, Henry 87

Konungs skuggsjá 3
Laing, Samuel 51; *Heimskringla* 51, 93, 107n
Landafræði xii, xv, 35
landnám 2, 10, 12–14, 21
Landnámabók x, xivn, 11, 14, 31, 38, 63n
landvættir 11, 20
Lang, Andrew 106
Lanier, Sidney 117, 120, 144; 'Psalm of the West' 118, 131–4
Larsson, Mats xviin
Laxdæla saga xin, 57, 142
Laxness, Halldór xvn
Leifr Eiríksson x, xiii, xvi, 3, 5, 6, 12, 14, 21, 22, 24, 25–6, 29, 32, 37, 44, 46, 49, 58, 60, 62, 67n, 68. 69, 75, 110, 114, 116, 119, 127, 129, 144, 145
Leifr Eiríksson statue 56, 67–9
Leifsbúðir 12, 17, 21, 25
Levin, David 86n
Lewis and Clark 120
Liljencrantz, Ottilie 120, 144; *Randvar the Songsmith* 126, 135, 136, 139–40; *The Thrall of Leif the Lucky* 135–7, 138; *The Vinland Champions* 135, 136, 137–8; *A Viking's Love* 135
Litzenberg, Karl 51n
Lodewyckx, A. 30n
Longfellow, Henry Wadsworth 54–5, 66, 117, 121, 127, 144; *Song of Hiawatha* 120; 'The Skeleton in Armor' 122–5, 126, 127, 139; 'The Saga of King Olaf' 122; *Ballads and Other Poems* 123–4
Lowell, James Russell 62, 66–8, 117, 120, 131, 144; *The Biglow Papers* 127–8; 'The Voyage to Vinland' 128–30, 131; 'Columbus' 128
Lyschander, Claus 71, 79; *Den Grønlandske Cronica* 71

Mackenzie, Sir George 38; *Travels in the Island of Iceland* 38
Mackay Brown, George 145; *Vinland* 151–3
MacLean, J. P. 63–64, 69n
Maddox, Lucy 86n
Manning, Val 149; *Valkyrie Queen* 149–50
Markland xi, xii–xiii, xv, xvi, 12, 13, 20, 26, 30–2, 35

Marsh, George Perkins 46, 47, 51–3, 57, 60, 61, 62; *Compendious Grammar* 53–54, 57
Massachusetts Historical Society 46–7, 55, 68–9
Mather, Samuel 41
Matthías Þórðarson 6n
McDougall, Ian 28n
Metcalfe, Paul 145; 'Shick Shock' 146–7
Micmac 15–16, 17n, 30n, 31n
Mill, John Stuart xiv
Möhler, Johan Adam 75
Moldenhauer, Joseph J. 118n
Montgomery, James 89; *Greenland* 89–90
Morris, Charles 85, 86n, 87
Morris, William 68, 118
Morris & Co. 67, 68, 87
Moulton, Joseph 42, 82
Mueller, Erasmus 52
Murray, Hugh 41, 82, 84

Nansen, Fridtjof xv
Navigatio Sancti Brendani xv, 19
Neukomm Edmond 103, 107; *Les Dompteurs de la mer* (*Tamers of the Sea*) 103–6
Newfoundland xvi–xvii, 71, 72
Newport Tower 74–5, 104, 122, 125
Norton, Charles Eliot 62, 128
Norumbega 65–66, 139, 140

Óláfr Haraldsson (King) xn
Óláfr Tryggvason (King) xi, 3, 5, 29, 75
Óláfs saga Tryggvasonar en mesta x, 3, 7n
Óláfur Halldórsson 1
Olson, Charles 145; *Maximus Poems* 145–6
Ormr (foster-father of Guðríðr Þorbjarnadóttir) 28
Ortelius, Abraham 65
Ostrbyggð (Eastern Settlement of Norse Greenland) 14, 35

Pagden, Anthony xix
Parkman, Francis 86
Pàroli, Teresa 2
Percy, Thomas 38, 81; *Five Pieces of Runic Poetry* 38; *Northern Antiquities* 38, 51
Peringskiöld, Johannes 37, 41, 42, 82n
Perkins, Richard 4n, 10
Pike, Zebulon 120

Pocahontas 142, 143n
Pontoppidan, Erik 41, 72
Poole, Russell 110n
Prescott, William Hickling 47
Priest, Josiah 48
Pynchon, Thomas 145; *Vineland* 151, 153–4

Rafn, Carl Christian xvii, 44, 46, 47–50, 51–6, 69, 74–5, 76, 80, 104, 127, 132
Rask, Erasmus 52n, 53
Reeves, Arthur M. 56, 57, 59
Reman, Edward xviin
Rhode Island Historical Society 46–7, 54
Robertson, William 41
Robinson, Kim 145; 'Vinland the Dream' 145
Rolfe, John 142
Rosen, David 136n
Royal Danish Society of Northern Antiquaries 44, 53, 55

Saga Óláfs Tryggvasonar (by Oddr Snorrason) 8n, 30n
Sale, Kirkpatrick 68n
Sayers, William 2, 14, 19, 25, 74n
Schoolcraft, Henry 48, 49, 53–4, 88
Schröder, Johan 42
Scott, Walter 90; *Illustrations of Northern Antiquities* 90; *The Pirate* 90
Seaver, Kirsten 78n
Sephton, John 58
Sertima, Ivan xviii
Shipley, John 64, 78
Shipley, Marie (née Brown) 61, 64–5, 67, 76, 77–8
Shute, Nevil 110, 116; *An Old Captivity* 111–14, 115, 138; *Vinland the Good* 111, 114–16, 151
Sigourney, Lydia Howard 125; 'The Newport Tower' 125
Skálhóltsannáll xiii
Skálhóltsbók xi, 13n, 27, 98n
Skrælingar 14–17, 19–20, 22, 27, 29, 32, 33, 84, 86, 101
Smiley, Jane 153; *The Greenlanders* 150–1, 155
Smith, Charles Sprague 56, 58
Smith, John 142, 143n
Smith, Joshua Toulmin 45, 50, 83, 86–7, 90
Snedden, Genevra 135n; *Leif and Thorkel* 135n

Snorri Þorbrandsson   12, 33
Snorri Þorfinnsson   25
Snorri Sturluson   63
Strömback, Dag   20n
Sveinn Estriðsson (King)   xii

Taylor, Bayard   126; 'The American
    Legend'   126, 130
Tegnér, Esaias   117; *Frithiofs saga*   117,
    123, 124, 125
Tocqueville, Alexis de   87
Torfæus, Thormod   38, 41, 72, 74, 75,
    82n, 104; *Historia Vinlandiæ Antiqvæ*
    38, 72
Torres, Luis Vaez de   16

Þjóðhildr Jǫrundardóttir (wife of Eiríkr
    rauði)   5, 7
Þorbjǫrg (*spákona*)   7–8, 10, 27, 30, 32,
    90
Þorbjǫrn Vífilsson   7, 28
Þorfinnr Karlsefni   xi, xv, xvii, 1, 4, 5,
    9–10, 11, 12–13, 15, 16, 18, 20,
    22–7, 28, 30–1, 32, 36, 49, 67n, 77,
    84–5, 110, 131, 144, 145
Þorgils Leifsson   29, 101
Þorgunna (of the Hebrides)   29, 32, 114
Þórhallr Gamlason   33
Þórhallr veiðimaðr ('hunter')   9, 26–27,
    30
Þorlákr Rúnólfsson   1
Þórir (first husband of Guðríðr
    Þorbjarnadóttir in *GS*)   28
Þórr   4, 9
Þorvaldr Eiríksson   6, 13, 14, 16, 19, 24,
    25, 27, 32, 80–4, 85, 119, 123n
Þorvarðr (husband of Freydís)   23, 26
Þorsteinn Eiríksson   6, 8–9, 25–6, 28, 32

University of Wisconsin   57, 58, 66

Verduin, Kathleen   62n
Verrazzano, Giovanni   16n, 18, 19, 21
Vestrbyggð (Western Settlement of Norse
    Greenland)   14, 35
Vilhjálmur Stefánsson   ix
Vínland   *passim*
Vínland Map   ix, 76, 78, 88
Vollman, William T.   145; *The Ice-Shirt*
    151

Wahlgren, Erik   xixn, 6n, 26n
Ward, Sam   124
Wawn, Andrew   92n, 109, 117n
Webb, Thomas   46, 51
Westrem, Scott D.   xix
Wheaton, Henry   40, 42, 60, 72, 75, 82,
    104; *History of the Northmen*   39–40,
    42, 52, 62, 82, 84
White, George LeRoy   124n
White, Horatio S.   55n
Whitney, Anne   67
Whittier, John Greenleaf   66, 117, 124,
    144; 'Mogg Megone'   120; 'The
    Norsemen'   121–2, 126
Williams, Stephen   46n
Williams, William Carlos   134; *In the
    American Grain*   134
Williamson, Hugh   41
Winsor, Justin   58–9
Wolfe, Catharine Lollard   67, 87

Qrvar-Odds saga   33